A BREED

A BREED APART

THE HISTORY BEHIND TYNESIDE'S MOST NOTORIOUS FAMILY

Eddie Lennie Jr
Tony Sayers Sr

mediaarts

First published in 2019 by Media Arts

All enquiries should be addressed to: Newcastle Legends Ltd

ISBN-13: 978-0-9927023-8-0

Cover design by Neil Jackson Media Arts

CONTENTS

FOREWORD
ALBERT SAYERS

For many years, I've wanted to record the struggles endured by my family; to put down in words what they went through just to earn an honest crust on the streets of Newcastle. I wanted to make sure our fight for the legalisation of street trading was documented for future generations of our family to read.

I approached Steve Wraith, who had successfully helped my nephew, Stephen Sayers pen his memoirs, as I felt he'd be the right man for the job. I didn't know he'd already spoken with two of my nephews; Tony Sayers and young Eddie Lennie about a similar project. It turned out Eddie had been harbouring the same thoughts on the subject for decades. He and Tony had started to put together some of his ideas back in 2016. It turns out Eddie has a talent for writing and was only too happy to turn years of notes and ideas into something like this - and so the process began.

Eddie has put a lot of time and effort into the writing of this book; working with Tony on gathering stories and family recollections, memories and anecdotes spanning generations of our family. Personally, I think he has really done a wonderful job, and has been supported throughout the process ably by Tony and Steve.

I have filled in as many blanks as I could and Eddie's mother, my cousin Mary Lou – now the oldest living member of our family – has been a source of invaluable information, and deserves a lot of credit for her input.

Our lives have been very different. I always remember from a very early age loving the street life. They were hard times, especially in the winter when it was snowing blizzards, but we'd still be out there with the old women, helping to sell and giving a hand where we could. Buying and selling, ducking and diving – you did what you had to in order to survive.

My mother's family was big. They were street traders and all with different pitches around the city centre, but it was a lovely, close community. I suppose you look after your own, and that's the way it's always been with us. You watch each other's backs.

I don't think any of us had a formal education. You don't have to be educated to be intelligent, do you? I think the way we were brought up was with a sort of 'street' intelligence.

The men in our family were all great characters. When I was very young I always picked things up from them; their mannerisms, style, and how they conducted themselves. You would never have heard those guys swearing in front of a woman or anything like that, yet these days, in some quarters it seems more acceptable. But the people we knew were all respectful. Good memories, good people.

Over decades, and despite much harassment from the police, our family fought a campaign to legalise street trading. There were many times when they'd take you off Northumberland Street and bang you up in a cell just for selling a bit of fruit. It's always been tough for us. We never had anything easy, but I suppose many people can say that, because life is hard. It has its highs and its lows. But we continued to fight and campaign for years for what we believed in.

There are some great characters in this book, many of them women. You will hear about my brothers Frankie, John and Peter – a fruiter and motor dealer for most of his life who, like my brother Frankie, started out on the barrows, just as we all did. We always looked up to my brother Frankie, I suppose with him being the oldest brother he was a bit of a role model. I got into boxing because he boxed. I guess I wanted to be like him, I suppose we all did really, because he was a great guy. He was a tough fella and didn't stand any nonsense, but he was also a gentleman.

John Brian, my other brother, was I guess what you would call a villain, with no respect for the law. The infamous 1960s 'Battle of Percy Street' which is covered in this book, gave John, Frankie and their team a reputation and 'the Sayers' stigma was born.

So who are the Sayers family? You might be picking up this book for the first time having never heard of us. You may have read news reports over the years about my young nephews John, Stephen and Michael and could be forgiven for thinking we're some sort of Tyneside Cosa Nostra. Or you could just know us from buying your fruit and veg from the barrow on Northumberland Street, which is where I still work today.

They say the apple never falls far from the tree; and I guess when you look at the amount of time my nephews John Henry, Stephen and Michael have served behind bars, then that saying rings very true. But it wasn't always that way. I remember how they'd all hang about my stall as I was working, along with the writers of this book, Tony and Eddie. They used to keep their eyes open. They would watch everything. That's where they got that street mentality from, which I suppose has served them very well in later life. They all went their different ways in life, but they're all good lads, and they're not mugs. The boys still come down to see me regularly at the pitch, and I like that. I have an awful lot of time for those lads, as I do for all of my nephews.

Let's not deny it; the Sayers family has a reputation. People who meet us for the first time have a preconception. It's a stigma that the whole family has to live with. It comes with the territory and it's the same with all families like ours. Sadly, the public opinion of the Sayers family is fairly one-sided. Reputations always evolve around people who can look after themselves, but there's always the myth – and the truth – behind the reputation.

We do suffer in many ways because of the stigma attached, but having said that, I am very proud of my name; and of all my family. At the time of writing this, I am in my 70th year and I wouldn't change one thing in my life. I've been very fortunate. I've got a wonderful wife and a wonderful daughter, and I love them both very much. You don't need tons of money to be happy. Of course, we all strive to get more money, and it's important isn't it? But as I said, I'm very, very proud. Proud of the boys; there's no pretence, you either accept it or you don't. We like who we like, and we dislike who we dislike because, at the end of the day, it's them and us; that's the way it's always been, and that's the way we look at it. We are survivors. We've all had to survive on the street, but there must be boundaries that people don't cross. I'm proud to say my family has never crossed those boundaries. Of course, authority has always been on the opposite side of the coin to us, going back over the last 130 years, and that is what this book is all about. Putting across our side of the story and making sure our history is correctly documented and ensuring the family is remembered for the right reasons.

I am so proud to have my name associated with this book; an honest and fair account of our family's history, and a document that our future generations can refer to in order to understand what made us the kind of people we are.

INTRODUCTION
EDDIE LENNIE JR

This story, in which some names, characters and events have been combined or altered for dramatic, legal, and interpretive purposes, is based on actual events, with dialogue added believed to be consistent with the events.

It is a story dedicated to 'our family,' both past and present. It is *their* story. The story of how *their* ancestors arrived in this city over 130 years ago, from the bandit border country of Ireland. How, from the humblest of beginnings, they rode their luck and made their name on the streets of Tyneside.

A name that would be recognised throughout the North, and in some cases, throughout the country.

Today these people blend into all walks of life and are woven into the fabric of society in all areas. From involvement in street trading to crime on many levels, some now proudly hold positions within the medical profession and the armed forces, from public services to business of all kinds and all sizes, and all manner of things in between.

For everyone from Hewson to Sayers, Kelly to Patterson, Baird to Chapman and Donnelly to Cruddas, and for all the blood that comes from them; this is your story.

We may no longer share one 'family' name, but in one way or another, we all share the mark from the same mad dog that bit us.

A BREED APART

Rome wasn't built in a day. Empires aren't created overnight. Respect and reputations are earned over generations.

In this dramatic true story, and precursor to the bestselling crime book *The Sayers: Tried and Tested at the Highest Level* we take a revealing look inside an extraordinary family that lived outside the law.

In an epic saga spanning three centuries we discover how, during a treacherous crossing of the Irish Sea in the late 1800s, a chance encounter between two kindred spirits became the life-blood from which a tide of one family's rivalry, revenge, scandal, betrayal, deceit and deception would flow as wide as the famous river upon which stood the streets of the city they later came to dominate.

Who would have known that wee Sarah 'Sally' McGurk, a teenage tinker from the Fenian stronghold of Carrickmacross – just south of the Republic border – and Paddy Kelly, a Hawker from Irish Travelling stock would become the rebellious forebears of a breed of people whose attitude to life and how they chose to live it would ultimately set them apart from everyday society? A family whose notorious endeavours and infamous exploits would become the stuff of Tyneside folklore. A breed whose burgeoning reputation would become renowned in underworld history. A family who simply were *a breed apart.*

This colourful tapestry of a life less ordinary takes us on a breathtaking journey with an unconventional family, through five generations. With unbelievable highs and unimaginable lows, unexpected twists and devastating turns, their story of survival may make you question many of your own values.

There is, so they say, a little devil inside us all, which most people, thankfully, keep out of sight. But when your livelihood is at stake and your liberty is on the line, you will live and die by the choices that you make and, when needs must, the Devil often drives.

If wee Sally needed, then Paddy Kelly must, and although it may never have been planned, the Devil began to drive a force of a family that would eventually become as much a part of Tyneside as the fog that sits upon it.

So much could have been different. So much could have been achieved, and so much could have been avoided had different worlds collided, but at every turn, through every generation, the plots began to thicken as their notoriety reached ever greater heights.

Like birds of peculiar feather, a dangerous flock they formed together, and the Devil picked up the pace. As their breed grew in size, the Kelly name became diluted, failing to propagate one 'family' but undoubtedly enhancing their reputation as a 'firm'.

As loyalties became stretched and divisions grew deeper, greed set in and jealousy began to take root. All which was once valued gave way to bitterness and betrayal, and as the level of their notoriety increased, their battle to succeed as a 'family' was tearing their breed apart.

But this is no ordinary family. Theirs was no ordinary life. And when survival is all you know, then survive is what you will do, whatever the cost.

LUCK, PLUCK AND VIRTUE

The excitement and anticipation was palpable. The noise almost deafening, as Paddy scurried along on the damp, steamy, bustling boardwalks of Belfast Dock. The year was 1886, almost 40 years after the Great Potato Famine and Irish natives were still heading for distant shores in their thousands in search of a better life.

The world was opening up to patriots of the Emerald Isle and depending on how much someone could pay for their fare, and how long they were prepared to be at sea, then Europe and the Americas were seen as the destination lands of milk and honey.

Patricci Kelly, or Paddy as he was known, was a chancer; half Gypsy and a hawker by trade – if indeed hawking is a trade; more of an art, and he was undoubtedly an artist. The son of an Irish Traveller and a countrywoman, he lived on his wits and did whatever he had to in order to survive. After upsetting a tearaway in Limerick, who definitely wasn't the type he'd want to upset, Paddy decided it was time to take a brief leave of absence and see what all the fuss was about across the Irish Sea.

Armed with little more than what he stood in, and virtually nothing in his pocket other than a copy of Horatio Alger's *Luck and Pluck*, which he always kept with him even though he couldn't read, Paddy set off in search of adventure and safety. He knew the tale in his book was one of a rise from rags to riches based on luck, pluck and virtue, and Paddy felt he definitely had at least one of those qualities as he set about trying to jib his way on board a steamer bound for Fleetwood. He had little choice, as he had no money to pay for a ticket.

Sarah McGurk, or Sally as she was known, came from a troubled and poverty-stricken background. She was daughter to a tinker mother, and a drunkard father who had given up the fight to maintain any sort of family environment. In a desperate bid to escape from a tortured home life, her extreme situation called for equally drastic measures. She wanted something more than the life she'd been living; just about anything would be better than that, and Sally was determined to go out and get it. Courage and determination, she had in plenty. A plan, however, she did not.

A raven-haired teenager with the gift of the blarney, she found herself at the quayside of Belfast Dock with a tatty old carpet bag containing all her worldly belongings, along with a few lucky charms, a clutch of handmade pegs, a handful of cloths made from the famous lace of her hometown and a well-thumbed 10 shilling note – a week's wage for a working man of the day. She was determined to head for English shores, even if just for the winter, as so many Irish folk did at the time.

The 10 bob note she carried was her world. If she broke into it, her world would start to fall apart, or at least that's what she convinced herself of. She would only ever add to that note and never part with it. It was her start, the passage to her new life, and she would guard it with her own life. She had to get to Fleetwood; she had to escape and carve out a new life of her own.

The deck of the Bazely Line feeder ship, the Albert, was as thick with passengers as it was the broad Irish accents that rang out from it. The ship's crew were less concerned about who was on board as they were about how many. The identity of passengers was, fortunately, less of an issue embarking, as that had to be proven once they reached English soil. Tickets were bought and sold, some were checked, and some were not. If the odd one wasn't, then the ticket holder had either wasted the price of their fare, or better still, they'd get themselves free passage, but even if that were the case, they'd have to slip the net at Fleetwood or talk their way out of trouble.

Paddy didn't have a proverbial pot to piss in. If he'd had the cash he'd have bought a ticket. The last thing he wanted was to get left behind on the dockside at Belfast. The fella he'd had over was a rough giant of a man with an even more prominent family, and being stitched up by the likes of Paddy Kelly wasn't something that they would want talked about in every public house in Limerick. They might not have been hot on his tail, but Paddy had no intentions of hanging around to find out. Get out the way for the winter; that was his plan. Let the dust settle and see what was going on over the water. He had extended family who had made the journey and settled there, as much as Travelling people ever settle. The unknown prospect was far better than the alternative, as life back then in Ireland was hard enough without being on your toes.

Desperate to get on board the Albert, Paddy nodded and winked his way through the crowds on the boarding ramp. Head down and fumbling for a non-existent ticket, deliberately holding up the group of excited passengers, he was eventually ushered forward by a broad Ulster crewman.

'Herry the feck up, will ya?' yelled the steward, as a bottleneck rapidly formed on the gangplank. 'This things gonna feckin' collapse under the lot o' ya!'

With little time and even less patience, the steward urged him on board. 'Ticket,' he demanded.

Paddy searched himself nervously, knowing full well he was never going to find something he didn't have. He looked around at the impatient crowd gathering behind him as he fumbled, making sure to let the steward see his book. If the crewman thought this man could read, then he might believe he was educated and not some chancer trying to slip on board.

'Who're ya?' snapped the steward. 'What's yer name?'

Without thinking, and still rummaging for his make-believe ticket, Paddy replied, 'Paddy, erm, Paddy Kelly.'

'Oh, sure it is now,' replied the steward sarcastically. 'Could ya not have come up wi' something a bit more original than that?'

Paddy shrugged his shoulders.

'And I suppose it'll be John Smith by the time we reach Fleetwood, will it? Move on!' the inspector bawled, as he shoved Paddy onto the deck, allowing the crowd to move forward.

'I'll catch you later, Paddy Kelly!' he snarled.

Paddy breathed a sigh of relief as he shuffled aboard, thinking, 'I fucking hope not!'

It was going to be a long night, and Paddy needed somewhere to plot up. Somewhere out of sight of the screw that had his eye on him. After sneaking around the lower decks in search of sanctuary and coming across more than a handful of immigrants with similar intentions – some even clutching small children – he eventually found himself a little hidey-hole in a cargo room on a lower deck of the ship. Scanning his surroundings in the dim light, he spotted a tarpaulin draped over some furniture and shuffled underneath. He prepared himself for a rough night; happy that he had made good his getaway. The long journey ahead would provide him with plenty of time to figure out how he was going to talk his way onto dry land at the other end.

Sitting on the floor in near blackness, Paddy tried to make himself as comfortable as possible, and although he couldn't read, and there was no light even if he could, he pulled out his cherished copy of *Luck and Pluck*. It was his comfort blanket amid the darkness and discomfort.

'An educated man, are we?'

Paddy near jumped from his skin at the sound of a woman's voice. Before he could say a word, she spoke again, in a soft Irish accent.

'An educated man, but you can't afford the price of a ticket,' she said sarcastically. 'Some fella ya are.'

Paddy's eyes adjusted to the dim light and he could just about make out the shape of the young woman sat just feet away from him.

'I'm down here looking for it,' he replied with equal sarcasm, 'The same as you are, I'll wager.'

'The cheek of it!' sneered the woman.

'Well, I doubt this is where the steward told you to sit when you showed him your ticket darlin'!' he replied.

He was a little less anxious now he knew he was holed-up with a woman, but she gave him a start again as she snatched the book from his grasp.

'LUCK AND PLUCK!?'

Paddy was astounded. This creature could read!

'A tale of rags to riches? Sure it's just like the rest of the shite he writes about,' she laughed.

Paddy was now dumbfounded.

'Who?' he asked ignorantly.

'Horatio Alger, y'eejit!'

It was clear that the man beside her had no idea what she was talking about. She continued to tease him.

'Tis virtue that wins the day,' she declared, as she looked for his reaction while flicking the pages, but Paddy was having difficulty processing the situation he found himself in as she continued.

'Luck and pluck is all well and good,' she pointed out. 'But success, *he* says is earned by good virtue.'

Paddy was lost; he knew the story was a rags to riches tale, but that's all he knew, and that's why he kept it with him: a talisman, a reminder, a dream. But how did this faceless silhouette, of tender age by the tone of her voice, know so much?

'You can read?' he uttered in amazement. She looked at him sideways.

'No. I just took a stab in the dark,' she replied with further sarcastic wit. The young girl shrieked loudly as he snatched the book from her hands.

'For the love of God, will ya be quiet?' he snapped.

Undeterred, she reacted, 'Oh, will y' look at yerself. We're in the bowels of the ship ya gobshite, who'll be for hearin' us down here?'

Paddy thought for a moment before replying, 'Well, be sure to bear that in mind if you have to take to screamin''

'In danger, am I?' she asked inquisitively.

Paddy was putting his prized book back in his pocket and admittedly declared, 'No more trouble than I am meself.'

The Albert eventually left Belfast Dock and the voyage to Fleetwood was underway. Paddy had escaped, for the time being at least, and he was relieved. Safe in this knowledge, at least until he reached Fleetwood, he settled in for the crossing with his unexpected shipmate. The passage was anything but smooth, as so often was the case on the Irish Sea at the wrong side of summer, but at least Paddy had some company for the duration. The lady in the darkness was a strange one, and Paddy was intrigued. So young and yet so wise. Uneducated yet able to read. Alone and a stowaway, at such a tender age, a curious woman indeed was his mysterious companion, wee Sally McGurk.

They talked throughout the crossing and exchanged their reasons for finding themselves in the same predicament. Kindred souls on a voyage to a better life, with little more than their wits between them. She referred to the story written on the pages of his book, one of many written in a similar vein at the time by the author, and a symbolic possession Paddy prized so dearly.

'So,' she enquired, 'A virtuous man are we, Paddy Kelly? I'm to be safe down here with you, am I?'

'As safe as you'd be anywhere else on this ship without a ticket, Sally,' he replied with a wink.

As the ship rose and fell with the swell of an angry storm, the two stowaways huddled closer within their den, Paddy occasionally propping up the sideboard they were using as a backrest for fear it would topple over and squash the pair of them. During one such crashing swell Paddy inadvertently manhandled Sally. Both awkwardly aware of the misdemeanour, he apologised immediately for his accidental fumble, and Sally coyly remarked, 'A man of virtue after all, Paddy Kelly.'

There was a spark. There was common ground; they had made a connection, and now they were somehow in this thing together, as if thrown there by some strange twist of fate. By the time they were approaching Fleetwood, they had hatched a plan that would hopefully get them onto dry land at the other end. Cooped up in their hideout for what seemed like an eternity, they had got to know a great deal about each other and sensed that maybe they would stand a better chance of getting off this ship together, rather than risking it alone. After all, the eagle-eyed steward was looking for a lone passenger in the shape of Paddy and, to Sally's knowledge, none of the crew had even set eyes on her when she sneaked aboard at Belfast.

The plan was to fasten themselves on to a family with children as they were due to disembark. They reckoned they would look far less conspicuous if they had a child on the end of their arm and, if it came on top for them, then it would be a scatter, and each for themselves. But as both of them were inherently aware, a little bit of front can get a person just about anywhere.

They snuck out of the storeroom and mingled with the hordes of excited passengers on deck, holding hands together so they looked like a couple, with Paddy keeping his head down to avoid making eye contact with his nemesis. They looked around for a family with children – the more kids the better would undoubtedly help their plan. Cosying up to a couple with a chaotic brood of screaming kids, they nestled in amongst them as they shuffled down the gangplank.

Nearing the dockside, Paddy reached down and held the hand of one of the excited young boys of the gaggle, while Sally offered to carry one of the smaller children for the increasingly stressed mother of this noisy little clan.

'Families with children this side, single men and woman over there,' came the directions shouted from the onshore officials.

Paddy clocked the steward he had sidestepped at Belfast, who was monitoring the line of single men being asked to produce their paperwork; and probably wondering when Paddy would show up.

As they approached the front of the line and the table where the officials sat checking tickets, it was time to make their move. Sally took an inch of flesh from the side of the toddler in her arms and nipped it hard. (Sly munjering,, as they would call it, had been done to her many times as a child, often to create a distraction if the situation called for it, or by way of a discrete and painful chastisement.) The little girl began to scream hysterically as the rest of her family clambered around her in panic.

The chaos was sufficient enough to distract the officials so Paddy and Sally could slip off amidst the commotion. Thankfully, the plan unfolded without a hitch and they mingled into the excited bustling crowd beyond the checkpoint.

But what next? It was never going to be easy for either of them, landing in a strange country, with heavy Irish accents and not the price of a meal between them. Sally made sure not to mention her 10 bob note to Paddy, after all, she had only just met him, and even though she too had jibbed her way across the Irish Sea, he had done the same, so the jury was still out on the strength of this man's virtue. What they did agree, however, was that maybe they stood a better chance together than alone – for the time being at least.

The West Coast of England offered many opportunities to the Irish immigrant of the day; with work available to weavers, mill workers, longshoremen, stevedores, and navvies. But the Irish weren't always welcomed with open arms in every port. Immigrants had been pouring into the country for decades and many villages in England had already become seen as unhealthy cesspits of disease having been seen by many to have put a strain on the health systems of cities like Liverpool a few decades earlier, following their exodus from their homeland's Potato Famine.

Paddy had no trade to speak of. Sally was equally unskilled. They stood little chance of survival, making their way in a new land; one which looked down on their kind. But they were streetwise, with cunning and guile, a nose for a deal, and, between the two of them, more front than Brighton.

In the relief and excitement of having made it safely to England, they decided their first port of call in this foreign land should be the nearest public house. They both deserved a drink, even if they were likely to be looked upon as unwelcome strangers.

The public house was like a tourist information centre for the likes of these two. In no time at all they heard tell of a Travellers' camp, not a mile from where they were enjoying a drink, paid for by Sally in exchange for a Carrickmacross lace cloth – ensuring no money changed hands.

There was no guarantee that Paddy would know anyone on the camp, but having been told there were some of 'his lot' on there, he was confident he would at least half-know somebody.

The roadside camp spilled onto an adjacent piece of wasteland. Several bow-topped wagons, a couple of tethered horses and an old juckle (dog), a smoking fire with two scruffy urchins poking sticks into it, and one young chavy (lad) chasing a chicken about the place; this was the scene that welcomed Paddy and Sally. Sally was as close to these kinds of people as you could be without actually being one. Tinkers were the settled Gypsies of the day, and Paddy was what some might call a half-breed, having one parent of Gypsy heritage, so they had little to fear in rolling up there uninvited.

After speaking to one of the women on the ground, Paddy learned that a possible relation of his was camped there and, after a welcoming cup of tea from a Romany chal (woman) named Tillie, Old Freedom appeared on the scene. The belief amongst Irish Travellers is that somewhere down the line they are all related, more often than not by drink, but as tradition and respect would have it, and although he'd never met the man in his life, this was now Paddy's Uncle Freedom. The evening was spent around a crackling stick fire, as rabbit and tatties were cooked in a stew on the old kettle prop, with ale and whiskey to wash it down.

Paddy felt at ease, and his new companion seemed to take to the situation like a duck to water. Soon the conversation turned to what Paddy's plan was. The truth was that he didn't have one. Freedom explained that the type of work around the West Coast wasn't the kind of thing for the likes of them, and due to so many Irish flooding in, there were just too many of their type around to get a decent living.

Freedom often travelled hundreds of miles hawking, away for days or weeks at a time just to keep himself. This was giving Paddy much to think about, but just like his book says, luck and pluck are the roads that lead from rags to riches, and as luck would have it, Uncle Freedom was heading cross-country the very next day on one of his trips away.

Freedom had obtained a load of American oilcloth, courtesy of a crooked dock worker at Fleetwood who he had straightened. The parcel stood him very little money, but knocked into a score of quids, and in 1886, £20 was the best part of a working man's wage for a year.

Freedom was bound for the North East, hawking his way to a fella he knew of in Gateshead who he could serve with whatever he had left when he arrived there. Freedom would be glad of the company and invited the pair to join him, especially since the journey to Tyneside would take the best part of a fortnight. Paddy thought this was a sign.

Gateshead lies south of the river from Newcastle; the heart of the shipbuilding industry and home of the coal miner. Newcastle was also the name of the town in Limerick that Paddy's big rough pursuer came from, a sign surely.

As the bow-topped wagon left the camp the following morning, heavily laden with a half-ton of oilcloth, or 'pongo' as they called it, the long and otherwise lonely road was all that lay ahead of them. It would be a hard old road at that time of year, but Freedom wanted to get this trip under his belt and be back before Christmas with the prize in his pocket to keep him over the winter.

Freedom had stayed on the camp near Fleetwood with two other families, as he had no family of his own.

He was a bachelor by choice, an unusual thing among Travellers of the time, but Freedom liked to live up to his name, and nothing and no one laid claim to him. However tough the journey might have been, it was made all the more difficult by the presence of Sally. As they pulled up to camp for the night, Paddy, for the first time since he met her, regretted having Sally in tow. As the evening around the stick fire drew to a close, it was clear that with a woman in their midst, the two men would *really* have to rough it.

The wagon had room for all three of them at a push, but it wasn't right, and without a word spoken between them on the subject, they knew what had to be done.

Sally was to sleep in the wagon while the two men made the best of what they could from what little hay they had for the horse, a couple of blankets, and two lengths of pongo. This makeshift bed would be laid out on the ground beneath the wagon, and before the pair of them tried to get some sleep the talk turned to subversion over Sally. Some two or three days into the journey, life under the stars was starting to lose its sparkle.

As the sun rose over the Pennines on a fresh, crisp autumn morning, Paddy stirred from yet another dreadful night and woke to relight the fire. He straightened himself out with a quick swill of cold water from Freedom's milk churn, and after taking a quick lag (pee) behind the hedgerow, he gave Freedom a little kick to wake him up. He must have been spark out, thought Paddy, as he gave him another nudge, but Freedom wasn't having any of it.

He let him sleep while he took a cup of tea to Sally and explained that Freedom was having a lie in. They laughed at the thought of it; neither of the men had hardly slept for days in such rough conditions, so they didn't pay too much attention to Freedom nicking a little extra shut-eye. But by the time they'd drunk their tea and made enough noise to wake the dead, they realised something wasn't right. Paddy knelt down to wake Freedom up properly, but the man was out cold. In fact, the cold had taken the man out:

No matter how much noise they made it wasn't going to wake him, old Freedom was dead. Panic ensued as the feckless pair processed the gravity of the situation. What were they to do? What the fuck were they supposed to do? Informing the authorities was out of the question. Try explaining it to them: a deceased Irish Traveller with two illegal immigrants and a wagon full of stolen cargo. They'd finish up on the next boat back to Belfast if they were lucky, or stuck in the nick for God-knows-how-long if they weren't. Should they take him back to the camp? Should they take him to a hospital? Where *was* the hospital? A doctor? But what would be the point? He was already dead. Take him on to the next village? What, and leave him on the green?

Their minds were running riot as questions and pitfalls fired out of their mouths like bullets. Every option would inevitably result in trouble and complication and would undoubtedly put paid to any kind of plan they might have had. Thinking on their feet is part of what people like them did instinctively. When you're in a corner you need your wits about you, and wits were all these two had, and they had them in abundance.

'This is your luck, Paddy!' Sally exclaimed in a eureka moment. Although he couldn't see it at first, she made him see some clarity amid the chaos, explaining how this tragic turn of events could alter the course of their lives. One man's loss can be another man's profit. Sally was very persuasive, and she played on Paddy's belief in his beloved book.

The luck part had been meeting with Freedom, and the events that had unfolded now required the pluck to do what was right, both for him and themselves if they ever wanted the life they had come in search of. Their destiny was in their own hands, if they were game enough to go through with Sally's plan.

But where, Paddy thought, does virtue come into burying a man at the side of the road?

As Paddy said a few words over the shallow grave in which Freedom now lay, wrapped in a length of his own oilcloth, Sally convinced him that he was indeed a man of virtue and had done the right thing, and as their prayers were offered up over the dear departed soul they felt the best and only conceivable thing had been done, under the circumstances.

Freedom had no family to speak of, or none that Paddy knew of in England. The two lots on the camp they'd left in Fleetwood weren't guaranteed to be there for any length of time; and faced with all of the other unworkable options, they felt that what they were doing was their only solution and, in some way, justifiable. After all, they hadn't killed the man. Freedom had lived by the road, and now he had died by it, and although not the best of funerals, it was a fitting way for a proper old Travelling man to go. His loss was indeed their gain. The horse and wagon were now their home and transport, and the half-ton of pongo was their start. Could this be right? Did this *feel* right? Paddy and Sally convinced themselves this is what they *had* to do, in view of the other options available. What was meant for them would not pass them by.

With mixed emotions they hit the road, and just as Freedom had intended, hawked their way across the spine of England en route to the industrial port of the Tyne. Freedom had told them of the dozens of pits weaving their way beneath the ground of the North East, and of how the shipyards rang with the sound of a million rivets being banged into the hulls of countless ships along the banks of the Tyne.

They felt excited and optimistic about the prospect, and although sparing many a thought for Freedom along the way, they agreed he was now freer than ever. They thanked the Lord for their blessing and moved on with wind in their sails, and a prayer for Uncle Freedom.

They'd shifted about half of the pongo by the time they reached Gateshead, calling at farms and businesses along the way. As they drove their wagon up the Durham Road their excitement was palpable. The Tyneside air was thick with the smell of coal and molten steel; a thriving city enjoying the rewards of industry, and a million miles away from the small villages they had left behind in Ireland. This was surely a place where Paddy and Sally could carve out a living. The ill-fated pair had, it seemed, cemented their relationship on the road to their utopia.

They had only met a week before but had been through more together than some couples had in a lifetime. They were partners in more ways than one. Little did they know, but the firstborn child of this match made under a tarpaulin was conceived beneath the roof of a bow-topped living wagon somewhere over the Pennines, and would be born on the banks of the River Tyne.

Paddy didn't call to see Freedom's mark (customer) for the pongo, he didn't want to arouse any suspicion as to the whereabouts of his benefactor. He made himself busy along the Teams and into the evolving Jewish quarter of Bensham. Before their journey's end, he'd cleared the boards of every last length of pongo and felt like a man of means with his horse, living wagon and what was now the best part of £25 in his pocket – a small fortune for a working man of the time and more than enough to put a roof over their heads.

As they set off across the Tyne for Newcastle, one of Europe's largest industrial cities, crossing the High Level Bridge for the first time and taking in the wonder of their new world, Sally and Paddy could never have imagined that they were on the brink of an amazing adventure which would leave their mark on Tyneside for generations to come.

For the time being they would live in their wagon, however, Sally was insistent that they have a proper place to live before Christmas. Sally had no idea of the impending addition to their union, until a woman on a camp they'd found outside the city intuitively asked her when the baby was due. Sally dismissed the question and took no heed, but the seed had been planted in more ways than one; and as the weather began to deteriorate and the nights grew long and cold, she began to think there was something in the old girl's perception.

As tell-tale signs of Sally's condition became apparent to her, she urged Paddy to get his act together and find them a proper roof to put over their heads, but she didn't give him any clue as to her delicate predicament.

Paddy was familiarising himself with his new surroundings and sussing out where might be the best place to settle. The hustle and bustle of the city was like a magnet to him. The pickings could be plentiful if they knew where to look, and cashing up the living wagon would get Paddy more than enough money for a cart, enabling him to hawk the surrounding area more efficiently.

The festive season was approaching, and Sally realised that the old girl on the camp was bang on the money. Frustrated with the lack of progress from Paddy, she put it to him bluntly, that if he expected her to spend the winter in a bow-topped wagon, then that was one thing, but to expect their unborn child to do the same was a different kettle of fish.

The news sprang Paddy into action. It was the first week of December as he walked Sally into the festively-decorated Newcastle city centre and through the fruit market on St Andrew's Street. Sally's eyes sparkled at the hustle and bustle around her. The town was alive with activity, and the smell of Christmas was in the air as barrows were unloaded with sacks, baskets, and trays brimming with goods.

Paddy was showing out to the one or two faces he'd familiarised himself with during his recce of the town, and Sally felt like this was where she was supposed to be. She breathed in the life that this place exuded, and linked Paddy's arm even tighter as she felt the buzz of the city reverberate through her young body. They took a left off St Andrew's Street onto Stowell Street and continued down.

'So what d'ya think then, Sally?'

Sally looked back over her shoulder, beguiled by what she had seen and how it made her feel. Smiling as she turned to him.

'Think o' what, Paddy Kelly?' she loved to give him his full title. He stopped in his tracks and turned to face her.

'This place.'

Hands on her hips she indignantly asked, 'What place?'

Paddy leaned across her and put what looked like a jailer's key into the lock of a small wooden door. She looked at him with a mixture of uncertainty and anticipation as he unlocked the door and pushed it open.

'*This* place,' he said proudly.

The look on her face was priceless as he stepped inside, taking her by the hand and into the small passage on the ground floor of a two-up two-down tenement that he'd managed to rent the ground floor of for two bob a week. Unlocking the second door to his right, he pushed it wide open and announced with pride, 'Your new home, Sally!'

She followed him through, almost in a trance-like state, shell shocked by all that was happening and what she had just experienced walking through the city. There was a small front room with a shabby old bed up against the far wall, crumbling plaster, and a table with two rickety chairs in the centre of the small space, parked firmly on a piece of oilcloth which covered part of the bare floor. Sally was speechless. This little girl from Carrickmacross had arrived at a place she could never have imagined just a few months earlier when she'd slipped onto the Albert at Belfast Dock, yet here she was; a mother-to-be with a man she met stowed away on a steamer.

She was intoxicated by it all.

'So, what d'ya think then, Mrs Kelly?' asked Paddy with a cheeky smile. It was all just too much for her by now, but this cack-handed attempt at a proposal brought her back to her senses.

'Mrs Kelly?!' she replied indignantly as she gave him one of her sideways looks. 'Kelly, you say?'

'Well, what name d'you think I want my child to carry?' he enquired.

Sally hesitated, her mind swimming as she looked around the room with the sun shining through the grubby net curtains hanging in the window, and taking all things into consideration, she knew that what he was suggesting was the right thing to do. It was the cherry on the cake she was thoroughly enjoying.

With a wry smile on her face, she looked at him warmly, looked down at the oilcloth covered floorboards before finally turning to him with her answer about their child's given name, wittily replying, 'Pongo?'

PADDY AND SALLY: WHAT'S BRED IN THE BONE?

Paddy and Sally thrived in their new environment. Theirs had been an unusual relationship from the start, and things had moved quickly. Paddy sold the living wagon, bought a cart, and hawked fruit and veg around the more remote communities surrounding the city, acquiring a regular pitch at the city's Quayside Market. The hawker became more of a costermonger as time went by and, although with child, Sally made use of her time, feathering their little nest and making a home of their two small rooms in the heart of the city.

Such was her confidence and charming personality that she soon made herself known to many of the local salesmen and traders in the nearby fruit market. She loved this place. It was a hive of activity, and full of colourful characters; everyone was hustling, and she knew it wouldn't be long before she was.

Armed with an inherently keen intelligence, Sally marked out people she could make use of, always looking for an opportunity. The moves are always there, but sometimes they take a little work, a bit of time and attention, and Sally was blessed in the art of cultivation. These kinds of talents are the backbone of any entrepreneur, business person or trickster for that matter, the lines between which are often blurred depending on what side of the deal they're on.

With Christmas out of the way, winter rolled on, and the annual lull in business activity kicked in. It was kipper season (the slack period after Christmas), things were slow, people were spent up, and the weather was terrible, making hawking by cart less practical for Paddy. The contacts they were building around the market and city centre bars weren't regular folk. Paddy didn't drink with the miners or shipbuilders, the associations he made were of a different nature and vital to keeping things ticking over for him. Simpsons Bar and The Bacchus were regular haunts for local spivs and wide-boys, as well as a few who held down proper jobs, like the market salesmen, but they weren't really bars frequented by the kind of workers that were stuck in a shipyard from dusk 'til dawn or trapped down a mine shaft in the bowels of Northumberland. Those types were what Paddy and Sally considered as 'grafting pecks'; straight-goers, marks for the likes of Paddy and Sally; the people they kept company with were their supply chain.

Paddy and Sally had enough to keep them while things were a bit skinny, thanks to Freedom and the pongo, but the idea was not to spend what they had; it was to add to it, to advance, to improve and get fat, not in the physical sense but in terms of increasing their wealth. At the end of the day, no one was going to give them a pay rise or a promotion, no bonus was going to come their way unless they had a touch (financial windfall). Paddy would often buy the odd bit of merchandise from likely lads that would cross his path, some trinket, counterfeit coins or a bit of hoist (stolen goods) they needed to sell in order to put food on their own table.

Often something as basic as a bed sheet could provide an opportunity to get a penny when things were really tight; some people would wash their bedding and pawn it for a ha'penny and, if they didn't return to repurchase them, the pawnbroker, or money lender, would sell them on for tuppence. Paddy may have been doing the odd dodgy deal, but felt he was displaying some kind of virtue, helping the less fortunate in some small way, while utilising the less legal by moving a bit of hooky gear. He too had to put food on his own table after all, and with the imminent arrival of their first child, Paddy did whatever was necessary – without risking his liberty of course, jail was definitely not a feature in any plans he had.

Sally, not being a shy girl, had invested a bit of time in straightening one of the salesmen at Moody & Evans wholesale suppliers in the fruit market. The hapless fool thought he was making an impression on this petite Irish girl and was looking for a way to impress her. What he *was* in fact doing, was falling into her trap. Her beguiling charm in the presence of this deluded sap was not so much an invitation of any kind of friendship;

more a request to step into the parlour, as the spider said to the fly.

Sally procured a tiny handcart from the dreamer at Moody's. Funnily enough, the term 'Moody & Evans' became a phrase that she introduced to her descendants in reference to something not being right, it being 'moody'. Moody & Evans, as a result of the way Sally kidded to the salesman to get what she wanted. The handcart was part of a plan to compensate for Paddy being unable to get out hawking in the winter. Sally had been taking stock of what was happening around her and realised that people shopping in the town were buying their fruit and veg from shops in the city's Grainger Market.

The fruit market at St Andrew's just around the corner was for traders only, so anyone wanting a half pound of mushrooms or one head of celery had to pay the shop owner's top dollar just 500 yards away in the Grainger Market. Sally reckoned that if she could cop on a little bit of gear from her deluded salesman, she could plot her small handcart up somewhere between the fruit market and the Grainger. She could literally fill a gap in the markets and, with no rent to pay, she could undercut the retailers and serve the smaller quantities to the punters, which they couldn't buy from the wholesalers.

Paddy liked the plan. He knew the game Sally was playing with the salesman, and knew it was being played with nothing but financial benefit in mind. And so it came to pass that in the early winter of 1887, Sally appeared on the streets of Newcastle for the very first time, selling whatever produce she could beg, steal or borrow. With no other overheads, it was a tidy little earner, and Sally had to travel no further than a few hundred yards from their home to set her stall out.

As Sally was with child, Paddy would pull the cart around to her pitch on Newgate Street, where she would peddle her wares until she cleared the boards then push the empty cart back home, on the odd occasion that Paddy didn't surface to do it. That happened from time to time, as Paddy spent more time in the city's drinking dens buying anything from bed sheets to curtains, wedding rings to pocket watches and anything else in between.

The going was good, considering the hardship of the times, and the pickings were often rich. But the garden rarely stays rosy forever, and when some young boy burst into Simpsons Bar one bright, crisp February day looking for Paddy, the flaw in their business model became arrestingly apparent.

Sally had been nicked!

Obstructing the public highway and peddling without a licence turned out to be the charges. Understandably, the event didn't go down too well with young Sally, as she argued the point fiercely with the arresting officer, almost bringing the street to a standstill.

The die was cast. Sally's little plan was, as it turned out, an illegal activity. The very thought of arresting a woman for trying to earn an honest crust, especially one in her condition, went not only above her head, but vehemently against her grain. What harm was she doing? In *her* eyes, she was providing a service; filling a gap in the market and trying to earn a shilling. What compounded the situation even further, as she later found out when Paddy arrived at Pilgrim Street nick to bail her out, was that resisting arrest had now been added to her two other charges.

It transpired that the local authorities did not issue licences for street-trading in the city, due to some long-standing by-law, but would do so for sites outside the town, or itinerant peddlers. This was fine for hawkers like Paddy, or those happy to get by on an out of town street somewhere, but no use to Sally and her new city based scheme. This incident could have put an end to Sally's plan right there and then, however, such was her resilience that the arrest was to be the beginning of a conflict which would rumble on for generations between the local authorities and the Kelly family.

Sally was determined to carve out a living with her little cart. A brave and bold approach for a woman of her time, particularly one so young and fresh off the boat. This was a time in British history when women were primarily kept in the shadows. The suffragette movement was in its infancy and women were as close as we've ever seen in this country to being second-class citizens.

Unless a woman were an academic, from the upper classes, or cleaned for them, then often the only real profession available to the 'weaker sex', and recognised to be the sole domain of women, was the age-old trade of flesh. Prostitution: the oldest profession and one that was openly plied on the Victorian streets of England.

Sally, however, had ideas of an alternative street trade, and she was going to make that trade her own in this town. Her suppliers were on her doorstep, her punters lined the nearby city streets, and there was plenty of bunce (profit) in the game – particularly when she could charm a bit of gear from a gullible salesman. It was an earner, and she wasn't about to give it up. So, this game of cat and mouse with the authorities continued. Sally certainly wasn't the kind to roll over, and the powers that be had no intention of changing the law just to accommodate her. So, she went to work, sometimes without any aggro, but kicking up an almighty stink if she did get caught in the act, which wasn't too often as she quickly learned how to play the game. If she weren't actually serving, and so long as she weren't stationary when a copper rolled up, then there was little they could do about it. But having to shut up shop and move her cart every time they did show up was not just an inconvenience, it was a wee bit hazardous, especially for a woman in her condition.

Sally could have employed a toot, someone to keep an eye out for the law, but she was too frugal for that and barely earning enough as it was. But after having to push her loaded barrow all the way back to Stowell Street one morning just after setting up the stall, she began to reconsider the idea. An enthusiastic young bobby, the same one who'd pinched her before, knew how to play this game as well. She spotted the lanky streak of piss one day as he came down Darn Crook beside the Co-op stores, so she chased the punter she was serving, covered her wares with her shawl and started to move the cart from her pitch. This copper knew the dance. Some of the local bobbies were less concerned about her activities and would occasionally look the other way in passing, while she attempted to conceal what she was up to, knowing full well that as soon as they were out of sight, Sally would be back to graft. But this sneaky copper was onto her. As she pushed her cart away, he slowly followed in the same direction. So she continued. And he followed. He knew what he was doing, but so did Sally. If she stopped, this horrible jobsworth would nick her for obstruction. As long as she kept moving, however, there wasn't a thing he could do. He knew it, she knew it. And so the slowest police chase in criminal history unfolded, terminating in the back lane of Stowell Street. No words were exchanged until they reached the yard at the rear of Paddy and Sally's tenement.

'There you go, Sally. Back home safe and sound,' the copper sneered. She gave him one of her trademark sideways looks as she pulled the cart into her yard, and realising she'd lost this battle, sneered back at him with utter contempt, 'Thank you, officer.'

He doffed his hat and replied, 'Just doing my duty,' before smugly walking away.

Sally followed him out of her yard and into the cobbled back lane before yelling at the departing constable, 'A nice job you got!' she declared. 'You wanna go and catch some real villains'. As he looked back with contempt she muttered the Irish words 'Tuki-alla'. Our day will come.

The authorities had a battle on their hands with this young, fiery Irish girl. Not only was she an immigrant, and a pain in their arse, but she was a determined, driven individual and a real contradiction to the female gender of the day. She was bold, brash and spoke her mind. She was definitely not going to sit in the corner and play second fiddle to her man, or keep her mouth shut and do as she was told by Paddy or anyone else.

She was not a woman from the standard mould of that time. Sally had risked life and limb to get to where she was, and she wasn't about to be stopped in her tracks by this latest setback. She had no family here, other than Paddy, yet she was steadfast in her belief that she could make something of herself. The law was merely going have to get used to this little Irish thorn in their side because she wasn't going to go away.

What could never have been envisaged, however, was just how much of a thorn in their side her arrival on Tyneside would turn out to be. This pair of Irish chancers were on the first steps of a remarkable journey that would see their mark left on the city they now called home, for generations to come.

In the summer of 1887, Mariah Kelly came screaming and kicking into the world at the hands of a couple of maternal neighbours, as was the norm at the time, and by the following summer her daughter became a regular feature at Sally's pitch, wrapped up in blankets and placed neatly in a wooden banana box underneath the barrow.

Talk about being born into something.

The name Mariah Kelly would grow to become synonymous with the barrows throughout the city, and a name that would become revered, respected and reviled by many in equal measure. This little girl would grow to take the art of street trading in Newcastle to a whole new level.

All the while Sally sly pitched with her barrow, suffering the occasional pinch, which she now considered an occupational hazard. Paddy seemed to spend more and more time ducking and diving in the local pubs than he did out hawking, but still loved to get out on his horse and cart. Sally was bringing money into the home and, as a result, Paddy felt the pressure was off him a little bit. This was a big mistake. Spending so much time in watering holes frequented by many of the town's undesirables wasn't the ideal environment for a married man with a young family, at least not so far as Sally was concerned.

They had a son, Frankie, in the years that followed the appearance of Mariah; his charge sheet for theft later in life shows his year of birth to be 1896 however, there is uncertainty about the accuracy of this. Parents back then often neglected to register the birth of a child upon its arrival, sometimes months or even years would pass before they got around to doing it. So with unpaid fines building, Sally had much on her plate, becoming more and more frustrated with the situation, while Paddy was taking more time out and more drink in, becoming oblivious to much of it.

By the time Mariah was a young girl, she was regularly seen keeping toot for her mother and helping out on the barrow. Every now and then Paddy would take Frank out hawking, but more often than not he ended up in the boozer, while young Frank was sat outside like an anxious puppy. This became the subject of many rows, and Sally would remind Paddy at every opportunity that he lacked the virtue, in reference to his beloved book, needed to become the man he so wanted to be. He had ridden his luck and was starting to lose his pluck, and when Sally wasn't happy, she wouldn't hesitate to tell him that she had more virtue in her little finger than he had in his entire body.

After losing a third child mid-term, the cracks in the marriage were beginning to show, and Sally started to care less about her good old Paddy Kelly and more about educating her daughter.

He was happiest holding court in Simpsons Bar where the craic was good, the pickings could be had, and the drink was always flowing. He loved the merriment of the city bars, the characters that frequented them, and the fact that he had become one of them. Just as people were taking notice of Sally, he made sure that all and sundry knew who Paddy Kelly was. He wasn't a shy lad, and the bar would often be on wheels when Paddy took to giving his favourite song, to the tune of *Clap your hands for Daddy coming down the Wagon Way*:

I'm a travelling boy from Ireland, and I haven't got a job,
I'm hawking bits of pongo just to earn an honest bob.
I rise up in the morning, I get up with the lark,
And as I'm walking down the street, you can hear the girl's remark:
'Hello, Paddy Kelly! You're the apple of me eye.
You're a dacent boy from Ireland, there's no one can deny.
Hello Paddy Kelly! You're the apple of me eye
You're a harem scare'm, divil may care'm, dacent Irish boy.

It's fair to say he had a bit of a tip for himself, did Old Paddy Kelly.

Sally had been shrewd with the money she earned, and careful with how she used it, never having to break into her prized 10-shilling note.

Her presence on the streets of Newcastle brought her into contact with all walks of life. Some of her punters were well-to-do folk from Gosforth and Jesmond, the more affluent suburbs of the city; but she also rubbed shoulders with many of the less fortunate and down at heel. She would hear countless sob stories from hard up customers in the hope of getting an extra apple or a bigger cabbage when they spent a few pennies at her pitch. Everyone was 'at it' in one way or another, but no one was going to pull the wool over Sally's eyes.

What they did, however, was open her eyes to another potential earner. Sally began running a tic book from her pitch, loaning the odd penny here and there, a half-crown or couple of bob to people she'd got to know. She would get a little return of course but was by no means a shark. She knew, as a woman, how difficult it could be to manage a home with children and a man that wasn't always pulling his weight. On many occasion she would only take back in return from people the money she'd lent out in the first place, standing judge and jury over the severity of the borrower's plight as to whether or not interest was applied.

On the other hand, she knew she could rely on Paddy for one thing; he would give a proper talking to anyone who tried to have Sally over, or even a slap without a seconds' thought, only if she looked like getting bumped (not paid) and the situation required it, and only if the debtor was a man. The women were Sally's to take care of.

Sally and Paddy lived lives that gradually became more distant as the years passed. Although they were earning, they were by no means well off and, by the time Mariah became a teenager, Sally had put her out with her own barrow on Nun Street, by the Grainger Market. Their son, Frankie, had become disillusioned with life sat outside the bars, and the Devil found work for his idle hands. He ran with a couple of delinquents from the West End and got pinched a few times for petty larceny and theft. After a short spell in jail, long before approved schools and borstals were thought of, Frankie left the city for the East End and his family later moved out to the coast and lived in Whitley Bay for many years. Mariah, however, remained steadfast to her mother, and the two women were becoming part of the fixtures and fittings in and around the city at the start of the twentieth century.

The young pretender to Sally's throne was getting an education far more valuable than the stuff they were teaching at school, not that she attended much. She was never going to be an academic, no more than she was going to work in a factory or a shoe shop. Not that there's anything wrong with any of those career paths, but young Mariah was born into a way of life that was lived out on the streets, and one that required a particular type of education where survival of the fittest was the rule of the day, and the laws of the jungle applied. Maybe those early days in a banana box were a metaphorical clue to that.

By the time she reached her teenage years Mariah was a regular sight at the fruit market, as Sally would march the length and breadth of the place, striking deals with salesmen and making sure she got the best prices for what she needed to stock her two pitches. The nicking job was still an ongoing threat, and even by the age of 13, Mariah often had to hold the fort while Sally spent a night in Pilgrim Street police cells, or even a few days in Durham Jail, for outstanding fines. It wasn't that she couldn't afford to pay them. She simply refused to.

Sally continually pestered the authorities to be considered for a street trader's license but was constantly refused. This to her was becoming a pointless standoff: if it was about money she thought, then let me pay for a license? If it wasn't about money, then why make me pay a fine? It just didn't make sense to her, and she'd be damned if she was going to give up an honest living because the authorities didn't have the brains they were born with. In fact, if brains were dynamite, she would say, those useless bastards in the council couldn't blow their hats off.

So, Sally marched on. Her campaign for legalisation would gain momentum with her daughter. Young Mariah was picking up every trick of the trade and by her late teens was pretty much running the show. Long winters on the cobbles, cold nights cleaning celery in wooden barrels of ice cold water in the backyard, and too many spells in Durham were beginning to take their toll on Sally, not to mention Paddy who was enjoying city life in the town and all it had to offer. Mariah loved the man, as a daughter loves her father, but her view of men like him, her brother, and most of the company they kept, was one of growing disdain. If Sally didn't suffer fools, Mariah couldn't abide the sight of them. Not all were like that, but the wasters who would come to her mother, and later in life to her, to borrow a few bob because they'd blown the housekeeping money playing cards or pissed it spectacularly high against the wall, were beginning to scunner (repulse) her.

Where were all the decent people? Where were the nice guys? *Were* there any nice guys?

Billy Fleming was a nice guy: a mild-mannered gentleman, a straight-goer who tickled Mariah with his soft-spoken voice and humble demeanour. He visited her pitch almost every day to buy an apple, an orange or a couple of ounces of mushrooms. She would tease him about his meagre purchases and always ask jokingly if he was having a party. The jibe went over his head as he'd just reply, 'No.'

This tickled her even more. He was the kind of man that was everything Mariah wasn't used to, and this intrigued her. He was a handsome man, clean and tidy, and he seemed to be a gentleman; although as her father had always told her, 'You can never judge a sausage by its skin.', the irony of which wasn't lost on her in relation to her dad. If she were to judge Paddy by the cover of the book he held so much value in, she'd be a tatey field away from what the man was really about.

The sun was still shining as Mariah was packing up the pitch for the day in the spring of 1906. She'd had a good day, as strawberries were in season and she'd secured a deal for half a gross of Punnett's from the soppy salesman at Moody & Evans, managing to clear the boards before the day was done. She was reckoning up her change on the barrow when Billy Fleming rolled up. They chatted for a while and, out of nowhere, as if there was something more than spring in the air, she asked the man what his intentions were. Mariah wasn't one to beat around the bush, and her threshold for tolerating fools was lower than a snake's belly.

Embarrassed by her straightforwardness, Billy stuttered and stammered, and in a convoluted roundabout way appeared to ask Mariah to go out with him one evening, or at least that's what it sounded like. Mariah agreed to the awkward invitation and Billy was more flabbergasted that he'd actually asked her out, or at least he thought he had; or had Mariah manipulated the entire situation to get what she wanted? Either way, it was on.

Unbelievably, Billy courted Mariah throughout the summer of that year, and before the end of 1906 made a proposal of marriage to the fresh-faced street girl whose intoxicating lifestyle was everything he'd never dreamed of, but everything he fell truly in love with. Sally was pleased that Mariah had found a decent man, but had reservations about her daughter marrying outside of her own. People from different cultures can often clash, and what seems right in the beginning can often to turn sour over time.

'What's bred in the bone,' they say, 'comes out in the marrow' or as Sally would put it 'What's in ya, comes out ya!'

But who was Sally to pass judgement? She had married someone with whom she had a million things in common, and look how that was ending up. They say opposites attract, and if ever two people were at different ends of the spectrum, it was these two. Ultimately, one way of life would inevitably swallow up the other and, just like in the jungle, the strongest would survive, and that persons way of life would prevail. And if that were to be the case, then there was only ever going to be one outcome. Mariah had found the type of man she wanted, and would no doubt manipulate the situation to suit her desired result. The outcome would be the one Mariah wanted, whether it was her way of life or his.

Billy and Mariah married in the early part of 1907 and went on to produce seven daughters by 1921, losing two children to miscarriage along the way. The seed that Paddy planted under the stars and beneath the cover of a bow-topped wagon somewhere over the Pennines some 20 years earlier was now beginning to flourish.

With seven granddaughters in quick succession, like a bunch of beautiful roses, Sally predicted there would no doubt be a few thorns between them along the way.

MARIAH KELLY AND THE MAGNIFICENT SEVEN

Paddy was becoming content with his life in the city. Contentment is the enemy of ambition, and Paddy had all but lost the plot of his treasured book. In short, he'd ridden his luck, used up his pluck and lost his virtue somewhere along the way.

Maybe his Achilles' heel was that the sheer strength and fortitude of his partner had somehow made him feel less vital in her life. Or maybe, like his father before him, he just liked a drink too much. Whatever the reason, Paddy had seemingly lost much of his gumption. On one, less frequent day, working the Quayside Market – one of the few pitches he had managed to keep hold of over the years – he set off for home after finishing up, with his faithful old horse and cart, cracking open his silver hip flask of Irish whiskey on the way. By the time he reached the Groat Market, heading up to Newgate Street and back towards home, he'd finished the flask but sadly, he didn't complete the journey. At some point along the route, Paddy drew his final breath and passed away silently perched on his cart with the reins in his hands. Incredibly, this was how Paddy was found as his trusty old gallower (horse) instinctively made the journey home, calmly taking Paddy and his cart back to the family that awaited him.

His passing was mourned in a manner that reflected his chequered life, both as a character and as a father. A decent turn out on the day of the funeral, considering they had no other extended family in the city. A few attended from the fruit market, as well as a handful of faces from the drinking dens of the city. Although deeply saddened by his death, the hole Paddy left in his family had been growing for many years, and his absence certainly didn't create the inevitable devastation that usually accompanies such a sudden loss.

Sally had become hardened over the years and now turned her focus to the outright preservation of herself and her daughter. She had been the young girl from a staunch Catholic village in the bandit country, south of the Republic border, with a dream of a better life. Self-taught in every respect, with the belief that she was cut out for better things, she wasn't going to let Paddy's demise stop her. But by the time she had laid Paddy to rest, she was dealing with Mariah's impending marriage to Billy Fleming.

Reflecting on how things had turned out between herself and Paddy, Sally put up little resistance to the unlikely union, secretly hoping that Billy might bring a little calm to a turbulent sea. What she really felt was sorry for the poor soul. He had no idea what he was letting himself in for. Oil and water just don't mix. Oil always rises to the top and, in Mariah's case, Sally knew the man would get swallowed up.

Mariah Kelly was the image of her mother, long black hair as thick as a horse's mane, she had that same persuasive Irish charm, but with twice the front and half the patience. Her dry wit and fiery temper were legendary by the time she reached her late teens. She'd been born into a world where times were hard, poverty was rife and survival came at any cost. She had been given an education that wasn't available in working-class households, hers was an education that not even money could buy. Schooling only became compulsory in the 1890s, and even those that attended could never have hoped to receive the kind of tutoring she had been given by her parents. Mariah knew the game, how to play it, and wasted no time in rolling her sleeves up and getting stuck right into it. No surprise then, when the announcement of Sally's first grandchild was made within a year of Mariah being wed.

From the year 1907 right through to 1920, Mariah fell pregnant almost every year. By the time this cycle of motherhood began, she was already forging a reputation as a formidable character on the streets of Newcastle. Her mother and mentor had taught her everything she knew: a great deal indeed, but far less than Mariah would come to know herself.

As Mariah grew up alongside Sally on the streets, she'd had to learn quickly, and even as a young woman she knew that the trick to getting a shilling wasn't about working hard – almost all work on Tyneside was hard back then – the trick was to work smart. Although there was no denying that the game she was in could be tough, it certainly beat knocking her plug in for somebody else while living on the breadline; that was for mugs. This street trading prodigy had her sights on getting this game boxed off in the city.

Even though the trade she and her mother plied was illegal in the eyes of the authorities, and the occasional night or two in the cells was part and parcel of it, she had a self-preserving belief that she could change things. She could straighten this game out, just like the many salesmen her mother had straightened at the market, or the couple of decent bobbies that would turn a blind eye for the price of a pound of bananas. She was going to turn this barrow girl game into a family business.

The arrival in 1907 of Mariah's first child Sarah, named after her grandmother – even though Sally never used her birth name – signalled the beginning of Sally taking more of a backseat as far as the barrow business was concerned.

Billy Fleming worked in a nine-to-five position as a clerk. This meant no one was available to look after the child through the day. Mariah often took Sarah to work with her, and she too would be seen wrapped up warm in a banana box beneath Mariah's barrow, just like her mother before her. And so this went on with each of the girls that followed, and both Sally and Mariah were often seen out with a child apiece under their wing. Billy Fleming had succumbed to the pressure from Mariah to give up his tuppence ha'penny job and help them with the business.

He wasn't much use as a salesman; he just didn't have the spiel or salesmanship required to be on a barrow. But as well as helping with the growing family, Billy had a passion for horses and could drive a cart. They had kept their hand in with the couple of farmers that Paddy used to hawk for a bit of gear, and if Billy could go and source a bit of stuff before it hit the market, then there would be more bunce from it when they sold it on the street. More profit meant more money, and the difference would more than compensate for Billy's loss of a wage packet. Although they were earning, Mariah and Billy were by no means well off. She worked hard and paid a hefty price for doing so. She was raising daughters and put them all to work in the family business as soon as they were able. The Kelly girls would each be working away at their own wooden beer barrels in the yard, scrubbing, cleaning and washing the earth from heads of celery, ready to be sold on the street the next day.

They could be the happiest of times for this band of cheeky sisters, but they were the hardest of times as well. The fun wears off quickly when it's dark, wet, windy, and so bitterly cold that the water in their barrels became frozen solid. But this is what they did. This was all they knew, this was their way of life, and this was their family.

All the while, and even when heavy with child, which she frequently was, Mariah would patrol the wholesale market at St Andrew's as if she owned the place. Everyone there knew her, they had watched her grow up in the place. The daughter of an Irish immigrant; once a child clinging to her mother's pinny, listening to her negotiate with the salesmen, Mariah had grown into this astute and driven young businesswoman and mother. She would drive the hardest of bargains, but if they were soft enough to get caught for a tanner (tuppence ha'penny) on the price of a pallet of plums, then she'd be there to catch them out. Most of the salesmen had a great deal of time for Mariah. She was an excellent buyer, and a better payer, even if every time she had to part with money she made them feel like they were stealing her last penny. Her reputation on the floor of every warehouse preceded her, and only certain salesmen knew how to, or could even begin to, deal with her. Some say she commanded respect, but many knew she had earned it.

Outside of the market she was equally as well known around the heart of Newcastle. She was a familiar face in the town, as was her mother and her rapidly arriving children. Her regular punters had a great deal of time for her, and the more familiar ones would even turn to her for help when times were hard, which they nearly always were. Her mother had run a tic book for years, and Mariah had followed suit but, unlike her mother, Mariah never wrote anything down. She had a built-in ability to recall, calculate and regurgitate numbers with total accuracy. Before a salesman could reckon up her bill, she would tot up in her head and tell him exactly what she owed, to the penny. If a borrower missed a payment she would know it, without any records to rely on, and she'd quietly bring it up when next she saw them.

Mariah was firm but fair. She knew just how tough it was to raise a family, keep a roof over their heads and put food on the table. Her fairness was always appreciated, and as a result, she rarely got bumped. If she did, she'd have something to say. If that meant sharply warning someone that they were now taking food out of the mouths of her daughters - the same food she'd loaned them money for to put in the mouths of *their* children, then she would do so in no uncertain terms, but this happened rarely. In some cases, when she believed the oversight was genuine and the hard luck story was true, she would offer a period of grace, so long as the debt was paid at some point. She was firm but fair, and as loyal as an old dog, but God help anyone who dared to treat her like one.

Hers was a colourful life, and vastly different to that of most young women of the time. She met and dealt with all walks of life. From prince to pauper and anything in between, Mariah could hold her own with anyone. From shoplifters who'd head to the barrow if they had a bit of hoist to sell, to famous actors of the day who would be performing at The Stoll on Westgate Hill or the Theatre Royal on Grey Street. She even had a couple of regular punters who worked in the council, buying fruit and veg from a barrow that was deemed illegal by their employers. Unfortunately her face was equally as well-known at the city's magistrates court and Mariah followed in her mother's footsteps by serving time in Durham.

This life may have been colourful, but some of those colours were darker than most regular people would ever wish to see. The streets could be cold and seedy, while the mines and docks were harsh and dangerous places, but life behind bars at the turn of the century was a cruel and harsh environment by anyone's standards, let alone a woman. Most folks on Tyneside were rough and ready people with little in the way of comforts, either at home or in the workplace. The thriving coalmining pits, and the many shipyards on which Newcastle made its name were treacherous and often deadly, yet real men worked there, risking their lives on a daily basis to provide for their families. But few got to see the inside of a cell in Durham Jail. For most men, risking their liberty to get a wage was too much of a price to pay, even if risking their life down a pit wasn't. Hard and honest work was the order of the day for most at the turn of the 20th century, but Mariah knew that working smart was the order by which she lived. Even with the risk of occasional incarceration, her way of life offered more freedom, opportunity and at times more money.

Billy Fleming resigned himself to playing second fiddle to Mariah, as the oil had eventually risen to the top, just like Sally had predicted. Even Sally herself became more of a passenger as the years passed. Mariah instilled in her girls a particular set of morals, codes and principles, as well as a healthy work ethic, along with the importance of respect, all of which hold great value. She also taught them to understand that a little bit of skulduggery was part of everyday life, and that everyone was 'at it' one way or another in the real world; as long as there was some degree of honour to what they did, and no one was getting hurt, then bending or breaking the odd rule was just an accepted fact of their life.

Trying to get an honest living by carrying out an honourable trade that the authorities considered illegal was a bitter pill for Mariah to swallow, so supplementing it with the odd bit of shady business seemed justifiable to her. Why be scared to do something they might nick her for, when they nicked her for doing something that she shouldn't get nicked for? 'You might as well be hung for a sheep as a lamb' that was her view. At the end of the day, Mariah and her girls were hurting no one. Their barrows provided a service to the punters, and the money lending was more like a community service than shylocking as far as Mariah was concerned, so if moving on a little bit of hoist helped pay the blisters (fines) for working the street, then so be it. Not that she paid many fines. She used them to cover up the cracks of the crumbling plaster walls of the two-up two-down on Stowell Street, which she and her family now shared with her mother.

Mariah was an unfathomable character. Was she a hard woman, or was she a hard-working mother of a growing family? Was she, or any of her girls, a welcome addition to the city streets? Or was she a belligerent thorn in the side of the authorities? Did she take advantage of anyone, or did she help them when they needed it? Whatever she did, and however she chose to do it, she would be judged by her peers. Which side of the fence they were on would determine how they saw her. What people heard was rarely what they knew, and she cared as little about the judgement of such people as she did about those who passed the laws which judged her. She had no time for fools, yet seemed to spend a lot of her time in the company of men she thought were prize ones.

Many of the men she came into contact with were of questionable character; slippery salesmen, thieves, pick-pockets, drinkers, ponces, villains, the police, magistrates or even screws. Not a great selection. It was this very thing that first attracted her to Billy Fleming. He was everything that these men weren't, everything her father, brother, and their cronies weren't, and he wasn't on the 'other side' either. He toed the mark. He was there when Mariah needed him, and happy to stay in the background when she didn't. He wasn't a big drinker, he didn't lift his hands, and he certainly wasn't a womaniser. He was a devoted husband and father to his adoring girls, but the one thing he'd failed to do for Mariah was provide her with the son she yearned for. Mariah had lost the two she'd carried for a while, and this upset her deeply; she longed for a son and heir. But she had her girls,

Sarah, Eliza, young Mariah, Mary, Joss, Chrissy, and Bella, born between the years of 1907 to 1921.

These years spanned the Great War, and for so many men of Billy Fleming's age, the call of King and country beckoned. At the age of 29, Billy left Newcastle to defend his country.

'You should be here defending me and your family,' Mariah would tell him.

But Billy was a decent citizen, a civilian and soon to become a soldier, that was what straight people did, no questions asked.

But Mariah asked plenty.

'Why defend the King and country that sends your wife to prison?' referring to the 'fools' who made the laws that would see her serve time for selling a bit of fruit and veg.

'They're the dogs that take me away from the kids I'm trying to raise!' she would remind him.

'But they're the people that keep peace on our streets,' he'd reply.

'Archie Bell and Big Bobby Tulip keep the bloody peace on our streets!' she'd yell at him, in reference to two local hardmen of the day.

Billy and Mariah were undoubtedly from different worlds, and at times like this, she would wonder what she'd ever seen in him. But then she'd stop and consider the alternatives. At least she wasn't getting battered, Billy wasn't pissing money up the wall or handing it over to a bookie. He wasn't a bad man, and she was able to go about her business as she saw fit. Any other man, particularly the kind she encountered in her world, would hardly have been so reasonable and could have presented any one, if not all of those problems had she married one of them.

Besides, she was a devout Catholic of full-blooded Irish stock born out of the Provo stronghold of Carrickmacross, and the idea of defending the oppressors was a contradiction to her Irish heritage.

But she accepted her husband's belief in carrying out his patriotic duty and, in the summer of 1916, along with almost another million second-round conscripts, Billy Fleming answered Kitchener's cry for help and headed off to battle. He could've chosen not to if he'd wanted to, but it was Mariah who was the conscientious objector, not him. He had a duty, and he was going to fulfil it and Mariah wasn't going to stand in his way.

By the time Billy marched off to war, young Sarah, their eldest, was nine years old and already a regular sight at the city's fruit market, watching and learning from Mariah's every move.

She knew which salesmen were good to deal with, just as she learned which ones were the nauses (awkward people), the contemptuous pukes that had no time for Mariah's manipulative ways. She was learning fast and growing up quickly. Ahead of her years, she was a captivating young girl with long flaxen hair and a hint of Irish charm that her soft Geordie accent failed to disguise. Sally was spending more time loaning money and taking advantage of the wartime black market, as well as helping raise the girls: Eliza, young Mariah, Mary and Joss as she was known, never getting her full title Josephine. Mariah was now becoming the matriarchal figurehead of the family.

So much had this woman grown to overshadow the quiet man in her life that she was rarely referred to as Mariah Fleming. She was known as Mariah Kelly, and her daughters were the Kelly girls. Anyone who worked in the fruit market or frequented the streets of the city, would see the Kelly girls every day around the town; miniature versions of the two women that were their greatest influence. Like a mother hen with all her little chicks in tow, they would follow Mariah through the fruit market. They weren't like regular little girls, but they weren't street urchins either.

Mariah made sure they always had decent shoes on their feet, petticoats under their dresses and ringlets in their hair, which she would create with twisted rags if the some of the girls needed curls they didn't have naturally. They were always clean and tidy and learned to carry themselves like their mother.

'We mightn't have much,' she would say, 'but we've got plenty to look at.'

She was a very proud woman, and few women around the area carried themselves like Mariah Kelly. She dressed tidily for the day and appropriately for the work she did. Not flash, but certainly not poverty-looking and whatever she wore, she would always have her shawl and her pockets; hand-stitched, leather cash pockets, made by a tanner in Blackfriars, were tied continuously around her waist and woe betide anyone who put a hand anywhere near them, even the girls. She also carried a shillelagh, a small Irish stick used for clumping people, though she never had to use it to defend herself. She wasn't a movie star looker of the day, but she was a head turner. She walked tall, proud and straight. Her sturdy gait had developed over years of carrying her groceries on her head in a woven basket. She would tightly roll up some newspaper into a hoop and perch it on her head like a crown, on top of which she'd place an apple basket filled with whatever she was carrying. This was a seldom seen throwback from a time gone by, and Mariah carried it off with aplomb, much to the fascination of all around her.

One such fascinated individual was a young boy from over the water. Frankie was the son of Peter Hewson, a hawker and pedlar from a well-heeled family in Gateshead. Just like young Sarah and her mother before her, young Frank would accompany his dad to the market, learning the game from an early age. Raised in a large house called Hawthorn Villa in the Teams area; the Hewsons were shrewd people and not short of money. They had stables for their horses, fine-looking carts, their livery was monogrammed, and they even had staff, well, a cleaner really, but nonetheless, she was someone who got paid to help around the home. Peter Hewson would be a regular at the market just like Mariah, and they would often be in the trade for the same gear on a daily basis.

Sometimes Peter would give a little more than Mariah would pay for whatever the line of the day might be. The salesmen would play one off against the other, what they call a Dutch auction, in pursuit of getting the best price. If Mariah was trying to squeeze them on a deal, they would tell her Hewson had already bid more money and was happy to take the gear if she refused to up the price. If she didn't, she'd lose the line to Hewson, and she didn't like that one bit. Mariah encouraged the one or two salesmen she had straightened to make sure they put her ahead of Hewson in the buying stakes, and to mark her card about any handy stuff coming in. But as loyal as they might have been to her, everyone has a price, and she would not be pleased if one of her salesmen let a bit of cheap gear go in Hewson's direction.

There was no love lost between Peter Hewson and Mariah, and he would often be heard name-calling her to his son Frankie, painting the picture of a tyrannical woman who'd be better off at home looking after her children instead of 'putting the man out of herself' in the market. But this only served to intrigue Frankie even more. He would watch Mariah gliding through the market and was amazed at her balancing act when he saw her with a basket on her head. On more than one occasion he would, without thinking, be so captivated by her that he would wander away from his father's side and find himself following her around the market. He was spellbound by her, how she reckoned up so quickly, how she kept everything in her head, and how she treated people, as well as how they treated her.

Another reason why he would often slope off and tail her around the market was that she always had her oldest daughter in tow. Sarah was around the same age as young Frankie, and although there was some business rivalry between their families, he was in awe of Mariah, and fiercely attracted to the pretty little red-haired girl that shadowed this enigmatic woman.

By the time the war was over, Mariah had given birth to five girls, from the oldest, Sarah aged nine, to little Joss who, at the age of about 18 months, had spent many an afternoon in a banana box.

Billy Fleming returned from his post badly wounded and seemed even more lifeless, having witnessed so much death during the Great War and having almost met his maker on the field of battle. He'd miraculously survived a bayonet wound that cut him from the base of his spine to the nape of his neck; a war hero with little to show for it other than injury and trauma. Surprisingly, however, he and Mariah went on to have two more girls, Christina and Isabel before the end of 1921, by which time young Sarah had her own pitch on Nuns Lane opposite the Empire Theatre Hall on Newgate Street.

Sarah had just turned 14 and was running her own barrow in the city centre, exposed to the daily threat of arrest from an early age. She would work her pitch and take her sister Eliza, or Liza as she was known, to keep toot. She would be the one keeping an eye out for the law, sometimes perched halfway up a street lamp to gain a better view, and if a copper did appear Liza would give out *their* whistle to let Sarah know it was time to hedge up. 'Hedge up' is a term used by street traders; simply meaning to get rid of the punters and stop serving before the police show up. The 'hedge' was the crowd of gathering punters, and like it or not, they would have to up them and shift if they didn't want to run the risk of getting pinched. This tactic of having a toot helped avoid many a nicking, and the fines that came with them. But even Sarah, Liza and some of the other sisters did get collared occasionally; and just like their mother and granny, as they got older they'd do the time rather than pay the fine, even if it was just overnight in Pilgrim Street. It was a matter of principle and a battle of wills. Mariah Kelly was adamant that she would get the authorities to change their minds before she and her girls would change their ways, and as her family grew, so did her barrow girl business.

As soon as each daughter came of age, they were given their own pitch, selected ahead of time by Mariah, who knew the city and which streets presented the best chance of making money. Until that time, each of the girls would get their first taste of the game by keeping toot for one of their sisters. Not only did this keep expenses down, as no one outside the family was getting paid from their take, but it was also part of the education.

In the world she had brought her girls into, she had to make sure they learned all the survival skills they needed. Billy Fleming could instill a sense of understanding and compassion into his daughters, but the tools they needed to survive on the streets came from Mariah, and she taught them all well. So, as time went by and more pitches sprung up with a Kelly girl at the helm, toots became employed more often, as they would double up as a schlepper doing all the humping, fetching and carrying as well as pulling the barrows to and from their pitches.

Mariah had now decided to rent a warehouse at the back of Blackfriars, just around the corner from Stowell Street where they all lived. She was buying stronger in the market and supplying her own chain of barrows, ran by her daughters, and although she was concerned about the expense of the warehouse she knew she had to speculate in order to accumulate. They were beginning to get a regular income. The game, after the war, wasn't as hard as it had been during; however, they were still getting arrested, but that was now part and parcel of what they did.

Her yard at the back of their home simply wasn't big enough for her growing number of barrows, and she had to stable the horse elsewhere. Her increased buying power gave her more pull in the market, enabling her to step on the toes of Peter Hewson and the like, and she now had a home-grown workforce of the most trusted kind in the shape of her own offspring; so if she was going to grow her business she needed to make the move.

Renting a warehouse around the corner from her home made absolute sense to Mariah, and she'd be able to ply her trade in the surrounding streets. With three or four pitches between her and the older daughters, and more in the pipeline with the younger ones coming through, Mariah had the chance of earning a tidy living at this street trading caper. Yes, it was tough being up at the crack of dawn for St Andrew's Market to make sure they secured a line to go to work with. Neither was there anything glamorous about washing mud-caked heads of celery in the backyard on dark, cold nights in the depth of winter, and although they were at work in all weathers and ran the constant risk of getting lifted, it wasn't a bad life. A tough one maybe, and a risky one, but it was the only one they knew.

Sally had circulated much of Newcastle over the years and knew a lot of people. During a trip one day to Byker across in the East End, she met a friend who sold flowers on Shields Road. Sally mentioned that her daughter might be able to help set her up in the town. The seed was firmly planted. If Mariah could rent a barrow to this girl and serve her with the stock, she'd be copping on from both ends; supplying the gear and charging rent for the barrow. It's what we'd call a franchise today, and Mariah was cultivating the idea in her own small way in her mid 20s, almost a hundred years ago.

'There's no flies on you.' Sally would tell her daughter,

'Nah,' Mariah would reply. 'Just the marks where they've been.'

With so much going on in her life, Mariah spent less time with Billy Fleming and more time running the warehouse. He knew the girls, and even his wife, were referred to by the surname of their father Paddy, which did little for his self-esteem and probably sapped what little life the war had left him with. But they wanted for nothing, he made sure the stock got to the warehouse from the market; he went out hawking now and again and was a good husband and father. He knew that he no longer matched up to Mariah's expectations and hadn't done so for a long time. It felt like the only private time they ever spent together resulted in the arrival of another child.

Was this because Mariah so desperately wanted a boy? Was he now no more than the live-in-lover and father to her children? Was he the love of her life, or simply becoming a pawn in whatever game she was playing? Whatever he felt he was, he was to find out exactly where he stood in time, and no one could have ever seen it coming.

Frankie Hewson had long since struck up a friendship with young Sarah. The two had become pally during their early days following their respective parents around the market. They would laugh and giggle as kids at how their mam and dad didn't like each other. 'That flash bastard from over the water,' Mariah would call Peter Hewson. 'That Gypsy faced cow from the town,' Peter would call Sarah's mother. But like Romeo and Juliet, the love-torn offspring of two rival families seemed destined to be together. He wasn't a soppy kid from the school playground, and she was no Shirley Temple. They were products of a different mentality. Sarah had seen, with her mother and father's problems, the importance of 'speaking the same language' as the person they were going to spend the rest of their life with. This metaphor had literal connotations too.

Much of the vocabulary used by people like them was a mixture of rhyming, street or back slang, with a bit of polari, pig-Latin, Yiddish, Gypsy Cant or Romany thrown in; the last thing they wanted to be doing was having to spend their life explaining what they were saying to their other half every two minutes. If they both lived a similar lifestyle, then they'd both know what to expect from it. There would be fewer surprises, and neither one would be consumed by the other – precisely what was happening to poor Billy Fleming.

Mariah was lending money left and right, wheeling, dealing and picking up the rent on a couple of barrows while her growing breed of girls went through stock on the street like a plague of locusts. Business was good, and she was making the most of it. Billy had become lost in her slipstream, and she had become distanced from the man who'd failed to give her a son. She was a woman of substance with plenty of life left in her and no shortage of attention from anyone, male or female. Many men flirted with her and, more often than not, would be put firmly in their place. Many women wanted to befriend her, but her tolerance of fools hadn't softened with the passage of time.

More and more faces would land at her warehouse, where she now spent most of her time. Anyone wanting to speak with her knew where she would be. She didn't have to make herself busy around the drinking dens in search of a bit of swag to knock out like her father had done; the swag would eventually find its way to the warehouse. She had carts and barrows of all shapes and sizes, a stable for the horses and a makeshift office with a desk and a tatty old leather captain's chair next to the fire at the back of the building. Just the one chair, and it was hers; she didn't want loafers sitting around the place all day.

If someone landed at the warehouse they were either doing business, or they were working, not sitting on their arse. Stock would come in and out daily, and whether she rented a horse and cart to someone to go tatting with (rag and bones was always an earner) or rented out a barrow to a would-be costermonger, she was steadily creating her own little empire, just the way she wanted. She ran the show with a firm hand and liked to keep abreast of everything going on in the town. If she could get an earner somewhere, then she'd be on it. The comings and goings were constant, colourful and always profitable.

Every character in Newcastle probably had cause to visit her warehouse at one time or another, and despite all of her legit and not-so-legit activity, she still kept everything in her head, nothing was ever written down. Her daughters would be out running their pitches while she would be holding court in the warehouse and dealing with any rogue or tinker that came in to see her. In some ways, she was like a Dickensian character, a female Fagin in an almost romantic kind of way, with her girls out working the streets while she was operating from her back-street warehouse. The girls and her business were her life; although which order they came in was up for debate. But her marriage was becoming lifeless and along with work, educating her daughters was where she fulfilled herself.

But as her mother had always told her, 'what's for you won't pass you by', and during the summer of 1922, just months after giving birth to Bella, a big raw-boned young man with dark wavy hair and a cheeky smile turned up at the warehouse. Jimmy Cruddas, known as Big Tom, was a West End lad and a bit of a cheeky chap. He was looking to rent a cart from Mariah to do a bit of tatting. After introducing himself he tried to talk his way into some graft, showing a bit of initiative by helping her take in delivery while he was there.

She liked the cut of his jib, and he made her laugh with his cheeky chat. Mariah was quite taken with this young fella and felt something she hadn't felt for a long, long time. He'd relit a spark inside her that she thought had long since gone out. Was her life about to take a turn she could never have imagined?

Was this the arrival of her Artful Dodger? Big Tom, or had Bill Sykes just appeared on the scene?

JUDGE, AND YE SHALL BE JUDGED

The Kelly girls were a familiar sight in the city. Everyone knew about Mariah, the old girl with the barrows, and her young daughters who were following in her footsteps, and the girls enjoyed the bit of notoriety it gave them. Mariah was becoming a well-known face, not just in the city, but all over Newcastle, particularly the West End where they lived.

By the mid-1920s she controlled half a dozen pitches in the town, four of which were family-run, and a couple that she served and rented barrows to. She was respected by many who knew her, but also by many that didn't. Her frequent spells in jail were documented and talked about in the bars and drinking dens of the city, as well as the wings of Durham Jail. She was becoming an infamous character in more ways than one and, just like Sally, she knew the value of a penny, and more importantly, how to get one. She also knew that if she looked after them, then the pounds would take care of themselves. She hated breaking into a note, a throwback from her mother, who to that day still had the half quid note she boarded the Albert with. It was one of the only things that Sally could always put her hands on, without having to think about where it was.

Sarah had started meeting up with Frankie Hewson on the quiet, and the two were getting along famously, despite their family rivalry. They weren't so sure it would be all the same if their parents found out about them however, but for the time being that didn't seem to matter. The younger girls were growing up fast and learning the ways of the street from their mother, granny and older sisters. As well as Sarah, both Liza and young Mariah now had their own pitches; Liza on Percy Street and Mariah on the corner of Clayton Street and Fenkle Street near the Central Station. Old Mariah would occasionally work her own pitch on Newgate Street but began to spend more time at the warehouse, letting Sally run her pitch whenever she was able. Sally, now in her late 50s, was white-haired, weather-beaten and growing weary.

Early signs of what we now know as dementia were starting to appear, although no one around her understood this. The young Kelly girls thought their granny was hysterical when she kept on forgetting things and talking nonsense every now and then. Mariah, on the other hand, just thought her mam was growing old and forgetful. The realisation that it was a little more serious dawned on them when Sally simply abandoned Mariah's pitch one day. She'd been talking to a punter and commented on the woman's lovely shawl. The punter told Sally that she'd bought it at Fenwick department store, not far from where they stood. Keen to go and get one for herself, Sally headed off in the direction of Northumberland Street in search of the shawl, without a second thought, and completely abandoned the pitch. This wouldn't have caused nearly as much fuss, had she not left baby Bella in a box underneath the barrow.

Billy Fleming was doing what he could, when he could, like the decent man he was, but his get up and go had got up and gone a long time ago. Serving in the army had given him some kind of purpose for a while, but he'd certainly paid the price for that. Like so many men in the prime of their lives who'd seen action on the fields of Flanders, he carried the physical and mental scars of war.

His girls were growing up fast and were caught in their mother's wake. They were young, strong independent women, and some of the older ones were already attracting male attention. Billy hoped they'd pick the right kind of men who'd be able to deal with the type of women they were sure to grow into. He knew first-hand what life was like in the shadow of a Kelly girl, he'd married the boss of them all, and he pitied any poor fella that wasn't up to the job.

Despite his time at war, Billy Fleming had maintained all the qualities Mariah had first seen in him and he remained the quiet, unassuming gentleman she'd met 20 years earlier, yet now she had somehow become disenchanted with him. Secretly, she'd hoped that Billy would have had more of an influence on her life. She had initially believed that this man, being from a different mould to the spivs and wide-boys she'd encountered all her life, would hopefully have changed her view of the opposite sex, but it hadn't. Something was missing and had been for a long time, and it wasn't just the son she yearned for. Maybe if they'd produced a boy, he might have grown into the son of her dreams: the ideal man, a product of a shrewd fiery Irish matriarch and a civilised gentleman with a formal education. That might have been enough, but she would never live to know that, and neither would Billy Fleming. Despite her hopes for a son, or even a husband who may have restored her faith in men, she now found herself wishing that Billy Fleming had a little bit of devilment in him. A hint of roguish charm that would have kept her on her toes, a little bit of rough about him; in fact all the things she hadn't wanted two decades earlier. But, that wasn't the case, and she had just gotten on with her life, and her Catholic upbringing made sure she got on with her marriage.

But her life was far from over, and as her mother would always tell her, 'What's for you won't pass you by'. The year was 1926 and Mariah's warehouse was a hive of activity, and the go-to place if you wanted a quick shilling.

Most things could be bought or sold there. A man could get a day's work with a handcart and a bit of gear, or a horse and cart if they wanted to do a bit of hawking or tatting. Around that time, one such likely lad rolled up at Mariah's door with his two sisters, all looking to go to work. They were fresh out of the Mile End Road in London's East End. They had been street traders down there but left London during the Great War and, after moving around for a while, ended up in Newcastle.

They were looking to rent a barrow from Mariah, or anything else that might be available so they could go to work. They would frequently call in to Blackfriars, sometimes getting a start and sometimes missing the boat, but the boy Maurice – Morry as he was know – began to be a regular visitor at the warehouse, feeling at home in this hustling environment. His slight cockney accent was the subject of much piss-taking and imitation, usually not the most flattering, and mostly by lads that hung around the place. He took it all in good humour, telling them that he at least spoke the Queen's English, not the German/Scotch sounding Geordie cobblers that came out of their mouths. He was a lairy little geezer, a proper cheeky cockney chappy, and Mariah liked his style. She had also been keeping an eye on her firstborn, Sarah; a beautiful young woman with a mane of auburn hair and an elegant way about her.

Mariah knew that Sarah and the young pup from the Gateshead firm had been friendly from the time they were kids, growing up around the market in the footsteps of herself and Peter Hewson. She had never disguised her contempt for the Hewsons and saw them as rivals within the trade. But she had a gut feeling that Sarah and young Frankie Hewson were still pally, and possibly becoming more than just friends.

The summer of 1926 was a pleasant one, and love, it seemed, was in the air. The memories of the Great War were just that and, although still fresh in the minds of many, a brave new world was coming out the other side of it. Times had changed rapidly since the turn of the century, and the results of the industrial revolution were now beginning to filter into everyday society. Motor cars were starting to appear more frequently on the streets of England, and electricity was reaching more and more people, even in parts of Tyneside. In fact, one of the most critical developments in the history of modern life took place there as Newcastle became the very first city in the world to be lit with electric light bulbs. The light bulb factory at Benwell, in the city's West End, was the first of its kind in the world. Mosely Street, not half of a mile from the warehouse, was the first street in the world to be lit up by such bulbs. The light bulb had been invented by a Sunderland lad, Joseph Swan, about a year before Thomas Edison claimed to have come up with the idea. The city Paddy and Sally had chosen to take root in was witnessing the dawn of a new era. Just the kind of fertile ground for the entrepreneurial Kelly girls.

The shipyards and armaments works lay along the River Tyne, to the West End and Elswick, close to where they lived. Vickers-Armstrong and Parsons, the steam turbine plant in the East End, were both building ships and powering stations for the rest of the world. The coal mines and pits of Newcastle were heating homes and firing furnaces all over the country, a couple of them at Gallowgate and Pitt Street were just a stone's throw from Mariah's warehouse. And the world famous Tyne Bridge was about to begin construction just half a mile away.

All of this was going on under Mariah's very nose, and it smelled good. Working people were beginning to feel the benefit of Newcastle's industrial success, and Mariah had to capitalise on this economic shift.

The town was always busy, people had a bit more money to spend, and Mariah and her girls were waiting on the streets to help relieve them of it. Exotic fruits were coming into the country more frequently now, and stuff was landing on the warehouse floors of the fruit market, the likes of which most people had never seen before, let alone handled. Full fresh pineapples, passion fruit, watermelons; all manner of weird and wonderful produce was becoming readily available, things that Mariah could charge well for on the barrows, as long as she could manage to get her hands on them at the market.

It was on one such day around that time, having lost out on a load of Costa Rican pineapples to old Peter Hewson, that Sarah decided to front Mariah up about her relationship with her rival's son. Had she known her mother had been gazumped by her boyfriend's old man that day, then she might've chosen another time to drop the bomb, but she had no idea. What she *did* know, however, was that Mariah had gotten wind of her friendship with the 'flash bastard's' son from over the water, and Sarah knew that she'd be better off fronting her mother about her clandestine relationship with Frankie than letting Mariah get to find out from someone else.

'I wouldn't like to think so,' Mariah sneered as she gave Sarah one of her Old Sally's sideways looks; a look Mariah had now developed into a trademark expression of contempt.

'No lassie o' mine is gonna have anything to do with that old bastard!' she exclaimed.

'He's the same age as you,' Sarah stated innocently.

'Ah don't care how old he is! No lassie o' mine!' Mariah didn't even need to finish the sentence.

But Sarah was a smart young woman in more ways than one, and confidently stated, 'Well this lassie of yours is mother, and he's coming here to see you tomorra.'

Raising her eyebrows in disbelief, Mariah said inquisitively. 'Coming here to see me, is he?' She was getting wound up by now.

'Frankie, mother. Not his dad,' Sarah pointed out patronisingly. Mariah glared at her daughter.

'Get out me sight,' she barked.

'Please ya self mother,' Sarah replied, very matter of fact, as she turned and headed out of the warehouse.

It was all too much for Mariah. 'Silly little woman,' she thought, before yelling, 'Gedd'aahdovit!' in Sarah's direction, flinging a peach the size of an October cabbage at her. It hit the wall right above her head, bursting to pieces. Sarah continued gracefully through the double doors of the warehouse and out on to the lane, without so much as batting an eyelid.

'This is bonny,' Mariah continued to mumble to herself as she reached for her snuff, something she had started to use regularly. She continued to grumble and curse away to herself when out of the corner of her eye she noticed someone walking through the doors her daughter had just swanned out of. She thought that Sarah had come back, so she straightened herself up with a start, ready for round two.

But it wasn't Sarah. It was Big Tom.

This well-built bruiser from the West End was looking for some work. Like everyone else who didn't shovel coal or pop rivets for a wage, he knew about Mariah, and how she might be in a position to help him out if he needed a shilling. Hoping to hire a pony and trap to go tatting, Big Tom tried to sweet talk Mariah, who was ten years his senior. She was having none of it at first, still boiling from the argument she'd just had with her daughter. But as he busied himself helping unload a delivery from the market, she began to take stock of this young charmer.

He had a way about him. He carried himself well and wasn't a bad-looking fella. Rough around the edges and a little bit lairy, but not the usual wide boy type that rolled up to the warehouse, and certainly nothing like Billy Fleming.

Mariah had nothing for him that day, but she could tell he had something about him, so told him to come back tomorrow and she'd sort something out. The truth was, whether she had something for him the following day or not, she was keen to see Big Tom again.

As he left the warehouse, Mariah sat herself down in her rough old captain's chair and took out the old silver hip flask she kept in the drawer of the desk, the same one her father had in his hand when his horse brought his lifeless body home from the Quayside. She felt like she needed a drink, her head was swimming. Not so much with the bombshell Sarah had dropped on her, or the fact that she'd been outbid by Old Hewson at the market, or that she'd nearly taken her daughter's head off with a giant peach – she'd almost forgotten about all that. Her head was awash with how she was feeling about this young chancer.

'Silly old cow,' she muttered to herself as she took a sip from the cut and carved hip flask, trying to rationalise what she was thinking. She looked toward the doors as the sun shone through them, noticing the splatter of flesh on the wall from the peach that could have taken the head clean off her daughters' shoulders. She shook her head, looked at the pretty hip flask on the desk and, picking it up again muttered to herself, 'Silly old, stupid old cow,' before taking a second nip.

Mariah was by no means a regular drinker, she was a staunch Catholic and a devout churchgoer. She had a sharp tongue but not a foul mouth. She was God-fearing and principled. She attended mass almost every day and paid her tithe; a percentage of income donated to the church, usually by the most devoted parishioners. It is practically an outdated custom now, but strong practicing Catholics would pay a tithe to the church religiously. She always accepted the body of Christ during mass and repented her sins every week.

The local clergy were on first name terms, and the parish priest was a frequent visitor to Mariah's home, which was where her weekly confession took place. And as luck would have it, she was due such a visit that evening. Perfect timing. The Lord works in mysterious ways.

Mariah needed to talk to her clerical confidant. She needed spiritual guidance. The events of her day had given her much to consider, and direction from the church was exactly what she needed. As long as that direction was the one Mariah wanted to go in.

Father Michael Flynn, from St Mary's Cathedral, the family's parish church, was a wily old soul. He was a trusted friend and a respected man of the cloth, yet wise enough that he understood the ways of the world. He had blessed each of Mariah's pitches, as well as her home, and was vocal about her harsh treatment at the hands of the law. He liked a drink, smoked like a trooper, swore like a sailor, and forgave Mariah every one of her moral indiscretions, not least of all because he never left her home empty-handed.

She was sat by the fire in the front parlour of her home on Stowell Street when Father Michael arrived. Chasing Bella and Chrissy out of the room to allow some privacy, Mariah poured the priest a drink as they sat by the warmth of the coal fire. Mariah had a tankard of stout by the hearth, which she drank each night habitually. The house smelled of good home cooking and freshly baked bread, just as it always did, something Father Michael would remark upon every time he came to visit.

Despite everything else Mariah did, she cooked proper food, every single day. Full-blown dinners of oxtail, or cow heel and black pudding pies, baked herring, pans of broth, Irish stew, legs of lamb and ham shanks, with every fresh vegetable imaginable. Homemade rice, bread and butter puddings, pies and tarts of every description were commonplace in the Kelly household. Foods that most families of the day might enjoy once a week were prepared and consumed daily in Mariah's kitchen.

No expense was spared when it came to food. It helped of course that they had access to every conceivable fruit or vegetable available, and most of the other ingredients were bartered for in exchange for surplus stock, or came off the back of someone's lorry. She would bake bread three times a week using two stone of dough on the table in her scullery. Her girls would watch and learn, while the older ones, who'd seen it all before, would laugh among themselves, knowing their mother took great satisfaction in the process of punching the granny out of the stuff. She gave vent on the defenseless mass and, every Monday, Wednesday and Friday, Sarah, Liza and young Mariah would know that their mother was 'stuck into it' in the scullery, having a good old 'paggar' (fight) with half a ton of dough: Irish anger management.

The old priest sipped his whiskey as they talked of all things Holy and Irish for a while; they loved a bit of rebel craic. He'd ask Mariah how she was, and she'd give her usual reply.

'I'm alright Father,' she would say, with a wink of an eye. 'At least 'til the doctor sees me.'

Mariah would take the poker from the fire and dip the red-hot end into her tankard of stout sitting on the hearth. It fizzed and hissed, as it always did, as Father Michael watched the unusual ritual.

'T'will warm the very cockles of your heart, Mariah,' he'd say.

She had strange ways and old-fashioned antics and clearly believed there was some nutritional value in heating up her stout this way.

'Aye,' she would answer as she took a sip. 'As long as it doesn't put hairs on me chest.' Rapier wit was never far from her lips.

On this occasion, however, Mariah had much to confide in Father Michael, and the talk soon turned to the things that were troubling her. The fact that she was unhappy about her firstborn's involvement with her rivals from Gateshead; was it right to feel that way? Or should she be happy for her daughter? After all, Frankie Hewson was no slouch. He was a smart young man. He always wore a suit with collar and tie, a nice trilby hat and boots so highly polished she could see her face in them. He wasn't a straight goer, and so understood their way of life. He knew how to get a shilling and, if his old man was anything to go by, he'd be a good provider; an admission she made reluctantly to the listening priest.

'He drives a motor, the boy!' she exclaimed. 'And to top it all, he's got a look of Spencer Tracy!' as if that was the deciding factor.

She knew she didn't want Sarah, or any of her girls for that matter, marrying the kind of man she had. Billy Fleming had never brought a day's darkness to her door, but as much as she loved the man, there hadn't been many bright lights either. The straight-and-narrow type just didn't fit in with the Kelly way of life, and she could bear witness to the fact. But why the Hewsons?

'Like attracts like, Mariah,' Father Michael advised. 'And you've just given me the best argument in the world for the two of them getting together.'

Mariah had to concede that, all in all the priest was right, and it was merely her contempt and pride that poisoned her attitude towards her daughter's suitor. Perhaps she would just have to swallow that pride, for the sake of her daughter, and the fear that her objections might drive Sarah into his arms all the quicker.

But what of Mariah's primal awakening? What about Big Tom Cruddas? This was a horse of a different colour altogether. How could it possibly be right for a woman, in her mid-life years, to have her head turned by a virtual stranger? He was a man almost ten years her junior, and her a married woman and mother of seven? This was a tricky situation and, for Sarah and Frankie Hewson, it couldn't have been better timed.

Big Tom's appearance on the scene completely took the dairy (attention) off the two of them. The tricky situation, however, wasn't nearly as tricky as Father Michael. He didn't know quite where to go with this shock revelation from Mariah. He needed time to consider it, and she needed time to let her feelings pass, he told her. So he gave her three Hail Mary's and a couple of Our Fathers for her penance and said he'd return the following Friday to discuss it further, if she still felt the need.

Father Michael was taken aback by what he'd heard and felt it was time to make his departure; allowing him time to absorb her confession completely, and a chance to build his sermon for Sunday around the mortal sin of adultery. That's why sermons often sound like they are directed specifically to individual members of a congregation – the priests know what's on people's minds because they've heard all of their confessions – it's the oldest trick in the book. Besides that, Father Michael was keen to see what he'd be taking away from the Kelly home on this visit, and so declared that he had to be off to tend to other members of his flock.

Mariah loaded him up with tins of fruit, loaves of freshly baked bread, half a dozen eggs and a couple of roll mop herrings – it was never meat on a Friday: flesh of the Lord and all that. He always left her home a happy and contented shepherd, heavy-laden with a plentiful bounty and never asking where half the stuff came from. He would turn a blind eye to Mariah in light of her generosity to both him and the church, and judgement was not his to make, but that of Our Lord. He had done his job and eased the burden of one of his flock – as well as his conscience – in exchange for a bundle of swag, and Mariah was only too happy to pay the price for her private weekly audience and absolution of her sins.

Frankie Hewson, true to his word, landed at the warehouse the next day. He came alone, not wanting Sarah present in case things got heated; he didn't want his girlfriend to see him get a possible dressing down from her mother. Nor did he want Sarah to see him give Mariah a piece of his mind if indeed it came to that. The encounter was surprisingly civilised, probably as a result of her chat with Father Michael. Frankie offered his respect all the same and told Mariah that he saw a lot of her in Sarah and that he'd always thought highly of Mariah, regardless of what his father had to say; he never judged a sausage by its skin, something Mariah related to.

Mariah knew he was a money getter, and therefore would never look to rely on any of what she'd earned; a prerequisite for any man her daughters got involved with. Frankie, by the same token, had no designs on Mariah's, or her daughter's money; of which Sarah was certainly not short, thanks to her own prolific money-lending activities. His family had apparent wealth, Frankie had his own car from the age of 14 and he knew how to make a living without putting his hand out or having to put a haversack on his back. He and Mariah were never going to be the best of friends, opposing parents would make sure of that, but at least the honourable thing had been done and mutual respect was good enough for now.

And so it came to be, that Sarah Kelly – or Fleming to use her birth name – the barrow girl granddaughter of an Irish tinker and a Gypsy hawker, daughter of a direct rival to her boyfriend's father; and Frankie Hewson, the son of a horse dealing hawker from the wrong side of the river, became the first of many colourful matches that the Kelly girls would go on to make.

Sarah had teamed up with someone cut from a similar cloth to her, a recipe she believed would result in a future that would be more of a partnership than a contest. At least that's what she hoped, and after seeing what had gone on between Mariah and Billy Fleming, she was confident that she had made a good choice. The Spencer Tracy resemblance didn't do any harm either.

QUEEN OF THE BARROWS

Big Tom had got his foot in the door at the warehouse. He was the muscle around the place and soon became part of the fixtures. It was handy to have a strapping man around, for as game and fearsome as Mariah was, she was still a woman, and all walks of life could turn up at her warehouse. Big Tom used to carry a bullwhip, strapped to his side like an early day Indiana Jones. He often used it to entertain kids in the lane and to keep the gallowers in check, but horses and children weren't the only ones who got to see him use it. He was a rough and ready fella, and if he didn't spark someone with the first dig, which was usually the case, he'd think nothing of giving them the lickings of a dog with his whip if the situation called for it.

Chancers would walk by the warehouse now and again, little toerags from outside the town. Very few people who lived in the city would dream of taking a liberty with Mariah or any of her girls, even before Big Tom was on the scene. If Big Tom caught any little scallies skulking around the warehouse, he'd crack his whip to chase them off or wrap it around their neck if he found them trying to steal something. If the loafers were there to buy a bit of gear or sell a bit of stuff then they'd be asked inside, and as long as it wasn't something stolen from a home, something personal or of sentimental value, then they might have some trade and be made welcome.

But if they had designs on stealing from the place it was a different story altogether, and with Big Tom on the scene, God help the hapless mug who thought he could thieve from their warehouse.

Sarah was seeing more and more of Frankie as he was often seen at Blackfriars, seemingly spending most of his time on the Kelly's side of the river. He enjoyed the comings and goings that took place at the warehouse and even started to get on the better side of Mariah. He had a keen eye for jewellery, bits of which sometimes found their way to the warehouse, and Frankie clearly knew what he was talking about when it came to a bit of tomfoolery. He impressed this upon her one day while there to pick up Sarah. A local thief scurried into the warehouse looking for Mariah. He was known to them, so he was invited in. He asked if Mariah could do anything with a silver pocket watch he had nicked from a flash jeweller's shop in Durham.

He was asking too much money for it as far as Mariah was concerned, and she bid the little villain pennies for it, assuming he'd take her hand off as they usually did. He wasn't having any of it, however, and insisted it was worth a few bob. She'd made her bid, and he could take it or leave it. Not impressed with her paltry offer, he picked up the timepiece and headed off out onto the lane. Frankie bottled him off (followed), and when he caught up with him outside, he asked to see the watch. As soon as he opened the case and took a look inside he knew it was a good'un. He produced an eyeglass that he always carried, handy for just such an occasion, and took a closer look.

Recognising the maker's name as a high-class watchmaker in Bond Street, London, he offered the man double what Mariah had, but still far less than the fella was after. Two minutes later Frankie walked back in the warehouse with the watch. Mariah was none too pleased. Had he just stepped on her toes?

'Good kettle that, Mariah,' he pointed out, carefully placing the watch on her desk.

She looked at Frankie Hewson, thinking, 'The apple doesn't fall far from the tree, he's just like his old man.'

'No good to me,' she said begrudgingly, trying hard to conceal her contempt.

'Well, I'll have it if you don't want it,' Frankie continued, 'It's a Bensons of Bond Street, gotta be worth a couple a nicker.'

Her ears pricked up, but she remained poker-faced. Frankie picked up the watch, which she could barely look at and had hardly studied in the first place. She thought to herself, this Hewson's faced bastard is in my warehouse and still trying to step on me toes.

'I've got an old Frummer pal over in Bensham that'll give me 50 bob for that,' he said as he put the watch in his pocket. 'I gave the chavy half a dollar for it.'

Now, this when it was handy that they all spoke the same language. A Frummer is another term for a Jew, usually Hasidic or Orthodox; 'kettle' is a slang term for a watch, a 'chavy' is a boy, a nicker is £1, fifty bob is £2.50, and five shillings is 25p, or a 'dollar' to the uninitiated.

Even though she thought he was trying to be clever, Frankie was making all the right noises, and Mariah liked that about him, and she particularly liked the next sound he made. 'So I'll split the bunce with you, Mariah.' She was taken aback and suitably impressed in equal measure, half the profit on the watch for doing nothing, although her face gave nothing away.

'That'll do then,' she said, without batting an eyelid. Frankie turned to Sarah, holding out his arm for her to link, and the two walked proudly out of the warehouse, but not before he looked back and piped up over his shoulder again, 'I'll drop your corner in tomorrow, Mariah,' referring to her share of the profit.

Loves young dream eh? But who'd be next?

The rest of her girls were getting up in years now. Liza and young Mariah were in their late teens, and the rest were little women, 12, 10, 6 and 5 but all going on 20, or at least they were around those ages; it was never easy to know exactly. Mariah would often give one of her grafters the task of going to the registry office to record the birth of her daughters, and many a time the pennies they were given to carry out this duty would end up in the till of a bar, and the child would have no record of birth until this came to light, sometimes months or even years later. Half of them didn't know when they were born precisely; Bella never found out until she got married, having never been registered at all; quite a common issue back then.

By now, Sally was all but housebound as her memory was failing, and she was too much of a liability to be roaming the streets as she used to. Mariah was in the market at the crack of dawn, then could be found either on her pitch, at the warehouse or at home cooking copious amounts of food, baking enough bread to open a shop. Work, in one way or another, was her life. She had all but fallen out of love with Billy Fleming, and besides her weekly visits from Father Michael, and her hot stout of an evening, she was beginning to feel old before her time. She was never what you'd have called a real looker and rarely got the chance to get dressed up. She took snuff like it was going out of fashion and had a sharp tongue in her head.

So when Big Tom would pay her some attention, which he often did, she rarely thought anything of it and swiftly put him in his place. He had a cheeky sense of humour, and besides, what could a handsome young man see in this tough old boot? She was in her 40th year but looked at least a decade older.

Morry Sayers, the crafty young cockney who'd caught Mariah's attention, had been in and out of the warehouse many times over the summer, and she was sure he was sniffing around Liza. Everyone, it seemed, was having fun. The post-war years were happier ones for England, and Tyneside was booming in the years that preceded the depression. The brave new world her mother and father had come in search of was evolving all around her, yet she felt she was somehow missing out. Too consumed by work and money, she sometimes felt her life was passing her by. Billy rarely came to Blackfriars, he liked to stay at home or go out on his horse and cart, sometimes just for a drive and some peaceful time alone. That's how her life was, but at her age with a growing family, there seemed little she could do about it.

'If this cheeky Charlie gets fresh with me once more,' she thought. 'I'm gonna stop him right in his tracks.'

She had made her mind up. Father Michael, after much deliberation, had suggested that Mariah was going through the change of life. Her ideas or feelings about Big Tom were, he said, a chemical imbalance that would pass in time. They were not real feelings he advised her, and as a devout Catholic married woman, she would have to resist this false temptation and focus on what was real in her life. All well and good she thought, so she did just that in the weeks that passed. But Mariah had reached a decision. The next time Big Tom made any kind of advance towards her, she was going to see where it led. She was going to 'put the cock on him'; in other words do exactly what he wouldn't expect, and put him firmly on the back foot.

Big Tom was just heading back from putting the girl's barrows out at their various pitches around the city, part of the daily duties at the warehouse. It was the early autumn of 1926, and they were enjoying an Indian summer. Mariah had been at home, cooking after an early start in the market, and decided to pop round to Blackfriars with a bit of food for Tom. Sally was indoors, and Billy Fleming had decided to go for a drive.

He loved his horse and cart and would often take a drive through Gosforth, heading along the Great North Road, before turning back for home through Kenton and Cowgate, over the Town Moor, and back to the warehouse with his beloved horse, Kitty. He named her after his war horse, who hadn't been as lucky as him in Flanders Field. Kitty was his pride and joy, and she belonged to him and him alone. She was Kitty Fleming, not Kitty Kelly.

When Big Tom arrived back at the warehouse, he noticed the doors were open, and assumed Mariah must be there. He was taking off his hat and coat as he came through the doors and saw her sitting at her desk. Big Tom was not a shy lad, and such was his sense of humour that he continued to remove his waistcoat, flip off his braces and take the very shirt from his back. 'She's warm out there today, Mariah,' he said as he approached her desk, in little more than his vest, trousers and boots.

Mariah was very much a prude when it came to such public displays of flesh, but this time she said nothing. She had a plan.

If the lairy boy got saucy again, she was going to see where it went. She knew she was playing with fire, but she was feeling alive. This was entirely out of character and could all go horribly wrong, she thought. He's a good worker and handy to have around the place, but if this goes wrong, it could be red faces all around. Mariah didn't do 'ladgings' (embarrassing situations), avoiding them at all costs. But she was throwing caution to the wind, and as Father Michael had told her, it was the 'change of life' that was causing these feelings and not her, so really, she couldn't be held responsible for the outcome, whatever it turned out to be. Big Tom, however, knew exactly what he was doing when he perched his backside on the desk opposite Mariah.

'I'm sweating like a bull with this heat' he declared, wiping his brow and picking up a slice of corned beef pie she had fetched from home, wrapped up in a cloth on her desk.

Taking a bite, he asked, 'That is for me, isn't it?' knowing full well it was. This was all part of the game they were both now playing. Big Tom did this kind of flirting stuff all the time and knew he'd either get a bollocking for his cheek or just be ignored. He played the game with her, regularly. The only difference this time was that Mariah was playing a game of her own. She was always in control, even when he flirted like he usually did, because she was the boss, she paid the wages. And she was in control now. She could take his advances in whichever direction she chose. Even if it backfired she would tell him she was winding him up, in which case he'd probably just wind his neck in out of embarrassment, or she could take it as far as she wanted and still pull rank. He wouldn't kick off either way, he needed her and the money more than she needed him.

'It is,' she replied, answering his question about the pie. 'I just fetched that down for quickness,' she said, choosing her words carefully. 'I was gonna make you a sandwich, but I didn't know what you'd fancy,' she continued, leaving the door wide open for one of his usual saucy comments.

'You know what I fancy, Mariah,' he replied, true to form, with that cheeky smile of his.

'So you keep telling me,' she said, drawing him in. He was shocked by her response, more used to being told to shut up by this point, but not this time. He struggled to swallow his mouthful of pie, and before he could come back with anything, Mariah continued.

'In fact, you've been coming out with that nonsense for weeks now and not done a thing about it.'

She could hardly believe what was coming out of her mouth, and Tom couldn't believe what he was hearing, as Mariah was taking this sweating bull firmly by the horns. Getting up from her chair, she moved around the desk towards him, where he sat speechless, not knowing which way to take her.

'So, I think it's about time you either shit or got off the pot, Tommy Cruddas.' She had a lovely way with words.

She shuffled with her shawl as Big Tom rose to his feet, towering over Mariah as she neared him, her head just about level with his broad, sweaty chest.

Liza was at her pitch on Percy Street with her little sister Joss. She was fiddling away with a load of seedless oranges, six for a tanner. As Joss was keeping toot, she spotted Morry Sayers sauntering up to the pitch. She gave out one of their whistles and Liza looked round sharply, expecting to hear Joss yelling, 'Hedge up lively!' but Joss had a silly grin slapped across her face and pointed in the direction of the approaching cockney charmer.

He would often call by to see Liza, and they would laugh and chat about what life was like in London. He would tell her tales of the comings and goings on the Mile End Road and how just about every street corner in the East End had a barrow. The barrow game was a part of cockney tradition and Morry couldn't believe they nicked the girls for grafting one in Newcastle. Liza couldn't explain it either, all she knew was that her mother and granny had fought for years to get legal pitches and it had not made a blind bit of difference to the useless articles at the council.

He was always keen and willing to work, and he wasted no time in trying to draw the punters in by ramping up his cockney accent. Liza loved the sound of it and could listen to him all day. He even showed her a little trick he used down south. He pulled out a shiv (knife) and split a couple of the juicy oranges in half.

He then proceeded to squeeze every last bit of the sweet smelling juice over the rest of the flash of oranges.

'The smell draws'em in see,' he told her in his adorable twang. And he was right. The sweet aroma wafted through the warm breeze, and they could actually see people walking by the barrow then turning back once they'd caught a nose-full of freshly squeezed orange juice. Punters were being lassoed by the smell and hedging up around the pitch like bees around a honey pot.

Little Joss was watching all of this from her post, and even got sucked in by the whole scenario. She claimed she wanted an orange, having smelled the succulent juice, but Liza knew she just wanted to listen to Morry's cockney patter.

'You're nicked, bonny lad,' came a deep and sinister voice accompanied by a hand on Morry's shoulder. It had come on top while he'd been serving a crowd of punters and the girls were too busy watching him.

Liza saw what was happening and stayed out the way, holding onto her little sister and scolding her for not doing her job. Morry looked at her and shook his head, marking her card not to come over and get involved. The crowd dispersed, and young Morry was escorted away by two uniformed officers, who at least had the decency to let the girls keep their remaining stock and remove their barrow from its pitch. They knew whose pitch it was, and they knew both Liza and Joss. They just wanted the collar, and Morry took it like a man.

Mariah later discovered that one of the arresting officers had quizzed Morry, 'So the Queen of the Barrows is enlisting cockney spivs now, is she?'

Queen of the Barrows. It was a remark that amused her, and although it was the first time that title had been used to describe her, it wasn't to be the last.

Billy Fleming was making his way down Gallowgate towards Blackfriars to wash down Kitty and lock up his cart. The Libra sun was low in the sky and a tangerine glow hung over the city as he approached the warehouse. The doors were closed when he pulled up outside. He slowly climbed down from the cart, no longer able to jump down like he used to, and fumbled for his key. As he reached the double doors, he could see that they weren't locked. Somebody was obviously inside, so he pushed open the doors, and a beam of golden sunlight shone across the floor of the darkened warehouse.

Briefly, sun-blinded by the sudden contrast, Billy struggled to process what he was seeing. Were his eyes deceiving him? Was his war-torn mind playing tricks on him, or was he really looking at his wife – the mother of his seven children and 'Queen of the Barrows' – in a compromising embrace with Big Tom Cruddas?

FORGET ABOUT WALLIS SIMPSON

Frankie Hewson was now spending most of his time in and around Newcastle. He had paid his dues to Mariah with the Benson pocket watch and, although he wasn't her blue-eyed boy, there was definitely a mutual respect between the two. He had started to sly pitch on the corner of Nelson Street beside the city's Grainger Market. Morry Sayers and Harry Mouzon, a relation of Morry's, who's family also hailed from Londons East End, worked the same corner of that street. It was a busy pitch in-between the Grainger Market and Northumberland Street, just a few yards away from Grey's Monument; smack bang in the heart of the city, but not as hot as Northumberland Street for getting nicked.

Sarah was a fine, elegant young woman, and very shrewd. She worked her pitch on Newgate Street as often as she could. Sarah, it turns out, had been born with a hole in the heart, which was only brought to light as a result of a hospital visit. She'd regularly become short of breath and her lips would sometimes turn a dangerous shade of aubergine. She wasn't going to let this stand in her way, such was her determined mindset, and that of all the Kelly girls, thanks to the drive and education their mother had instilled in them. Sarah became an astute money lender, and a far more serious one than her mother or Sally had ever been.

She was also a regular at Miller's salerooms in Gallowgate, always on the lookout for a bargain or a particular piece she could turn over for a bit of profit. Her courtship with Frankie resulted in marriage by the summer of 1930, held at St Mary's Cathedral where Mariah and Billy Fleming had married, and Paddy and Sally before them, in fact just about every marriage in this family for the next hundred years took place there. All in the family were baptised into or buried out of St Mary's; hatched, matched and dispatched from the biggest Catholic Cathedral in Newcastle, only fitting for what was to become one of Newcastle's most prominent families.

Morry Sayers and Liza wed within a year of her older sister, and young Mariah and Mary were now young women with no shortage of attention from a variety of suitors, many with the hope they might wheedle their way into the Kelly clan.

The truth of the matter was, the Kellys were currently the subject of a great local scandal. People who didn't know them before were undoubtedly hearing about them in the aftermath of 1926. Forget about the Wallis Simpson carry some ten years later when the future King of the Country got involved with a twice married debutant from Pennsylvania. The 'Queen of the Barrows' was a big a deal in the West End of the town and beyond, and her marital decision making was every bit as scandalous in Newcastle at that time.

Billy Fleming's eyes had not deceived him on that beautiful autumn day when he and his beloved Kitty pulled up outside the warehouse. And the sight that he was presented with signalled the beginning of the end for this mild-mannered war hero. Not even the horrors of the Great War could have prepared him for that vision, and it was to be the final straw for Billy Fleming.

Whether it was the change of life or not, Mariah's actions with Big Tom Cruddas were to change the course of many of the lives around her and sadly bring about the end of her faithful husband's. Her tryst with Big Tom turned out to become a full-blown affair, much to the amazement of everyone in her orbit; not least of all her seven daughters who had always looked up to this strong matriarch, and adored their gentleman of a father.

Big Tom had lit a fuse, blazing a trail of destruction and division that would scar their breed for years. Whatever it was about Big Tom, Mariah wanted more of it, and with her lifeless marriage and desire for a son, mixed up with the physical and mental shifts that the change of life can bring about, her moral and emotional compass, it seemed, had become temporarily damaged.

She managed to keep her indiscretion with Big Tom between herself and Billy initially, trying to convince both herself and her husband that it was merely that, an indiscretion. But it turned out to be so much more. Big Tom was a vital part of Mariah's organisation, and she refused to let him go. She fought her feelings and struggled with her desires for months, receiving countless prayers of penance from good old Father Michael, who was hopeful that sanity would be restored in the fullness of time.

But before much time had passed, the unthinkable occurred. 1926 was all but over, and those aware of the impending situation were beginning to wish that it could come to a close sooner. Mariah was a practicing Catholic and contraception was never part of any physical relationship, marital or otherwise. So, when she made the earth-shattering announcement that she was again with child, it seemed the wheel was about to come flying off every barrow in Newcastle. Was this the son she had longed for? Had Billy Fleming, in a last-ditch attempt to salvage his marriage and his life, managed to produce another child, a son perhaps? Was sanity to be restored just like Father Michael had suggested, and prayed for religiously? Nothing and no one could have been prepared when Mariah announced that the child she was carrying was the actually seed of Big Tom's loins.

Shockwaves vibrated throughout the city amongst the people that knew her and her family, and they were plenty. Her girls were ashamed and confused, the younger ones in particular. Sally was merely confused most of the time. The older girls were embarrassed by the scandal.

Father Michael had taken to signing the cross on himself so much that the marks were visible, and poor Billy Fleming, the quiet, decent, honourable man that was father to these girls, had been tipped so far over the edge by the entire sorry affair that he passed away before the year was out. Many say he died of a broken heart. This may well have been the case.

Billy's spirit had long since been broken by war and the monumental Mariah. Battlefield injury had broken his body, so there was little left to break but the poor man's heart. The girls were devastated by the death of their father, and now the fella they had become accustomed to seeing around the warehouse, the man they had come to know and trust was now, to them, a different person altogether.

Was he no longer a friend? Was he now family? And more importantly, was he to become their step-father? Not if Sarah, Liza, young Mariah and Mary were to have anything to do with it. The younger girls were busy dealing with the passing of their father and for the time being didn't need to know the whys and the wherefores.

Big Tom had also fought in the Great War and served in the same regiment as a man called Victor McGlaglen, who later became famous for his role alongside John Wayne in the hugely successful film *The Quiet Man*. The very term used in remembrance of the man, the quiet, gentle man, Billy Fleming, whom Big Tom had so ceremoniously betrayed.

Billy Fleming was buried in the West End of the city, in a private ceremony attended by immediate family only. Her daughters consumed by grief, Mariah didn't want the recent scandal to overshadow Billy's interment. This was to be the only private funeral that this family would have for a long time. In the century that followed, the funerals of this family would be written about, televised, attended by hundreds and witnessed by thousands.

Incredibly, Mariah had decided that she was going to make a go of it with Big Tom. She could hardly disguise her predicament, and termination was unthinkable for this God-fearing woman. Unfortunately however, adultery hadn't ranked so high on her scale of mortal sins. The result of her actions rendered her incapable of taking Holy Communion each week at mass. All the Our Fathers and Hail Marys in the world weren't going to make a difference, not as long as the sin perpetuated. Her older daughters were vocally opposed to the unholy union and demanded that she take up residence with her fancy man away from their family home. She agreed, for their sake, and would eventually leave the older sisters on Stowell Street.

The younger girls were not to entertain Big Tom, by order of their siblings, and they eventually got farmed out to Sarah and Liza as they each flew the nest in turn. Initially, they all stayed together, but some of the younger ones were with family friends for long spells. It was a sad, difficult time for the Kelly girls. They were now divided in their number, but not yet as a family.

The winter of 1927 saw significant changes within this dysfunctional clan. It was almost as if a rot was setting in with Mariah. The fact that she couldn't take her sacred holy communion any longer hurt her deeply. Perhaps the absence of the Body of Christ inside her own body was leaving a space for the Devil to reside. Where there's a void, something will eventually move in. She was wrestling with many demons, and it came out in her with more frequency. The young girls would be encouraged by Mariah to be nice to 'Uncle Tom', but they were coached otherwise by Sarah and the older sisters. It was business as usual, but things were never the same. How could they be? Mariah had brought an uncomfortable spotlight on her family, but despite the impact on her girls, it only served to toughen these already hardened individuals.

Big Tom was now virtually running the warehouse. With Mariah expecting a child, and now in her early 40s, her tenth pregnancy in 20 years, including the two she had lost meant that the older girls in particular, had little choice but to see the man on a daily basis.

This wasn't easy for Sarah especially. Being Mariah's firstborn, Sarah felt the most betrayed by her mother's monumental indiscretion, and even more so by her mother's decision to embark on a relationship with Big Tom. This led to obvious friction between the two, as she had little time for the man that had not only stolen their mother from them but had, in her eyes, been largely responsible for her father's demise.

Mariah on the other hand, defended her actions at every opportunity, blindly loyal to her own sensibility.

To cow to public opinion or the aspersions of others would surely have been her downfall, and regardless of any wrongdoing on her behalf, Mariah would defend her actions to anyone daring to question them. Not that anyone did, at least not to her face; she dismissed all condemnation. Her chosen form of defense was attack. Whatever had happened, she could not lose face. She had to remain a woman to be respected at all costs, and her wicked tongue and fiery temper would go into overdrive if she thought anyone had anything to say about what was going on in her life. The line between respect and fear were becoming increasingly blurred.

After speaking with Father Michael, Mariah had decided that her best course of action was to marry Big Tom, albeit not under God's roof. That would at least take some of the sting out the tail of the gossipmongers, as well as easing her way back into God's flock. Big Tom, however, wasn't so keen on the idea. This surprised Mariah, but greatly angered Sarah. How dare this man rebuke her mother after what he had done? On one such day at the warehouse, Sarah let Tom know precisely how she felt. With her sister Liza by her side, Sarah questioned him about his reluctance to make an honest woman of their mother. His refusal to explain his decision, and his dismissive attitude towards his interrogators, incensed the flame-headed Sarah.

She screamed at him and called him from a pig to a dog, entirely out of character for this demure young lady. He just laughed and told her to go about her business and not interfere in his. But she persisted, as did Liza. They demanded an explanation. Tom was becoming irritated and refused to stand for the third degree from either of them, but Sarah was like a dog with a bone, and wouldn't let go. Big Tom eventually snapped, he wasn't known for his patience.

'Cos I'm already fucking married!' he yelled in her face.

There was a stunned silence. She looked at her sister, who stood wide-eyed with shock. Big Tom turned to walk away as Sarah reached into a stack of crates by the warehouse doors and, pulling out a beer bottle, proceeded to smash it cleanly over the back of Big Tom's head. Liza shrieked and went to pull her sister back as Big Tom spun on his heels and instinctively went for his bullwhip, pushing away Liza, who had jumped in between them.

'Touch that whip, and I swear to God I'll put the next one in your face,' said Sarah calmly, before Liza pulled her quickly out the doors and into the lane.

Bad blood was beginning to circulate, and the girls closed ranks. Mariah moved from the Stowell Street home, taking her mother, Sally with her. Sally's dementia was only getting worse, and she had little choice in the arrangement. The time before Mariah left home was a difficult one, but thankfully it was short. There was no mileage in prolonging anything, and with the impending arrival of Mariah's child to Tom, it was a case of the sooner, the better.

It was enough that the girls had to deal with their mother each day at work, let alone share a roof with her. And to make matters worse, having to see Big Tom at the same time served only to rub salt in the wound. The wounds were deep and very, very raw. All eyes were on them, wondering how they were going to deal with this scandalous situation. Was this going to be the ruination of this family? No men in the breed yet, to provide for and protect the Kelly girls, and no Mariah to rule the roost. Could they really hold things together? Was this going to tear their family apart? Or was it to be the making of them?

In the run up to Mariah's exit from the family home, Sarah, Liza and young Mariah would spend as much time as they could away from Stowell Street after work.

Sarah and Frankie Hewson were courting strong, and Liza and Morry would often be seen out with them, young Mariah even playing gooseberry from time to time rather than stay indoors while their mother was under the same roof. There was an unwritten standoff for a while. They all knew they had to somehow come out of this as a family, so they never discussed the situation for fear of bringing it all to an unholy end. She would be out of the home soon enough, and they could have space and time for their wounds to heal. Mariah had simply passed a point of no return where Big Tom was concerned. She had to be seen to do what she felt was the right thing. Two wrongs don't make a right, and that's how Mariah justified her choice.

Chasing him and having a bastard child under the same roof as her daughters seemed to be a worse option than leaving them all to start a new life with another man. It was a gamble Mariah was prepared to take. Perhaps she knew that her girls were made of stronger stuff than most. Maybe she thought it would only strengthen their already considerable resolve. Perhaps, she just knew exactly what she was doing. One thing was for sure, Mariah was in control, even in the face of such adversity. So, in the late spring of 1927, Mariah gave birth to her eighth child, her first out of wedlock.

Big Tom had yet to tell Mariah of his real reason for refusing to get married. After the incident at the warehouse, Sarah had struck a deal with him. If he were to move in with her mother, she would allow him to break the news to her about his wife, in his own time. If he didn't, she would let the cat out of the bag and let the chips fall where they may. Big Tom had a cushy number running the warehouse, getting involved in any deals that went on around the place, with a guaranteed income by the Queen of the Barrows' side. He may have even thought that he could end up taking things over instead of the girls, but that was never going to happen. The girls were dealt a further blow, when their mother decided to take up her new residence with Big Tom, moving into a house directly across the street from them.

This was enough to knock the wind out of anyone's sails. The rally of punches over the last year just kept raining down on the Kelly girls, but what doesn't kill you, as they say, only makes you stronger, and characters were being built that would turn out to be bombproof. Only Mariah would ever know if there was a method in her madness. But even if she didn't realise this would be a huge test of their metal, she did at least know that living on their doorstep meant she could still be watching over them; a possible act of veiled kindness and concern amid such seemingly selfish behaviour. She was desperate for a boy, and perhaps that clouded much of her judgement, so when Peggy was born, there was at least some balance restored to the situation. A son and heir would have put the Kelly girls in the shadow, even if Mariah's actions hadn't. There may have been a sigh of relief on the Kelly girls' side of Stowell Street, but if there was, Sarah made sure Mariah never heard it. Sarah was a perceptive and capable young woman. She had grown up quickly, in a world where who they were, what they stood for and how they carried themselves was everything.

Sarah saw it as her duty to show the watching world that the Kelly girls were not simply surviving this dreadful upheaval, but that they were stronger as a result; they had to keep face and remain united. They were respected, admired and revered by many, and Sarah would make sure it stayed that way. She kept on at Big Tom about sorting his situation out whenever she got the chance to. Tom, however, was dragging his feet. Sarah decided to do some homework and discovered that not only was he married, just as he had said, but he had two young children with his wife. What a scandalous situation this really was, and it was becoming more outrageous by the day.

A compromise was met. Big Tom would leave his wife and their two children, and reside under the same roof as Mariah, performing the duties of a husband in every other way until he could make an honest woman of her. He pursued a divorce from poor Mrs Cruddas, but she refused point blank. Inevitably, Mariah was made aware of Tom's wife and children and merely adapted the situation to suit what she saw as best for her, her girls, and her reputation.

She never stopped insisting that he badger for the divorce, but in the meantime, if anyone's family was going to be broken up by this affair, it certainly wasn't going to be hers. Mariah and Big Tom went on to have two more children together, and the sad truth is, they were only finally married when Mrs Cruddas passed away, denying him a divorce until the bitter end. She clearly had her own pride to consider too. Incredibly, this resulted in the marriage of Mariah Kelly and Big Tom Cruddas not taking place for another 30 years.

Stowell Street was now known as the place where the Kellys lived. A street that housed seven sisters fending for themselves on one side, living opposite the mother who'd effectively abandoned them to live with her fancy man; previously married to another woman with whom he had two children, yet had fathered another to Mariah. If they were a quiet, unassuming family that no one really knew much about then it might not have been so newsworthy, but everyone knew Mariah, and everyone knew the Kelly girls, and everyone had an opinion.

Those opinions were best kept to themselves or talked about only in conversation by outsiders and never with any of the family. In spite of everything, the Kelly's remained stoic on this scandal. Even in the face of such an earth-shattering event, one that might have destroyed any other family, it seemed to have the opposite effect on this breed, at least from the outside looking in. The girls would not hear of their mother being called by anyone, even if they criticised her to one another. And as for as anyone voicing their opinion to Mariah, if they weren't afraid of the dressing down she'd give them then they knew they'd have Big Tom to answer to, and that was deterrent enough for anyone choosing not to keep their own counsel.

Mariah continued conducting business from the warehouse, renting out a couple of barrows and supplying them with gear. Tom had a few regular tatters who would rent a horse and cart, and he would spend the odd day hawking. Sarah worked her pitch when she could and had her young sister Chrissy keeping toot, Liza took Bella to work, young Mariah took Mary, Joss would float from one pitch to another and thought she was the overseer, earning herself the nickname 'Joss the Boss'.

The younger sisters did attend school occasionally, so every now and then the older girls would have to work their pitch and keep toot themselves as the police continued to pinch them for plying their trade on the city streets, even though they were now running established pitches and becoming recognisable landmarks around the town. People loved to buy their produce from the girls. They knew they were hard working, they knew they were getting fresh produce at a reasonable price, and they loved the patter they would get from these colourful characters who were skirting with the law to provide their service. But the law didn't see it nearly so romantically. The coppers who loved their job would make a meal out of nicking any one of the sisters when they got the chance. They would be frog marched from their pitches and manhandled unceremoniously into the back of a police van, black Mariahs as they were known. In fact, many would refer to Mariah as Black Mariah on account of the amount of times she was thrown in the back of one. The coppers would confiscate the goods, compound the barrows and fine her for obstructing the public highway and trading without a license.

Fines were rarely paid, out of principle. When the fines started to mount up, or if any of the girls were arrested and had fines outstanding, it would result in a night in Pilgrim Street nick, or worse, a few days in Durham Jail. This only served to garner support for the girls and respect for what they believed in, as their plight and struggle for legalisation would often be documented in the local press, usually after Mariah had been locked up, or sentenced to a week in Durham.

Word of a Kelly girls' arrests would soon get back to the warehouse or the boozers frequented by friends of the family. A whip-round would be made to cover the fines and money would be sent down to the nick to get them released, but the girls wouldn't take the money; they'd rather do a night locked up than pay the fines. It was bad enough being pinched, but having their gear confiscated, having to pay to get their barrow back and sometimes being threatened with a charge of handling stolen goods because they couldn't produce a receipt for what they were selling, was seen as a diabolical liberty. It was a matter of principle, and the girls saw themselves as street suffragettes with a right to be heard, and certainly not deserving of the treatment they received by the oppressors who persecuted them so badly.

The fruit and veg the girls sold on the street was totally legit, but because Mariah had the unique ability to keep every transaction stored mentally, she would seldom ask for a receipt; everything went down in the salesmen's ledger as a cash deal, 'down to pal' as they would say. Why should she keep a legitimate record of her business when her business wasn't even recognised as legitimate? This also conveniently avoided any paper trail the tax man might ever want to get his hands on. She asked for nothing from the state, so she wasn't in any hurry to give them any of her hard-earned money paying tax or fines.

This was the way she saw things, frig 'em. That was her attitude, and that's the way she played it. It became a game and mindset that would see personal conflict between this breed and the authorities continue for generations to come.

AND THEN THERE WERE TEN

Peggy arrived in 1927, born across the street from her seven sisters to another mister. Sarah, Liza, young Mariah and the rest of the Kelly girls were managing to keep themselves well enough, and becoming more independent by the day. The older girls were all making a living, and they rarely went short, Mariah always saw to that. Sarah was a good earner herself, and with Frankie Hewson by her side she had a great ally, and would surely never starve.

Liza and Morry were as thick as thieves, and young Mariah had caught the eye of showman from Shields who had been chatting to them when they all took an annual trip to the Hoppings. This was a huge fair that converged on the town moor of Newcastle every summer, the largest travelling fair in Europe; a place where all the showmen would meet at the beginning of the summer season before heading off in all directions to fairs up and down the country. This historic attraction began its life just before Paddy and Sally arrived on Tyneside, and members of the family have always had some presence on there, working one line or another, even to this day.

Frankie and Morry were working there, and all the girls paid a visit on a balmy evening in late June, the week of the fair. The young ones loved the sideshows, like The World's Smallest Woman, The Bearded Lady and George the Gentle Giant, while they all blagged loads of free rides with the old 'pass a Traveller' spiel. A lot of the show-people would let someone ride for free, if it was a bit quiet and they said they were from Travelling stock, even though there is little love lost between show folk and Gypsies, so it was a great way of getting around the fair without spending too much money, as well as getting one over on the showmen.

The boxing booth was always a magnet for the local boys, and that's where Frankie and Morry bumped into Georgie Kelly, or Coronation as he was known. Coronation's family had shows down on the seafront, across the river in South Shields, but he often got into Newcastle, drinking in some of the same bars as the boys from time to time. He was a character, just like Frankie and Morry; people of a certain ilk will always gravitate towards each other. Folk like them could pick their own out in a room full of people, it's just how it is, and these three were all cut from a similar cloth. It seemed that the Kelly girls were only interested in the kind of men that their mother had tried to avoid in Billy Fleming; the straight-goers just didn't fit the bill.

These birds flocked together with men of a similar feather, men who were capable, sharp, determined and prepared to do whatever was necessary to put food on their tables. These were not nine-to-five people. They didn't look, dress or talk like nine-to-five people. They were wheelers, dealers, wide-boys and spielers, just the kind of chaps to give the Kelly girls a run for their money, and a mix that would ensure any potential offspring would benefit from an education only available from people like them.

Mariah tried her best to get the young girls on side with her new arrangement, 'Say hello to your Uncle Tom,' she would tell them, whenever they were in the warehouse. 'Not my uncle,' they would tell her, or him, without hesitation; the older girls had them well taught. Mariah knew what she had done was a source of great resentment among her daughters, but she was steadfast, her course was set, and within a year another child was in the pipeline.

A boy is what she had always prayed for, but yet another daughter, Muriel, arrived just before the end of the 1920s. With nine girls to her name, still out of wedlock and now of an age where further childbirth could prove fatally dangerous, Mariah was resigned to her situation, but still had one last go at producing a boy and, in 1931, he eventually appeared on the scene.

Albert was to be his given name. It had all began with Paddy and Sally meeting on The Albert at the Belfast dockside in 1886, and now Albert, her only son, was to become the apple of

Mariah's eye. By the time he arrived, Sarah and Frankie had been wed at St Mary's and would soon be expecting their first child. Liza and Morry tied the knot a little while after, and young Mariah was next to follow suit. The first three of the next generation were born within a year of each other. The three eldest girls would now add a Kelly, a Hewson and a Sayers to the bloodline, in that order. In a whirlwind of a year, the focus shifted from Mariah's own situation to that of becoming a grandmother three times over. Rarely a dull moment, with little time to dwell on the past.

Morry and Liza had been married under the roof of the cathedral, as was the family tradition, and both Frankie and Sarah were by their sides on their special day. It was a big wedding and well-attended.

During the ceremony, Frankie noticed some unwelcome guests at the rear of St Mary's. Several members of the local constabulary had arrived and were gathered in uniform at the entrance to the Cathedral. This wasn't only an invasion of the happy couple's privacy, but a cause of great concern for Frankie and Morry. There were warrants out for both of their arrests due to outstanding fines, and the worst thing was, the entrance through which the bobbies had arrived was also the exit. Frankie had to mark Morry's card during the service about the police presence, gatecrashing the service because they knew both men would be under one roof, with no way of escaping a pinch.

Once the service was over, Father Michael invited the bride and groom into the vestry to sign the marriage certificates. Morry chatted Frankie to follow them as he walked past the front row of guests. Frankie took the nod, following Morry and Liza into the private room at the side of the altar. Father Michael had noticed the unexpected visitors during the service and asked the chaps what it was all about. Upon hearing the their predicament, the priest immediately suggested that once the paperwork was taken care of, the two men had best leave by the side door of the vestry rather than re-enter the Cathedral and walk into the arms of the law, not on such a joyously sacred day. Good Old Father Michael, one of your own.

Liza and Father Michael reappeared from the vestry, minus the two men that went in there with them. A ripple went through the congregation as the penny dropped. The police presence hadn't gone unnoticed by the guests, and the realisation that Morry and Frankie had given them the slip sent a murmur of laughter through the Cathedral, spreading like a wave until it reached the back, by which time some people were now pointing and laughing directly at the confused police officers.

One soppy copper was shoved forward by his colleagues and was told to get to the vestry, quick time. He took off down the aisle like a child on an errand, to a barrage of heckles and laughter, while his oppos squirmed uncomfortably by the main doors, before bursting them open, screaming, 'Get round the back now!' The keystone cops were off, and out the way of the hostile congregation, many of whom by then were shouting and calling the slippery so-and-sos all the names they could, under the roof of God. The two wedding fugitives had indeed taken steppo from the scene, thanks to the collusion of Father Michael, and were now on their toes. It didn't interfere with their celebration plans, however.

They headed to a nearby boozer for a couple of beers before going to the reception venue, safe in the knowledge that the likelihood of the law turning up, after the hostile welcome they got at the service, was slim to say the least, especially as the guests were now plied with firewater.

'Who invited the gavas (police) then?' laughed Morry, as the guests welcomed the two lovable rogues to the reception. When they eventually landed, the celebrations went on long into the night, and into the following day for some. It was a growing tradition among the family to get married on a Wednesday, due to the fact it was always a half-day in business terms. An early wedding meant just half a day's work missed and a full day on the drink, or two or three for those who weren't so gainfully occupied.

The day had been eventful in more ways than one, and the night rolled on as the drink flowed merrily, with even the younger sisters getting in on the act. Mariah was in attendance but kept a low profile at first, not wishing to upstage her daughter on her wedding day, although she took to holding court with her small group of company throughout the evening. She eventually settled into the merriment and regaled the guests with one of her favourite rebel songs, which always got an airing when the craic was good and the drink was flowing, before belting out her signature tune, accompanied by her faithful daughters:

All me life I wanted to be a barrow girl,
A barrow girl is all I wanted to be
I push me barrow, through the streets so wide,
I'm a costa, a costa, from over the other side
I turn me back upon the whole society, take me where the ripe bananas grow
I sell 'em a dozen a shilling, that's how I earns me living,
I oughta been a barrow girl years ago
Get off me barrow
I oughta been a barrow girl years ago

The ink had hardly dried on Liza's wedding certificate when young Mariah announced that she was having a baby to Coronation Kelly, and before the dust settled on the latest Kelly revelation, Sarah announced the same news about her and Frankie.

Old Mariah was delighted at the news of two new additions to her breed and didn't have to wait long before Liza announced the arrival of a third. Named after his grandfather Billy Fleming, Billy Kelly was first to come into the world, born to Mariah and George in 1932. Billy was the eldest child of the new generation of the family, and Kelly was once again an official surname within the ranks, thanks to Coronation.

The first of Sarah's and Liza's bloodlines soon followed. Mary Hewson was born in the autumn of 1932, and Frankie Sayers just a short time later. Born of colourful stock, it seemed only right that colourful names were adopted to suit the three new offspring. They were known from an early age – and answered for the remainder of their lives to– Billy Buck, Mary Lou and Frankie Doodles, and not surprisingly, three unique individuals they all turned out to be. As their great-granny Sally would say, and still did when she could string a sensible sentence together, 'what's bred in the bone, comes out in the marrow'. With wheeler-dealers, costermongers, cockney street traders, barrow girls and a showman as parents, there was little chance of any of the three great-grandchildren becoming anything other than characters in their own right.

This was indeed becoming a notable family; loud, proud and firm in their beliefs. There were now six people living under one roof on Stowell Street in the home shared by Mariah, Big Tom, Sally and the three Cruddas children. The Kelly girls were now dispersed from the street but moved to places nearby, all within a stone's throw of each other in the West End, with Liza and young Mariah sharing a two-up two-down on Blandford Street, while Frankie and Sarah moved to Elswick East Terrace. Old Mariah, in spite of everything, was fiercely proud of her family, 'We might not have much,' she would tell people, 'but we've got plenty to look at.' And plenty more would follow.

That was a guaranteed fact, with three capable young women having children of their own, four that were growing up fast and sometimes furious, living with their older sisters, and the three young children under her own roof with Big Tom and Sally. Despite all the controversy over her and Big Tom, she always held her head high and rose above any condemnation. No one was going to tell Mariah Kelly how to live her life and, in turn, she was not going to run the rule over her daughters. She had tutored them well and instilled in them a set of morals and principles by which they all lived by, and regardless of those who stood in judgement of the way they conducted their affairs, they would continue to do things their way, as long as they weren't doing anyone else any harm.

Mrs Cruddas may not have looked at it that way, but in love and war all is fair, and Big Tom wouldn't be where he was if it hadn't have been what he wanted.

There were now ten direct decedents of Mariah, her prize being her one and only son and heir, Albert Cruddas. Although it was a close call, Albert was thankfully born before any of the next generations made an appearance, avoiding any further hereditary disorder to this controversial clan. Albert did, however, grow up alongside Buck, Doodles and little Mary Lou, more like a brother to them than the uncle he actually was. Albert was doted upon from the word go. Mariah had waited almost a quarter of a century for her boy, enduring 11 other pregnancies spanning 24 years, before he became part of the equation.

She was tenacious in her pursuit, and she eventually got what she wanted. That was her way, and the way she raised her family. Never to give up. To neither judge nor be judged. To do what they believed to be right, and if people didn't like what they did, then to hell with them and do it anyway. Mariah may have been many things to many people, but as with all reputations, they can vary dramatically depending on who it is you talk to. For everyone that thought she was a hard and heartless woman – and many did – there were half a dozen more who understood that her actions towards her family were always done out of some curious interpretation of maternal love. She watched out for them and watched over them, literally, when they all lived on opposite sides of Stowell Street. She protected them from the harm of any outsiders. She taught them self-worth, self-preservation and gifted them all with the ability to earn their own living, not depending on anyone else to put food on their tables. There was an attitude within her family recognised by all around them. They stood united against the world, regardless of their internal differences. Family was what it was all about, and no matter what was going on around them, nothing would ever expose any external cracks in their foundations. That was something only they could bring about themselves. However, their family name Kelly, even though not their birthright, was now being diluted by the introduction of new men to this breed.

There were now Hewsons, Sayers and another Kelly on the firm, not to mention the Cruddas branch, and the firm would only get bigger. With another war less than a decade away, this family would attract more men of questionable character into their ranks before 1939 as the younger girls became paired off, creating a cocktail of family intrigue and collusion that would escalate dramatically during the Second World War.

If your background was chequered, and your lifestyle was neither straight nor narrow, something like a war, and the inevitable blackmarket economy that comes with it, is like giving steroids to a bodybuilder; it may work wonders for your appearance but plays havoc with you on the inside. The hardship of the Second World War made an entire nation turn a blind eye to little bits of skulduggery and corruption, even straight goers. Civil servants and even the local plod would sometimes bend the rules just to get a little extra something during times of such great hardship and austerity, even if only to keep up morale within the home. It became generally accepted to look out for yourself during wartime, even if it meant bending or breaking the law. However, if you were crooked, or even half-crooked, wartime could turn you from a harmless rogue into a villain, and this breed had the bottle to make the very most of the impending situation.

In the early years that followed Albert's arrival, an array of other grandchildren appeared on the scene: Sarah and Frankie only ever had Mary Lou; Sarah, frequently plagued by her heart condition, feared carrying another child; Liza and Morry kept up the pace with the arrival of a daughter Sylvia, to join the young Frankie Doodles, and Mariah and Coronation Kelly produced

Vera and Georgie as siblings to Buck, all of whom arrived before the Second World War.

Joss eventually befriended a chap from the Big Lamp area of the West End, William Craig, who was tragically blown up during the war, carrying out his duties in the bomb disposal unit.

Mary paired up with another likely lad from the town called Joe Patterson, or Pow as he was known. Bella and Chrissy were the youngest of the bunch and were still single by 1939.

All the girls had their own pitches, scattered around the city centre, and were still trying to avoid arrest on a daily basis. Growing up in such a relationship with authority created a contempt for the law which was almost bred into them, so it was always a case of 'them and us'.

The law was the enemy in whatever way it presented, be it magistrate, screw or bobby on the beat. This family, although unconventional, wasn't made up of bad people. They were no worse than those who prosecuted, manhandled and abused them; they were just different, and their oppressors had made it a crime for them to be so. These were women trying to earn an honest living, they didn't ask for help from the state, they weren't hardened criminals robbing defenceless citizens merely to line their pockets. But this is how they were treated, and such treatment can only result in alienation from normal society, creating an environment of solidarity within their own ranks.

They would never rely on someone else to put food on their table, and they were never going to spend a lifetime knocking their plug in every day to line someone else's pockets, getting paid a pittance for doing so, and having no life of their own. That wasn't their way. They knew better, they wanted better, and they would make sure they got better.

WELL, HELLO MARY LOU, BILLY BUCK, AND FRANKIE DOODLES

While the Kelly girls were making their bones on the street of Newcastle, their sharp-suited, sharp-minded men were often plotting and scheming as to how they might get a shilling elsewhere.

The chaps always looked the part wherever they were. Made-to-measure suits, collar and tie, trilby, fedora or Homberg hats, good quality topcoats if the weather dictated, with hand-stitched leather brogues or highly polished boots; they were not just every inch the men about town, they were men of the world and had likeminded pals all over the country. They would often get word from friends in other cities about who and what was making money, and they would turn their hands to many things to make sure they got their share. If the chaps weren't on the barrows at Nelson Street, where there'd sometimes be three or four, side by side all selling a different line, then they'd be holding court in the Café Royal or Simpsons Bar near the city's Grainger Market. Wheeling and dealing in anything and everything was the name of the game, as long as there was a bit of bunce in it.

Frankie Hewson knew his way around a bit of tom, especially stones, or a bit of red. Gold, or 'red' as they called it, was always an earner. Frankie always carried an eyeglass for the stones, and a set of Troy ounce scales to weigh the red.

Morry would get handy lines from pals down the Smoke; silk handkerchiefs, scarves, leather purses or anything they could do a bit of pitch pulling with on the street. Pitching up with a suitcase on a box, and going to work with a bit of swag was often the call of the day for the boys, and a little touch early doors would often see them clear the boards by midday, freeing up plenty of time to plot up in the boozer with a few quid on the hip to deal up with; and if nothing was coming through the door, it gave them time to plot and scheme the next move.

Pow had secured a pitch on the Bigg Market, thanks to Coronation, and stuck a grafter on it so he could spend a bit more time in the bars looking for the next few quid, getting involved in whatever was going on with the chaps. Often they would shoot down the road to big race meetings and work the courses. They knew a couple of tricky bottle-merchants (pickpockets), and would take them to big meetings around the North. Frankie's dad had been a good pickpocket in his youth and schooled Frankie in a few moves, with Morry having learned the art on the streets of Whitechapel.

They also knew all the good grafters in the town, and the boys would often have a day or two away with a little firm, working the courses team handed. Only a decade earlier race courses had been the concern of many serious villains. Protection rackets and extortion were rife on the tracks and they could, at times, be dangerous places to be. Running battles between the Sabini's and one or two other London Firms, as well as The Brummagem or Birmingham Boys (Peaky Blinders), would often violently overspill in full view of the civilians attending the meetings. The majority of that business went on further south, and had since blown over. Our lads, however, were far more stealth-like, less conspicuous and not at all violent in what they got up to, slipping in and out of the courses without brining any attention to themselves, usually at least.

Their prey was always the big winners, especially those who were advertising their good fortune heavily at the bar. People who won big were people who bet big. People who bet big were people with money, not the working class man having a two bob flutter on a 33-1 shot. It was the Flash Harrys betting fivers and tenners on the same outsider or having a score (£20) or pony (£25) on an odds-on favourite. These types either had the money to lose, or they'd had their card marked and were buying money on a crooked race, making them no better than the boys when it came down to it. Either way, they were the ones who could afford a little light-fingered recession.

Looking very much the part, Frankie and Morry would wangle their way into the owner's enclosure or the grandstand bars looking for a mark; the loudmouth fool who was letting everyone know his business and flashing the readies like a red light in a brass nail's (prostitute's) window. They'd bottle (follow) him off to the bookies' enclosure and point him out to the rest of the firm. They would then continue to follow him to see what he was betting on, and see what his return would be if he won. If the fella had a touch, then they knew what he'd be holding as a minimum, and that, they knew, would at least be their prize. If the dippers (pickpockets) couldn't get to buzz (steal from) him after he picked up his winnings, they would tail him to the gents and work the lemon on him.

The 'lemon' was an old dipper's trick used during the war on officers and GIs. Often these flash types, just like the GIs and officers, were a bit more concerned about personal hygiene than the majority of the working classes in those days. The grafters would plot up in a cubicle and peek out when they heard someone flush a chain. If they were lucky, the mark would come from a cubical and approach the sink, often leaving his jacket off to wash his hands. It would be while he was having a wash, or a 'lemon squash', that they would seize their chance and grab the prize, leaving the soapy-faced mark high, but not so dry, and minus his recent windfall, usually along with the poor sod's jacket.

If he was a dirty bastard and left without a lemon, then they'd merely bottle him off back into the crowds and have a go at the bump stakes, the bamboozle, a nudge on the shoulder, a bit of manhandling, and before they knew it the double shuffle had been executed, and the hapless soul still lost his tank to the light-fingered tricksters.

It was a skill and an art, not the most noble, but an art nonetheless. They weren't robbing someone's home or nicking some poor fella's pay packet, they were preying on the wealthy, careless braggarts who could afford to lose the equivalent of a working man's wage for a year on one single bet. This may not have been everyone's idea of a day at the races, but they weren't everyone.

Many a day at the track paid as much as a week on the barrows, even after the divvy up between them, but it wasn't always a dead cert. Sometimes they wouldn't find a mark all day, or they'd get a scatter because it came on top for one of the dippers. Being a well-known pickpocket meant their face might be spotted, and if that happened at the track, then they simply had to be off. The barrows, however, were a banker, and whenever the chaps didn't have some move on the go or a bit of business down the road, they could be seen on the corner of Nelson Street shouting their wares and grafting a hedge.

In some respects it was a life of easy money for them; however, they were risking their liberty by doing many of these things, even by working the barrow, and the penalty for not doing their job well could be jail. All of the boys did a bit of bird over the years for one reason or another, but even jail time for them wasn't quite as daunting as it was for some, even though they endured the same harsh conditions.

When you lived like them, you circulated with people like them; so when they found themselves at Her Majesty's pleasure they'd tend to see a lot of familiar names and faces from within their world, and knowing the right people when they were on the landings could make life inside an awful lot easier. The problem with their way of life, unfortunately, was the curse of the 'easy come, easy go' mentality. When the money they got hadn't cost them blood, sweat, or tears, or they hadn't had to spend 12 hours down a mine shaft to get it, it seemingly became a lot easier to obtain; and because they thought it was there whenever they needed it, it certainly became a whole lot easier to spend. And spend it they did.

They dressed well, ate well and drank well, and never worried about tomorrow. They were never going to starve, and as young men, they believed they had all the time in the world to go out and get it, even the very next day if they wanted. A foolish notion, and a degenerative symptom of their own easy come, easy go mentality.

The scandal of Mariah-gate had blown over by the time Albert arrived. People accepted what had happened, they had no choice, it was behind them and the Kelly girls had survived the scandal with great dignity.

Mariah rarely worked on the barrow by then, spending her time either at the warehouse or in her kitchen, still baking bread, wholesale style, three times a week, delivering freshly made flat cakes to all of her daughter's households every other day. She had done this for as long as anyone could remember. Some of the younger daughters weren't so keen on eating Mariah's stottie cakes anymore though, as a couple of them had spotted Mariah dropping her snuff tin into the dough one time. She blew away as much as she could before kneading in what was left, probably giving the loaves a little extra kick. She loved a bit of snuff, and in her later years almost developed a brown moustache, she took it so often. But she still baked every Monday, Wednesday and Friday, even with three young children and the deteriorating Sally to look after, as well as Big Tom. The homemade stottie cakes would be wrapped in tea towels and placed on end between the spindles of her staircase to cool, in preparation for delivery to all of her girls the next day.

She was indeed a remarkable woman, identifiable in her local community as a woman that could be approached in a time of need. She was in a position to help someone in a tight spot, with friends in many places, and she was someone who could be turned to for a favour. Most favours would be returned if called upon, as often was the case; Mariah made sure that nobody mistook her kindness for weakness. She still supported her beloved St Mary's and enjoyed her weekly audience with the ageing Father Michael, although she had not been able to accept the holy sacrament of communion since she gave into temptation with Big Tom, and that pained her.

She had always kept her family well, and now they were keeping themselves in the manner to which they had become accustomed, and in which they had been taught to do so. She wasn't an incredibly wealthy woman at this point, but she was far from the breadline, and she intended to make sure it stayed that way. By the late 1930s, Mariah was a woman in her mid-50s, and still a proud and enigmatic figure. Mary Lou would often be playing on the rooftop yard of St Mary's school on Oystershell Lane, behind Buckingham Street, when she would hear the other school kids shouting, 'Look! Look! It's that woman with the basket on her head!' as they saw Mariah walking up the street. 'She's a funny woman, your granny,' they would say to Mary Lou, and they weren't wrong. What's more, Mary Lou knew they weren't.

Mary Lou spent a lot of time with her granny, she was the eldest of her granddaughters, and Mariah felt a little sorry for her as she knew her mother Sarah wasn't a healthy woman. Sarah often had Mariah look after Mary Lou when she wasn't feeling up to it. Mariah somehow sensed that Sarah might not be around for a lot of her young daughter's life, so tended to make a fuss of her. Mary Lou was oblivious to her mother's poor health as a young child, enjoying her privileged childhood growing up in this colourful environment provided by her many formidable aunties, unconventional uncles and likeminded cousins, not to mention her funny granny.

For all her sweet little girl looks, Mary Lou was a proper tomboy; she had to be, growing up with Billy Buck and Frankie Doodles. They would all run riot around the fruit market, where everyone knew them. They were the fourth generation of the Kelly's to tread the warehouse floors at St Andrew's. Mary Lou liked a fight, just as Frankie Doodles did, and when Buck had taken his fill of Doodles' jabs and right hooks, Mary Lou would step in to spar with her cousin, and gave as good as she got. Doodles, however, was a natural, and he soon earned himself a reputation as a fighter.

No one dared bully any of them at school, in fact school bullies were straightened out by Doodles. He hated them and would take pleasure in ironing one out in the schoolyard if he heard of one taking a liberty. He'd do the same thing many times on the cobbles and in the ring in the years that followed. Mary Lou was equally as feared among the female pupils because she fought like a boy. If anyone had anything to say or tried to take a liberty with her, Buck or Doodles, then they would have all three cousins to answer to; threat enough for people to stay on the good side of them.

If anyone picked a fight with one, they picked a fight with them all, and that was a principle worth noting when crossing swords with any of the family, from that day to this. Doodles, Mary Lou, Buck and Albert, their uncle of just a few months older, were very thick, close-knit, and were always seen together. Even though they all answered to different surnames at school registration, everyone knew they were one family, and everyone knew what their family were like. These children were not only born into a reputation, but they were also carving out their own from an early age.

Family reputation in their world was different. It wasn't restricted to their street or manor (neighbourhood), or even their town. Moving in their world resulted in meeting similar people from all over the country, not least of all when they were locked up. Their name could be mentioned in the right circles up and down the land, or the wrong ones depending on how you looked at it, and that was be a valuable commodity. On one occasion, the chaps were down in London doing some business with a good friend of theirs from Manchester, a big fine-looking fella they called Big Tim. Neil Timminey, who dressed immaculately, had plenty of style and a charming personality to match. Whilst in a bar in London's East End the chaps encountered some unwelcome attention from a little firm who seemed to have some influence in the establishment.

One of the group, the mouthpiece of the crew, didn't fancy the lads and accused Tim of being an undercover copper. This didn't go down well with Tim, and he let his accuser know it. Before they all knew it, Tim, Frankie and Morry were out in the lane with the other firm. The mouthpiece and Tim peeled off their coats and shaped up for a straightener. Tim was a lump of a man and knew how to hold his hands up, much to the surprise of his opponent. It was a tidy scrap until Tim seemed to be getting on top, and that's when the other two heavies tried to interfere. After some shouting and bawling, peace was restored to proceedings, following a short stand off and with apologies being made for the accusation of mistaken identity, they all shook hands and went back inside for a drink. New friends were made on that day, each realising they were dealing with their own kind, with both sides acknowledging the fact. There exists a mentality, an understanding among people of this nature, regardless of where they come from. The chaps couldn't have come from much further away (in distance) than the 'Old School' villains of East End, but the cloth they were cut from was very much the same.

Some years later, Frankie took Sarah and little Mary Lou back down to London on business, and they visited the same bar, as Frankie wanted to pay respect to his friends there. Mary Lou was made a fuss of, and bunged a nicker by the nice smart man and friend of her dad. Not until much later in life did she realise the nice smart man who'd given her a pound in that Mile End boozer was in fact Jack Spot, a man who became one of the most feared villains in London, long before the Krays had cut their teeth. This was the world the family lived in, and back up in the coal mining heartland of the North East it was members of this family who would later come to attract the same kind of notoriety in Newcastle as the leading faces in London did on their own manor.

The Second World War was looming, and had been ever since Germany were made to sign the Treaty of Versailles at the end of the Great War. Its harshness and the fact that the British and French saw Nazi Germany as the sole warmongers of

Europe had been eating away at the Germans for two decades. They were the villains of the piece; they had been paying for the damages of the Great War for too long, and Hitler wasn't going to stand for it any longer. He defied the treaty and made Germany strong again by rearmament. With arms they could take over other European countries and become even stronger. They invaded Poland in 1939, and the rest, we know, is tragic history. It's a jungle out there, and the laws of the jungle apply on every level of humanity. From the global governments that rule our countries, through the corridors of power and on to the streets we live in. The world is a dangerous place, and only the strong survive.

Survival was in the blood of Mariah Kelly's breed. It was in the air they breathed. It was bred into them, and their self-preservation and ability to survive would come into its own after 1939. The Second World War would become not just a turning point in history, but a watershed moment in time for the family. Things had never been straight forward growing up in their world, and the war was about to make it a lot less straighter.

THE TAKE AWAY

There's an old trick in the street trading game, it's called the 'Take Away'. It's something commonly used in all kinds of business, and it was about to be unveiled all over the country. It had already been carried out in America in the 1920s, and it caused absolute chaos.

Prohibition heralded the real outbreak of organised crime in the States, something which gripped the country like a plague, and it was about to happen on British soil. Not prohibition, but rationing and, in both cases, the principal caused the same effect. When you take something away from someone, they want it even more, and in most cases, they'll do anything in order to get it; hence why street traders often use the 'take away'.

During prohibition, the great American public became enemy number two. The Mob may have been public enemy number one, but the nations desire to consume alcohol formed the basis for organised crime. Bootlegging, illegal drinking dens, speakeasies, gang warfare and violence became prevalent on a scale not seen since the days of the Wild West. There was an insatiable thirst for liquor which required quenching on a grand scale, and if the government weren't prepared to permit its produce, importation, transportation or sale, then it was left to the profiteers to do so. It was business; one which the state had been party to up to that point but had now decided they wanted out, along with determining the same for the entire population. But the punters rebelled and decided they just weren't having it. The reality was, the public were not only the driving force behind organised crime, they were the footsoldiers. They broke the law every time they drank in public, and they did it regularly and blatantly. Many of those entrusted with upholding the law turned a blind eye to much of what went on during prohibition, most of them breaking the same laws themselves by using gin joints, blind pigs or speakeasies as they were called.

What the public wants, the public ultimately gets, one way or another, and if you take away something so fundamental to their lives, something that is such a basic need for a civilised existence, the public will proceed to bend as many rules as they can get away with in order to satisfy their need. Wide-scale criminality and organised crime was one result of taking alcohol away from the citizens of America, and the people of Great Britain were about to have something even more fundamental taken away from them. Almost every product deemed a luxury item was rationed by the Government; bacon, butter, sugar and even petrol, followed by ration schemes for meat, tea, jam, biscuits, cheese, eggs, lard, milk, canned or dried fruit and much more – the very things people were used to having, even if not all the time.

They'd had these things before, they wanted them still, and would continue to get them; anyway they could. These products weren't banned like alcohol had been in the States, but the government were dramatically reducing there availability, and taking these things away from people would inevitably create a black market. The profiteers would service the needs of the nation one way or another, and once again the people of the land would become the driving force of the dark economy.

By the time war broke out, the talk on the streets was all about call-ups. Frankie, Morry, Coronation and Pow were of an age to fight, and would no doubt get the letter in due course. The memories of the Great War were still fresh in the minds of at least two generations of the country, and horror stories from that dark period were now being recounted in bars and homes around the country as a new conflict loomed. Few people had escaped without some kind of loss or tragedy within their family or circle as a result of the First World War, and many men were now dreading the call-up this time around. The Great War had almost been seen as an adventure for many naïve young men at the turn of the century, they'd had nothing to measure the experience against. But the Second World War was pretty much on the back of the previous one in the scheme of things, and Hitler's Nazi Germany was well and truly on the rampage.

Vast numbers of men would have happily avoided conscription this time around if they'd had a choice, but without reasonable grounds they would have to don a uniform and fight, this time for a new King and his country. Going AWOL meant going on your toes. Working men, straight going people, simply couldn't do such a thing. How would they survive? They needed their jobs. If they went absent without leave then they were liable to be arrested, and they certainly couldn't go back to their place of work as their boss would be duty bound to inform the authorities. Their home would be visited by military police, they'd run the risk of being stopped in the street and asked for identification; they would basically be a fugitive and have to live on their wits, in the shadows. If, however, they already lived on their wits, were used to the law at their door and were avoiding arrest every day on the barrow, then life as a fugitive could almost be a busman's holiday, and a far better alternative to risking their lives like the unsuspecting lambs that had been sent to their slaughter at the Somme.

It takes a special kind of person to go to war, that cannot be denied, but the majority going to war in 1939 did so because they had to, not because they wanted to. Their efforts can never be played down, nor can the loss of life during conflict. Their bravery ensured our freedom. But when your memories of WWI are filled with dread and sorrow at the loss of family, and your existence is spent in conflict with the establishment that wants you to lay down your life for them, it becomes a conflict of a different kind, a conflict of interests, and the chaps weren't interested.

It also takes a special kind of person to be able to live on their wits, fend for themselves and be reliant on no person or state to provide them with an income, and to be undeterred by scrutiny from the authorities. If possessing this ability enabled them to avoid risking their life, a life that could at worst become no more than a number on a 'lost in battle' ledger, or at best a life that might be forever scarred, physically or mentally, with little more to show for it than a badge; then the prospect of war becomes one of choice, rather than one of necessity.

Where your duty lies is where you feel you're most needed. For some it was King and country, for some it was wife and family, and like it or not, these people were all about family. The country had never given them any breaks, every opportunity presented to them was one created by themselves, and they in turn, had not taken anything from the country by way of handouts from the state.

The Crown had never been that good to them anyway, although they'd given some of their time to it at their Majesty's pleasure, so there was no love lost on that score. They had little desire to abandon their families, or their way of life, in order to defend a system that persecuted them. They knew, just like the leaders of the world know, war is good for business. The decision was simple, either go to war and risk your life as cannon fodder for the upper-class, or stay at home to protect and provide for your family, while capitalising on the best business opportunity you are ever likely to be presented with.

Frankie, Morry, Coronation, Pow, the Kelly girls and their expanding breed were perfectly poised to make the most of the underground economy that WWII created. They were already crooked in the eyes of the law, and in the eyes of the local underworld of petty crooks and villains, they were as bent as a nine bob note.

As part of Hitler's War Directive No. 9, Newcastle was identified as the main focus for destruction in the North East, deemed as a strategic target with its important heavy industry. The bridges spanning the river Tyne, the steelworks at Elswick, the docks, shipyards, and Vickers-Armstrong naval yard, as well as the Wallsend slipway were all targeted for destruction by the Nazi German Luftwaffe. The city suffered devastating bombing raids, with over a hundred deaths when the High Level Bridge was attacked in 1940. Byker goods yard burned to the ground in

1941, when a seemingly relentless raid left hundreds dead and thousands of locals homeless.

Many of the family saw first-hand the devastation of the Newcastle Blitz; they lived in the bomb zone close to the city centre on the banks of the Tyne, some in Elswick itself. The novelty and danger of running to the air raid shelters soon wore off and, as the air raids increased, it resulted in some of the family being sent off to Aspatria, on Cumbria's west coast, in order to avoid the bombing. Over 30,000 people from Newcastle, mainly children, were evacuated from the city during those months, especially those close to the Tyneside target sites of the Luftwaffe.

Living so close to the focus of the bombing meant the Kelly girls and their kin didn't just see and hear the attacking Messerschmitts, but they witnessed the damage caused by their raids. Poor Joss had just recently been wed to Willy Craig, who at the age of 20, was among the first wave of young men drafted for war duty. He was only a few weeks into his service when he was fatally wounded in a bomb disposal exercise on the day of his 21st birthday. Not only was this a devastating tragedy for Joss and the young man's family, but it was another reason for the rest of the Kelly girls' spouses to take an even dimmer view of getting involved in this World War caper.

Billy Fleming had almost lost his life in the first war and came home a physically and mentally broken man. He did get a medal though, and a lot of good it did him. Some of the men's fathers and uncles had lost their lives in the First World War; factors which played heavily on the minds of the new additions to the Kellys. Due to their general age of around 30 or so, they were not in the initial draft category, and by the time Frankie Hewson got the call, he was busy nursing Sarah through a recent spate of scares with her heart. It was during this time of the war's first year, before the Blitz began in earnest, that Frankie took little Mary Lou and Sarah down to London.

A strange direction to head in when the Luftwaffe were at large, but the Blitz in London didn't really begin until September

1940. It was during the early summer, a period in time known as the 'phony war' on a visit to the capital with her mam and dad that young Mary Lou got to meet her old man's cockney pal, Jack Spot.

Liza, Frankie Doodles, and his younger sister Sylvia were packed off to Aspatria, along with Young Mariah, Billy Buck, his sister Vera and brother Georgie. Sarah didn't go, she needed to be close to a hospital that could deal with her condition, and Wingrove Hospital (now known as Newcastle General Hospital) was just up the street from where they lived. Sadly, in the late autumn of 1940, shortly after walking home from town with Mary Lou, Sarah suffered a massive heart attack. Becoming short of breath as they walked up Westgate Road past the Stoll Theatre, Sarah decided to make a pit stop at her sister Liza's on Blandford Street. They ended up staying the night rather than go back to an empty home, as Frankie had reluctantly answered the call-up. The following morning, Mary Lou was ushered to her Granny Mariah's, something that would happen many times to her over the next decade. She went without question, but the real motive was to get Sarah's eight-year-old daughter out of the way to allow the coroner to come and issue a certificate of death for Sarah Hewson, who had passed away peacefully during the night, aged just 33.

This sad and premature tragedy sent shockwaves through the family. The oldest Kelly girl was gone, leaving behind an only child whose father was away on army training. It triggered a series of events which would result in Frankie, following immediate compassionate leave, going AWOL to be by his daughter's side permanently. Mariah, however, had different ideas about where Mary Lou should be raised, and a tug of war rumbled on for years, seeing the young motherless child dragged from the West End to Gateshead and back again for much of her youth, even being kidnapped by her Aunt Joss at one point. Mary Lou wasn't so much a war baby, as a tug-of-war baby.

The Kellys wanted Mary Lou with them, and the Hewsons wanted her in Gateshead. Mary Lou got spoiled in both places, as you might expect for one losing her mother so young. But the two worlds were very different for the young girl, and she used the situation to her best advantage.

Life in Hawthorn Villa, her great-grandfather's residence, was strict. Tables were correctly set for meals. Fine china and silver cutlery adorned the crisp white tablecloth, set out like a fine dining establishment. Milk bottles and odd salt and pepper pots adorned Mariah's table in the scullery at Sunderland Street, where she had now moved to. Life in the West End was rough and ready, and the little tomboy loved it. All of her cousins were away to Aspatria, so when Mary Lou was at Mariah's she would be spoiled to death, and get away with murder. If she went too far though, she would be sent packing.

The same would happen in Gateshead, where she would have the best of clothes handmade for her, and different coloured shoes to match each outfit; one for every day of the week. Both families had money, but at that point, the Hewsons appeared to be far more affluent. If Mary Lou became too comfortable over the water, then the Kelly girls would conspire to get her back in the West End, and she was whisked away on more than one occasion by her aunties. This was never hard to do as Mary Lou would often run away from one family to the other whenever she felt she might get better treatment from the other side. Although but a child, Mary Lou knew the game and played it well; playing one off against the other to make the most of her unfortunate, yet charmed situation.

Frankie Hewson had been drafted into the army and was only a couple of weeks into his training when Sarah died. He was given leave, but made it permanent by failing to return for duty. He was arrested by the Military Police and sent to Fenham Barracks, where he was visited by his daughter. Frankie requested an exemption on exceptional grounds but was refused, so he made his leave permanent by going AWOL. After all, he had a young daughter to take care of; 'family first!'

Without Sarah, he would spend more time in Gateshead with his daughter, but even Frankie couldn't resist the draw of

Newcastle and the opportunities it presented. He still had contact with the family; however, his connection to them would become further convoluted in later years. But wherever he was, or wherever his daughter was, he made sure she wanted for nothing. Mary Lou would attend school wearing diamond rings on her fingers, gifts from her father's jewellery dealings. She would be paraded around classrooms because she was so perfectly turned out in her fine attire, tailored coats, fine dresses and Kiltie shoes. She was different from the other pupils in this way, but was as rough and ready as any one of them when she had to be. She was once relieved of her dinner money by the teachers at St Mary's, who contacted Mariah and asked why this eight-year-old girl had attempted to pay for her school meals with a pound note, enough to pay for her meals for a year.

Mary Lou could get whatever she wanted from both families, and either one would make sure she got it, if for no other reason than to show the other side that they could. The rivalry between the two families played perfectly into Mary Lou's hands. When her cousins came back from Cumbria she would spend most of her time in the West End, and be in her element. She'd take Buck, Doodles and the younger ones for days out, paying for taxis to take them to the Spanish City in Whitley Bay, simply because she refused to stand in a queue for the train at the Central Station. She would play the wag from school and take half the class to The Essoldo on Westgate Road for matinee screenings, paying for them all to sit in the Circle seats, where the posh people sat. She lived a charmed life did Mary Lou, as if it were some form of compensation for losing her mother so young.

Taking ingredients into school for cookery class during the war served as a bleak attempt at home economics for most people. The basic wartime ingredients of powdered egg, scrapings of flour, milk and butter were just enough to bake a paltry cake. However, when Mary Lou turned up with a basket filled with Bramley cooking apples, tins of fruit, a bag of flour, half a dozen eggs, a pint of fresh milk, a bag of sugar, salt and a quarter of butter, it was blatantly obvious to those around her that life in Mary Lou's household was utterly different to everyone else's, even the teachers. But by God, they all enjoyed one hell of a homemade apple pie when Mary Lou was in their cookery class.

The war was on, and the nation was feeling the pinch. Meagre rations meant every household, regardless of financial status, was restricted in what they could have, how much they could have, and how often they could have it. It was the 'Take Away', and you know how that one works. Mary Lou could only have provided such an array of fresh and scarce ingredients by some extraordinary means. Stuff like that didn't just fall off the back of a lorry, at least not directly into her school basket. She had access to everything that everyone else desired.

Her families made sure of it, and the West End faction made sure they had their fingers in more pies than Mary Lou baked in school. The black market was booming; not just in Newcastle but all over the land, and certain people around the country were making a killing. The Kelly family were doing precisely that their manor. They had the warehouse, the contacts and the infrastructure to put themselves on top, and Mariah seized the opportunity with both hands.

Morry Sayers had joined the Royal Navy but was returned from duty on account of a hearing problem, at least that's what he told them. Morry also told his kids that he was a decorated war hero, so somebody was being kidded to somewhere. Like his pal Frankie Hewson, it was a blessing, although unlike Frankie, Morry wasn't on his toes.

Coronation just ignored the call, and Pow decided he didn't fancy the war job at all after being conscripted. He'd lost his father at the Battle of the Somme, so once bitten twice shy was his attitude to the impending conflict. He was on the train to his post in Portsmouth and watched through the window as the south coast night sky was lit up by a blitzkrieg attack. Joe could be a bit of a stutterer, especially when he was excited.

'F-F-F-Fuck this for a game of f-fucking soldiers!' he muttered under his breath, and leapt from the moving train under cover of darkness.

Once back home, he would recount the vision that awaited him in Portsmouth and would frequently tell everyone about 'The b-b-bangs an-and the p-pows' that the bombs made as they hit the ground where he was heading. Some say this is where Joe's nickname, Pow, originated. Truth is Pow was actually called after his dad, a champion runner at the famous Powder Hall Stadium in Edinburgh. Whether that's where the nickname Pow came from or not, one thing for sure was that he wasn't having any of it, and he did a bit of his own championship running from the train bound for Portsmouth as he went on the trot from the army that night.

The boys, as it turned out, would all be around Newcastle for the duration, not just for their family, but for the pickings that were there to be made by people like them.

It was accepted to bend or break the rules within this family, but now the entire nation was turning a blind eye to many things. Almost everyone, in every town and city, from every profession or walk of life, became just a little bit crooked. A hooky tin of peaches, or half a dozen fresh eggs on top of their weekly rations would lift the morale of any household. Winston Churchill was keen on maintaining morale in the nation, and the Kellys, along with their likeminded partners, were every bit as keen, and provided as much morale as they could get their hands on.

Depending on how you view the wartime activities of the Kelly clan, you'd be forgiven for believing they were either a bunch of criminals or a forward-thinking crew providing a much-needed service to their fellow citizens.

They weren't, however, taking from the needy to line their pockets, that was never their style. They were getting their hands on goods that everyone wanted, and distributing them in the bars and on the streets of the city to the people who needed them. Jump-ups on trucks delivering to factories and distribution warehouses were often carried out by the boys and their cronies.

A jump-up is basically what it says, when a truck driver was absent from his vehicle, they would jump up and clear the wagon of its contents, or take the truck if they had to.

Little firms all over the city would be at it, and they knew where to go and get ready cash for their ill-gotten gains. Wholesaling to Mariah was far quicker than running all over the place selling bits and bobs; this way they could have the readies on their hip so they were free to go out and start again. Distribution was key, and that's where Mariah cornered the market. The warehouse was the perfect place for anything they took in. They would carve it up there and get it out on the street lively; any leftovers were quickly shipped to the homes of family members, who were far less likely to get a spin from the law than the warehouse was. Mariah's front parlour was also an Aladdin's cave, full of every conceivable rationed item.

Fresh fruit and veg had never been in short supply for the Kellys but now hundreds of cases of tinned fruit, canned meat, butter, eggs, jam or whatever was in demand, was available in abundance in her household. The turnover of stock was constant, and there were some very busy villains around town at that time, keeping Mariah supplied. All her daughters had well-stocked cupboards, there were no Old Mother Hubbards on their firm. Some of them couldn't help trying to cop on that little bit extra though. Joss the Boss had been given a lovely leather holdall by Mariah, and she carried it with her everywhere, especially when she went to visit her mother. As soon as Joss was ready to leave Sunderland Street she would pick up her leather bag, say her goodbyes, and head for the front door. She'd open the door, then close it loudly a second later without leaving the house. She'd then nip into the parlour and load up, before slipping out of the house silently so no one could hear.

Mariah was too wide for Joss's antics though, and would often remark to her daughter, 'That bag could tell a few tales if it could talk.' But Mariah knew that Joss had lost her young husband and didn't begrudge her daughter's light-fingered antics. After all, what's in you comes out of you.

Mariah was making money, lots of it, and fast. She may have done some questionable things in her time when it came to the parental treatment of her daughters, but she certainly had her good points. Each of Mariah's nine remaining children got £100 apiece for their Christmas box during the war years, a lot of money when you consider the average working wage was around six quid a week. Multiply that bung by ten, Mary Lou got a big note (£100) too in lieu of her mother Sarah, and you're talking about the equivalent of three years' wages for the average man, just in Christmas gifts to her kids. It's no wonder Mary Lou took pound notes to school.

During the war years, the rest of the Kelly girls found themselves perspective husbands, although Joss remained single for many years.

Several more grandchildren arrived on the scene. Liza had John, Peter and Albert. Mariah had Thomas, Marie and the twins Frankie and Jimmy. Peggy and Muriel went to work on the barrow just like their sisters, and Albert Cruddas, the apple of Mariah's eye, had all the hallmarks of a future playboy. Trouble was never far from any of their doors during those years. Frankie Hewson, Pow Patter and Coronation Kelly were all on the trot, and up to all sorts of skulduggery with Morry and several other local likely lads. If it wasn't the Military Police knocking at their door, then it was can bottles (uniformed police officers). Pepper pots and rolling pins were always at the ready for any of the law if they tried to muscle their way across a Kelly threshold. A dose of pepper in the face would be enough to slow them down while anyone who wasn't supposed to be there could make good their escape.

Mary, Pow's wife, even had two mattresses in the backyard beneath a high flat roof at the rear of her house on Westgate Hill. The kids would often see Pow and a couple of the others practising their jump so they'd be ready for a scatter out the back window if the time came when the law turned up at the door.

When all the younger kids were back from evacuation to Aspatria, they'd be dodging around the city and helping out at any one of their mothers' or aunties' pitches, keeping toot and learning the trade. The people of Newcastle had grown up seeing four generations of this family plying their trade in the city. They were a recognised family, respected by most, and treat with trepidation by some.

The men were not people to trifle with, and the youngsters of the family weren't scared of anything – other people, the police, or a fight – and that was just the granddaughters! Nobody messed with them. If they did, then they'd have to prepare for their own war. Picking a fight with any single one of this firm meant picking a fight with the entire breed. That's how they worked. They stood together against the rest of the world, and the world hadn't seen anything yet.

WHAT'S IN A NAME?

Desertion is a dirty word, yet over 150,000 British and US men did the dirty during the Second World War. The maximum penalty for deserting your post was death, with the Second World War's first, and only, execution for desertion taking place in January 1945. The most likely outcome for those going AWOL was dishonourable discharge, forfeiture of pay and a maximum sentence of five years' incarceration. That was the worst that could happen if you went on your toes instead of attending your post. The worst-case scenario for actually attending your post was death, either by getting shot or being blown up in the line of duty.

For many men it was a no-brainer, especially if they were the kind of man that lived outside the law in the first place. The truth is many men and women attempted to avoid conscription, offering up various excuses in an attempt to avoid conflict, hardship, capture or death at the hands of the Nazis during the Second World War. For members of the Kelly clan and others like them up and down the country, war, service, duty, obligation, whatever you want to call it, just was not on the agenda.

If you're anti-establishment and opposed to authority, then you look after your own – it's just you and your family, and that's exactly what they did; with the rationing of goods dictated by the government providing rich pickings for the duration.

This mentality wasn't lost entirely on men, and certainly not just the men of this family. Chrissy and Bella were called up for service during the war, but they didn't last long either. Slaving away for twelve hours a day in prime targets such as the armourment factories, like a sitting duck for the Germans, wasn't their idea of a shrewd move. As a result Mariah, Liza and Mariah harboured their younger sisters and were frequently fending off the Military Police. The number of times they would get a spin by the MPs or the old bill looking for any number of this mob during the war years was almost countless. It was a regular occurrence. Many times one of the lads, Chrissy or Bella would be there when there'd be a sharp rap at the door, and occasionally the search party would storm into the house while Mariah or the older girls would toss pepper into the eyes of the officers and give them a sly bat with a rolling pin while they were temporarily blinded. This would give their prey time to vacate the premises and avoid capture; the two mattresses at the back of Mary's house were used to break the fall of more than one or two of the boys on such occasions.

It was a time of much activity for the family, and life was lived at a pace, with one eye looking over their shoulder, and the other one on the prize. Chrissy had moved in with Liza, and Bella had been living with Sarah since Mariah's ignominious departure from Billy Fleming and up until Sarah's passing, before also joining Liza's household. They would help out on the older sisters' pitches and had to be even more vigilant than usual; a tug from the law would result in far worse than a fine for obstructing the public highway if they were to get captured for failing to turn up for duty in compliance with the war effort. On the upside, money was coming in thick and fast for the family, and whatever kind of wealth Mariah had before 1939 escalated over the next seven years to the point of considerable wealth before the war eventually came to an end.

The parlour of Mariah's home was awash with vast amounts of black market produce. The younger generation grew up not knowing the hardships of wartime rationing. Scarcity was alien to them, in fact, abundance was more of a common factor in the lives of this lot. The sweet-faced Mary Lou, with her poker-straight hair, curled to resemble Shirley Temple's, appeared as though butter wouldn't melt in her mouth, but she led her cousins into all sorts of mischief. She would sneak them into Mariah's parlour, where they would burst open tins of fruit from cases piled up with all the other swag. A tin of fresh fruit would be a welcome treat on anyone's table during wartime if they could get their hands on one, but such was the availability of the stuff in the Kelly household that the kids would wastefully pierce half a dozen tins just so they could drink the juice.

The young cousins would have bars of chocolate, sherbet dabs, and bottles of pop, even cigarettes at their fingertips if they wanted them. Much of this went on without Mariah's knowledge, but as she would often say knowingly, 'I'm not asleep when me eyes are shut.' She had a wonderful turn of phrase, but trusted no one. One of her favourite sayings was 'from Carrickmacross to Crossmaglen, there are more thieves than honest men, and I wouldn't trust the arse I sit on.' She knew what the kids were up to, but what could she do? She'd raised her family to know all the moves, so she could hardly complain too much when they put some of them into practice, even if it was at her expense.

On one particular occasion Mary Lou, young Sylvia Sayers and Vera Kelly snuck into the parlour while Mariah was out and their Aunt Peggy was looking after them. Keen to get on with her chores, Peggy chased the youngsters from the scullery so she could clean. The three girls made their way up the hall to the front door, and Mary Lou remembered what Joss used to do when she pretended to leave. She opened the front door then closed it again loudly without leaving the house. The three then crept into the parlour, not wanting to play outside in the freezing cold. They helped themselves to a tin of peaches each and pierced them with a pen knife so they could drink the sweet syrup, before creeping around the back of the old upright piano that stood in the corner. There was an old mattress behind the piano, and the girls made themselves cosy as they drank the juice from their cans.

Sylvia and Vera were only five or six years old, Mary Lou was around 11 or 12, the ringleader. Sylvia and Vera were making a noise and getting restless, as young kids do, so Mary Lou tried her best to keep them quiet, fearful of being discovered by Peggy, who was only about 16 herself and convinced they had gone out to play.

'Go to sleep,' Mary Lou whispered to them, blowing gently on their little faces and stroking their eyelids to try and get them over. She sang them lullabies and did all she could to get them to sleep, anything would have been better than being found out by Peggy, and probably slung outside in the cold, after a clip round the ear.

Eventually, they all nodded off, and in the quiet warmth of the parlour, in their little den behind the piano, all three were sound asleep. The girls snoozed well on into the evening, woken only by the noise of panic coming from the hallway outside the door. It was dark now, both in the parlour and outside the house, where anxious family members searched high and low for the missing girls. A search party was sent across to Gateshead, as they knew Mary Lou would think nothing of taking herself over there by taxi anytime the fancy took her.

Old Hewson's house had been screamed to the ground by Liza and Mariah looking for their kids. The flames were fanned by the Hewsons blaming the Kellys, citing their lack of discipline with Mary Lou as reason for the girls going missing. The men had been out on the streets looking in all the likely places for them; the search could have gone on forever outside the house, but nobody other than Mary Lou, Sylvia and Vera knew that. The three girls were now on their toes and terrified to hand themselves in. If the crying, screaming, shouting and bawling on the other side of the door was anything to go by, they weren't likely to get a warm reception when all came to light. But they couldn't stay there forever, even though there was enough supplies in the parlour to keep them there until D-Day.

They opened the door gingerly and took a look through the gap, witnessing a chaotic scene. The girls had been missing for six hours and panic was setting in with the crowd of family that had converged on Mariah's home. As the missing trio slowly crept into the hallway, the air immediately turned blue as the three deserters innocently emerged from the parlour.

'My baby!'

'Where've you been?!' cried Liza and Mariah, drowned out by the men cursing.

'Where've you been, you little bastards? Fucking murder you three have caused this day!'

A babble of abuse and consolation ensued, but the panic was finally over and the tears from the three fugitives eventually restored compassion to the situation. After all, girls will be girls. They were safe. They *were* little bastards. But they were safe little bastards, and that's all that mattered.

Mariah ran a tight ship and still kept all of her dealings in her head. Banks were never an option for her. She was old fashioned, trusting no one but herself with her money. Unable to invest on her own, due to the laws preventing unmarried women owning property, Mariah owned nothing outright, and would not be able to unless she married Big Tom, and Mrs Cruddas was never going to allow that to happen, so Mariah kept her money where she could easily access it.

In the parlour stood a tallboy dresser, and Mariah chose to hide her readies beneath a towel in the large bottom drawer. Throughout the war that drawer saw an awful lot of action, often filled with bundles of notes standing on end, rolled tightly and fastened with rubber bands, at times there'd be 30 or 40 fat rolls of white £5 notes packed in there, covered by nothing more than the towel.

This may not have been her only stash, but it was the stash that some of the family knew about. The kids may have taken the odd tin of peaches or bar of chocolate from the stock in the parlour, but no one dared touch Mariah's gelt (cash). She was buying contraband regularly, renting barrows out, supplying her daughter's pitches and money-lending all over town. Every transaction was made in cash, ready money, and it was coming from all directions. It paid for a big funeral with a horse-drawn hearse, a line of funeral cars and a flat-backed wagon laden with flowers for her mother's funeral. Sally also had sadly passed away in 1940. The fiery tinkers daughter and pioneering Mother of the breed, the young girl who'd risked life and limb to create a future, and had descended on Newcastle over half a century earlier, was no more. That era had come to its end, and in some ways, it was a blessing, as she was in the grip of late-stage dementia.

The second of two large funeral procession that year weaved its way through the West End streets of Newcastle before arriving at Elswick Cemetery, where Sally was laid to rest in a corner plot of land not more than a couple of yards away from her first born grandchild Sarah; bought by Mariah as the resting place for many of her own in the years that followed.

With the passing of her eldest daughter and her mother, it had been a year of great loss, but Mariah continued to rule her roost with an iron fist, however, she was becoming seemingly more generous with her family, making sure they had whatever they needed, and in some cases, the best of everything they wanted, with Albert being her primary beneficiary. He was the son Mariah had longed for, ever since she married Billy Fleming. It took 12 pregnancies - nine girls and two miscarried boys - before Albert came along, and Mariah thought the sun shone out of his backside. In turn, Albert thought the world revolved around the sun that shone out of his jacksie, and he had Mariah wrapped around his little finger.

Like the rest of the young generation, Albert knew about his mother's stash, and also knew how he could cream a little off it without being caught. He was a slippery little customer, which was no surprise really, as the apple rarely falls far from the tree. His cunning scheme came to light however, when some of the younger ones, after another hideout session behind the piano in the parlour, stumbled on his little scam. The back of the piano was made up of wooden slats with a hessian cloth covering the internal workings. But on one den-making expedition, some of the kids noticed a split in the cloth. It was just a small split, big enough to get your hand in, and when one of them did that day, they brought out a bunch of crumpled notes that had been stuffed down there.

None of Mariah's grandchildren would have dared steal from her in this way, they were terrified of her notorious temper. Getting on the wrong side of her for such a crime would have resulted in a sudden halt in her generosity, usually so easily bestowed when the fancy took her. You just don't bite the hand that feeds you. But Albert was not one of Mariah's grandchildren, he was her blue-eyed boy, and could get away with murder. He'd shrewdly been peeling the odd note from bundles in the tallboy. Had he simply stolen one of the bundles, Albert would've been found out immediately; Mariah would have known precisely how many bundles were in the drawer at any given time. But peeling a note from one bundle, or one from half a dozen bundles felt safe enough to Albert, the discovery might not be made for a long time, if ever.

Albert had developed a safe little system, and a passion for spending money; even at a young age he had all the hallmarks of a spendthrift. Immaculately dressed in tailored suits, with monogrammed shirts, beautiful ties and a diamond tiepin to finish off his slick appearance, Albert looked every inch a young man of means.

He only worked if he wanted to, not because he had to, and even then it was only to keep Mariah happy. When the younger children discovered the money in the piano, they decided to replace it and keep their mouths shut, but they knew someone was at it, and it was sure to come out eventually. Peggy, Albert's older sister, discovered the hidey-hole sometime later while cleaning the house, and the alarm was raised. Everyone with access to the parlour was quizzed, but the only likely culprit was Albert. He was the only one with the gall to do such a thing, and he knew he could sweet talk his way out of anything with his doting mother. He was found out eventually, and whatever went on between him and Mariah certainly didn't dampen his appetite for splashing the cash. His mother had plenty, so why should he live hand to mouth? He was the only son of Mariah Kelly, and *that*, he figured, gave him some degree of entitlement, besides,

Mariah would never have it said that her son was short of a few quid.

Frankie, Morry, Coronation and Pow weren't always around as much as they'd like to have been, still on their toes they often went down the road, working or doing some deal with a few cockney boys or pals in the Midlands. That's if they weren't locked up for the odd six months for a bit of nonsense or captured by the MPs.

They did manage to produce a few more children in between times though, by the end of the war: John, Peter and another Albert had come along to complete the Sayers family, little brothers to Sylvia and Doodles. Young Mariah had Marie, Thomas and the twins Frankie and Jimmy, on top of Buck, Vera and Georgie; making the full complement of the new Kelly clan. Mary and Pow produced Joseph, Michael, Patricia and Terry; that was the Patterson's register. Barrow boys and barrow girls in the making, every last one of them, born into a business and a family that were growing not only in numbers but in notoriety.

There were other family names of note in their orbit in Newcastle at the time; Findlay, Orange, Johnson, Quinn, Rigney, Balmer, and Drummond to name a few from the street trading and fruit game. There were other, slightly more nefarious, names like Tams, Snowden, Anderson, Shotton, and Conroy from the town; villains, vagabonds and hardmen of the first waters. These were all friends and associates of the men in the family, who, like some of their contemporaries, straddled both worlds: the straight and the crooked. Even though the Kelly breed now bore many different surnames, they were always recognised, if not as one family, then certainly one firm.

One incredible turn of events that no one saw coming was Frankie Hewson's realignment with the family. The son of a business rival, married into the Kellys back in the early 1930s, and since Sarah's passing at the start of the war, had continued to be around the rest of the boys; never really becoming a stranger.

With Mary Lou spending most of her time living with her granny due to Frankie's frequent absence, he still visited Sunderland Street and the warehouse in Blackfriars, socialising with the family as well as working with the boys from time to time.

Clearly, Frankie had become accustomed to family life with the townies, and in a dramatic turn of events which took everyone by surprise, he was about to re-enter the family as a husband for a second time. He had grown close to Sarah's sister Chrissy. Their friendship was kept quiet for as long as they could manage, but when they both realised that it was a serious relationship, he once again did the right thing, just as he had done some 15 years earlier, but this time he was proposing to Sarah's young sister Chrissy.

In the grand scheme of things, it wasn't such a bad move. Frankie was a good money getter, and had done right by Sarah for the short duration of their marriage, cut short only by her untimely death. He was a known quantity within the family and already had their respect, but this was another unexpected twist in the already convoluted family tree. Even if marriage to your deceased wife's sister was now acceptable by law, as it had not previously been, it had certainly not been permitted that long ago by the Catholic Church, and Mariah was already in the bad books on that front, since she was still living in sin as far as the church was concerned.

What now – might she have burst into flames if she dared to enter St Mary's Cathedral? Had it been a few decades earlier then possibly, but the church was moving with the times, and although Mariah was still blackballed because of her ongoing relationship with Big Tom, it transpired that her young daughter could actually sanctify her marriage under St Mary's sacred roof, much to Mariah's relief. Nevertheless, this relationship and impending union, or reunion if you like, was once again the cause of much debate within the family, and not everyone gave it their blessing initially.

But once more, love conquered all and, in the summer of 1947, a double wedding took place at St Mary's Cathedral. Bella had fallen for a young saddle maker by the name of Joe Baird. He was a law-abiding man, and very talented with his hands. He could carve the most beautiful things, such as a dapple-grey rocking horse with hand-stitched Western saddle, made for his only daughter Eileen. It was indeed something to behold; being handed down through several family members before being given as a gift to the children's ward in the Princess Mary Hospital on the Great North Road. Joe's manual dexterity was even more impressive given that his right-arm was deformed following an accident at birth. He was a pleasant fellow, not loud or brash. He wasn't the best dressed man in town, however, but Bella brought him up to speed and made sure he acquired some decent suits and trilby hats to fit in with the rest of the chaps in the family.

The double wedding was a big affair, attended by the whole family and their extended relations and friends. Many travelled the length of the country to put in an appearance, and the lavish reception was held at the function suite on the top floor of the Co-op building on Buckingham Street, in the Big Lamp area of the city, with little expense spared by the paymaster, Mariah.

One person feeling most compromised by this uncustomary union was the teenage Mary Lou. Chrissy had always been her auntie. Was she now to be her mother as well? As it turned out, it was not a harmonious arrangement. Mary Lou had spent the past few years living between Sunderland Street and Gateshead, but now she found herself under one roof with her dad and stepmother, Aunt Chrissy, back on Elswick East Terrace in the heart of Newcastle's West End. Mary Lou had been spoilt by both sides of her family for the best part of her life as a result of losing her own mother at such a tender age; but that was all about to change. Frankie and Chrissy would go on to have two children of their own, Frank Junior and Josephine, or Jo as she preferred to be known.

This awkward adjustment was natural to some degree, but Chrissy's favouritism towards her own children was obvious, and Mary Lou wasn't used to playing second fiddle to anyone.

Her dad had been all hers since her mother passed away, but now there was another woman, as well as two more children vying for Frankie's attention, and Chrissy would naturally ensure that her younger ones got the best of it. After all, Mary Lou was now a young woman and would soon be making her own way in life, so why should she be hanging onto her father's shirt tails? She shared a home with them, but it wasn't the best of times in Mary Lou's life.

After a while, she moved to Gateshead and stayed with Old Peter Hewson and her grandma and namesake Mary, before moving in with Frankie's sister Sarah in the Bensham area of Gateshead. She still spent a lot of time in Newcastle with her cousins, that's where her heart was, but she was happier living with her auntie in Gateshead, rather than her mother's replacement in Newcastle.

Mariah had accumulated considerable wealth during the war years, and although she was cash-rich, she had not invested her money in anything that would ensure her family's status in the future. She was a shrewd woman yet overly cautious. Big Tom was the father to three of her children, but she still wasn't Mrs Cruddas. Not all of her business dealings were entirely above board, even the barrow business was still considered illegal by the authorities in Newcastle. She had enough money to last her a lifetime, but she had a big family and a generous streak when it came to them, although as soon as her girls found men of their own, she made sure it was those men that kept their women and not the other way round; it was certainly never going to be her duty.

No man would be getting their hands on Mariah's dough, son-in-law, common law or otherwise. She rented the house she lived in, she rented the warehouse she operated from and had her name to nothing of substance, other than her reputation. The war years had been good to the family. The black market had enjoyed a seven-year boom, yet the end of the war didn't mark the end of money-making opportunities enjoyed by them, as rationing went on well into the 1950s. Hay was being made while the sun was still shining and long after the bombs stopped falling. New young barrow boys were on the street. Buck and Doodles at first, followed by Georgie, Thomas, Frankie and Jimmy Kelly, along with Sylvia, Peter and Albert Sayers.

John Sayers dabbled once or twice but had ideas of his own on making money, and as a result was never far from trouble. The boys were always seen in each other's company and were quite a little firm around town. Wheelers, dealers, fighters and, in some cases, stealers, but honourable with it. They weren't house burglars or bag snatchers, but they would creep the odd shop or screw the odd factory if they had their card marked, but never a person's home, that wasn't their way. They weren't liberty takers by anybody's standards and hated those who were. They looked after their own and were loyal men within their world, men who could be trusted to keep their mouths shut. Being a grass was the worst offence a person could commit in their world, and it was a line this breed had been raised never to cross.

Once you'd gone down that route, you would never be trusted and you would never be welcomed back into that world. Honour and reputation amongst these kinds of men was everything in those days, and staunch men were respected men. Fear of imprisonment for them was not the daunting deterrent it might have been for most people, yet they never swear another person's life away in order to avoid jail. Prison had been a constant in their lives. Lots of men might have been able to say their old man had done a bit of bird, or their brother or uncle, but very few could say that their mother, aunties and granny had also done time.

With most of Mariah's daughters now married, almost all of them wed to men of a particular character, two of them even marrying the same one of those characters, it left only Joss, a widow to Willy Craig. Joss eventually married again, to a local bookie by the name of Tommy Chapman; Peggy married his brother John Chapman, also in the fruit game, while Muriel, Mariah's other daughter to Big Tom, later married a fella called Joe Donnelly; a big bruiser of a man with a loud and gruff personality, earning him the nickname 'The Growler', and last but never least, in Mariah's eyes, was Albert. He married one Elsie Elsender from Scotswood.

Scotswood Road, made famous in the *Blaydon Races* song was about two miles long, running alongside the north bank of the River Tyne. The road had many streets running off it into the West End, and at one time there was a boozer on the corner of just about every one of them, no less than 46 pubs in its heyday. It was a lively place and the scene of many a wild night in Newcastle, long before the infamous Bigg Market gained its notorious reputation.

It was a time when bars were the hub of any local community. Television hadn't yet reached the masses, and the extent of home entertainment was the wireless radio, if you were fortunate enough to have one. The public house was the place to be; to socialise, relax, be entertained, and to keep abreast of what was going on in your world. They were vibrant, lively places filled with people from all walks of life. The stench of ale and smoke would hit you before you even walked through the doors, and once inside, the only noise would be that of laughter and conversation, no pool tables or fruit machines, no TV screens or jukeboxes. Other than a wireless, the only time music would be heard was if someone could play the piano, provided the bar was lucky enough to have one.

Certain pubs were used by the coal miners or the Vickers-Armstrong factory workers, others by the locals who lived in the rabbit warren of streets criss-crossing the great road, and some of the rougher bars were frequented by the more unsavoury types. They were all used from time to time by members of the family. Sometimes they'd be flooding the worker's bars with hooky gear, or visiting local pals, and sometimes they'd be there to do business with their crooked cronies. As a result, everybody in the area knew the men of this burgeoning family, generally recognised as one large firm, and one best not to be messed with.

The pickings were rich around the town, and their family numbers were growing within it. There may have been more mouths to feed by the time the war was over, but the increase in men from similar walks of life produced a new generation of characters born into the street life of their city. More numbers meant a greater reach, which meant more contacts, more grafters and more money. But like many others from that walk of life, the curse of 'easy come, easy go' money was often a factor perpetuating their existence. Crooked people would get it fast and spend it faster.

When it was gone, they'd be at it again, and again the same thing would happen, and it wasn't so different for the men of this family. However, if they did squander any money they got, they were fortunately not the types who had to go out and risk their liberty every day by thieving to keep their wheels spinning. They had many talents when it came to turning a shilling, and Mariah would gladly give any of her offspring a little start money so they could have a deal, buy a bit of gear to turn a profit, or supply them with a bit of stock for the barrow rather than have them out risking their liberty. This was a reciprocal arrangement of course. If she helped the boys out it kept them directly away from unnecessary danger, and hopefully out of jail, for which Mariah would receive a drink, a cut of any profit they might make as a result of her assistance.

This kept the chaps out of real trouble for the best part and kept the bottom drawer of Mariah's tallboy well stocked, although sometimes the temptation to carry out a little bit of naughty 'graft' was too great for some of the chaps to turn down, regardless of the alternative options available to them.

The house on Sunderland Street was always a hive of activity. Gear was coming and going, men would be there divvying up or talking business, while life in the house went on around them as though it was the most natural thing in the world.

The young ones had grown up used to this life, and were now beginning to emulate their forebears. Little boys quickly became little men, capable men in due course. The barrow game was and always had been an earner. If there was nothing on the go that could get them a better day's take than a few hours at a pitch then they would always be out on the barrow, sometimes up to seven or eight would be seen around the bottom end of Nelson Street as the family numbers grew, and other faces began jumping on the bandwagon. A good day at a pitch could get you as much as a tenner bunce, decent profit for a day's work, or sometimes just half a day if they cleared the boards early, especially since a working man would toil all week for less than a that.

So, the barrow job was decent more often than not, but if something better came along then some of the lads, particularly the younger generation, would dabble elsewhere in the pursuit of richer pickings.

The 1950s were looming, but life was still tough for most people in post-war Britain, as rationing continued long after D-day, and for the family at least, that wasn't such a bad thing.

Knowing as many colourful people as they did, opportunity was never far away. The 'faces' of the time were friendly with the younger generation now, Buck, Doodles and Albert; their reputation as hard, capable men would often attract the attention of villains if assistance for a particular bit of business was required. Not all of the chaps were game enough to put their liberty on the line if the stakes were too high though. Some, however, cared less and got involved with bits and pieces from time to time.

Doodles was making a name for himself in the ring, having already done so on the cobbles. He was a tough man and didn't stand for any nonsense, but he was a gentleman. He was a good boxer, but lousy management prevented him from earning any real money from the game. He boxed featherweight, about 9st 6lb, and the guy who looked after him, a fellow from Blackpool called Jim Turner, was matching him with fighters a stone or two heavier than him, and of course that didn't work out well. He went down to London, had some decent fights and won some trophies, but never earned any money at the game.

Real money, however, was readily available in the town, especially with a talent like his, and as a result, much of his was earned the other way. Doodles could quite easily have been a contender for a British title, had he been fortunate enough to have had decent management. He did have some notable boots to fill, however. His father's family tree revealed a relation by the name of Tom Sayers, a man who became heavyweight boxing champion of England back in 1857, even taking on American Champion John C Heenan for what was considered to be, at the time, the first world heavyweight championship contest.

The fight was ultimately called off by the referee due to crowd trouble, and the contest declared as a draw. Strangely, a man of the same name as Tom Sayers' opponent would later become a friend of Frankie's, and it was an ancestor of his that actually fought Tom Sayers; small world. Championship boxing, however, evaded Doodles, and like many men from similar backgrounds, he became involved with all the local villains. As a man of respect, he got rolled into many little moves and bits of work, someone who could hold their hands up like Doodles would always get a living in his world.

Right across the board, this breed were earning. The women of both generations still had a presence on the streets, and thankfully, as the 1950s approached, things for Mariah and her daughters had eased up as far as their pitches were concerned. The Watch Committee, an internal body of Northumbria Police force had unexpectedly declared a truce with them. Sense, it seemed, had eventually prevailed and Mariah and her girls were given a surprise amnesty. But it wasn't all it seemed.

So long had she, and now her girls, been present on the streets of Newcastle, and such had been their treatment at the hands of the local authorities, that the Watch Committee decided to allow them to stand their own pitches without further fear of arrest. This was a watershed moment for the girls and a victory of sorts for Mariah. She had continued her mother's campaign for legalisation and although the amnesty wasn't exactly that, it did mean that, for as long as they were alive, they could work their pitches trouble free. No such courtesy was extended to any of the chaps, however, and what was given with one hand by the Watch Committee, was taken away with the other.

Anyone other than Mariah, her daughters and a couple of the longstanding flower girls in town, was still fair game for the law, and with several men in the shape of Frankie Hewson, Morry, Pow and Coronation, as well as the younger ones coming through, the threat of getting nicked for sly pitching was still as much of an occupational hazard as it had ever been. A Special Patrol Group (SPG) was formed to keep sly pitching off the streets, and when the SPG did the rounds, everyone got lifted.

The warehouse, however, was still the centre of much activity and very much a meeting place for all the family. Mariah was the figure head, and the words she used to say were now more relevant than ever before, she may no longer have not had much, but she now certainly had an awful lot to look at. She had her favourites within her flock, and she had some that she was less enamoured with.

Making flesh of one child or grandchild and foul of another isn't something that most people would tend to do with their offspring, but Mariah wasn't most people, and if she liked one more than the other, then she would have no concerns about showing it. After all, you can pick your friends, but not your family, and it wasn't like she only had three or four to choose from, she had dozens of them, and they kept on coming with every year that passed. Getting spoiled, as far as Mariah was concerned, was no less character building than getting overlooked. Being used to nice things could encourage her offspring to make sure they continued to have them, if it didn't, it was their own foolish fault. She could be black and white in that regard, even though she loved all of her family dearly, she loved some more dearly than others, and besides; there were just so many of them.

Naturally, Mariah had a soft spot for Mary Lou. She was the only child of her firstborn daughter and had been left without her mother at just eight years old. Coupled with the fact that the other half of Mary Lou's family were 'that lot from Gateshead', Mariah made no secret of ruining Mary Lou. The other 'special one' of course, was her only son Albert. Albert was just a matter of months older than his niece Mary Lou, and in the months that straddled October 1952 to July '53, Mariah made grandiose gestures to the pair of them. Albert came of age in the autumn of 1952, and in keeping with his extravagant lifestyle, Mariah bestowed the young man with a cash gift of £1,000. Such a gift in modern day society would be considered substantial, but a grand for your 21st birthday in 1952 was like getting 40 or 50 grand today. But that wasn't the end of Mariah's extravagant generosity, at a time when many people would struggle to make ends meet.

Mary Lou had started to see a handsome young fella from the East End by the name of Tommy Lennie, although everyone called him Eddie. He was an apprentice floor-layer at W E Harkers in Newcastle. He was to all intents and purposes a straight goer, in as much as he did a legitimate job for his living. His family had originated from the West End, but his mother Elsie had moved to Byker after the death of her husband Tommy, who hailed from Scotswood Road, and she ran the Blue Bell bar at the top of Shields Road for a while. Tommy fought in the Second World War and had been a tasty pick-pocket in his day, sadly, he died suddenly of a heart attack at the dining table of their home in 1947.

Eddie, like his mother, had very sallow skin and jet-black hair which he wore in a quiff. With his sharp attire, he liked his tuggies (clothes), Eddie cut a fine young figure of a man, in the mould of Hollywood heartthrob Tony Curtis. His mother Elsie, however, was determined her boy wouldn't go off the rails and applied for him to get an apprenticeship at Harkers. She had fears about which way Eddie might turn in the absence of his father, and the fact that he spent his life in the snooker halls around town rather than school. He was a young hustler and would play grown men for money when he was just a lad of 13 or 14. Older fellas would take him to different clubs to play their best players for money, and Eddie would get a cut of all the winnings. So, Elsie was determined his misspent youth wouldn't turn into a wasted life.

Upon hearing of Mary Lou's involvement with Eddie, Frankie Hewson demanded to see the young man, not overly impressed that Eddie was working for a furniture and haberdashery store in Newcastle, laying floors for a living. This would have been welcome news to most perspective in-laws, but their world dictated different standards. Someone who stood on their own two feet, did whatever they had to do in order to provide for their family and didn't have to answer to anyone in order to put food on the table; that's what would fit the bill for Mary Lou. So when she produced a photograph of the two of them out with friends, Frankie Hewson became even more insistent on meeting this curious fella.

Mary Lou was a pale-skinned English rose, and Eddie looked, as her father put it at the time, like he had a bit of tar brush in him, in the picture at least, with his dark-skinned hand draped around Mary's alabaster shoulder. Eventually, Mary dragged her beau along to North Shields market, where Frankie had a pitch a couple of days a week on a derelict bomb site on the corner of Rudyard Street and Savile Street. His fears about Eddie's ethnicity were alleviated when he finally met him. He indeed was not, as Frankie had thought, a black man, and to make Frankie feel even better about the young fella, Eddie revealed who his father was.

Frankie knew of Tommy Lennie from his days as a dipper, and that certainly helped make Frankie feel a whole lot better about things. Madness when you think about it, but this was their mentality, their way of life, and if his future son-in-law's old man was crooked, then there was still hope for Eddie. By contrast, Eddie's mother Elsie had reservations about her son getting involved with this family. Before taking over the Blue Bell in Byker, she had served behind the bar of the Three Bulls Heads on Percy Street, just along from Liza's pitch. She knew who Mary Lou was, and knew of the family. Many of the chaps used the Three Bulls, and Elsie had seen first-hand how they went on. She knew what they were, how they lived, and she feared her son would not be able to keep up with their lifestyle, let alone keep one of their own in the manner she assumed the girl was accustomed to, at least not on an apprentice's wage.

It cuts both ways, the view of the other side, but in spite of their seemingly social differences, the two had undoubtedly hit it off. Eddie and Mary Lou courted strongly for the best part of a year after being introduced at The Westgate Picture Hall by Billy Findlay, a pal of Eddie's, and a friend of the family. They made plans to wed as soon as possible, and Mary Lou, being Mary Lou, wanted it to happen now, and to happen big. 'A rainbow wedding, I want,' she would tell anyone that listened, each bridesmaid in a different coloured dress, with a white silk and lace wedding dress for herself. She had grand plans for their big day, but not the grand money to make it happen, and Eddie wasn't getting any fortunes as an apprentice. Sarah, Mary Lou's mother, would have no doubt made sure her only daughter had all she wanted for her big day. She had been a woman of means herself, however, Sarah was no longer around, and Frankie Hewson's new wife Chrissy was less concerned about such extravagant desires, especially since Mary Lou wasn't actually her own daughter.

Chrissy and Frankie had two children of their own to take care of, and Mary Lou had no real mother to turn to. Frankie had to be diplomatic about the situation and do his best not upset either of the women over the forthcoming wedding. Mary Lou had been playing one family off against the other for the best part of her life following her mother's death, as well as her own passing around between the Kellys and the Hewsons. It was now time to have a quiet word with her fairy grandmother, and she knew just how to play the wily old 'Queen of the Barrows'.

Anything that might give Mariah a bit of one-upmanship over the Gateshead mob would go down well with her.

Upon listening to Mary Lou, how she loved young Eddie and wanted to marry soon but couldn't get her own way with her dad and Chrissy. 'Aye' said Mariah, as she corrected her ample bosom, never bridled by a brazier, which sat cradled in her folded arms. She told Mary Lou not to worry, reassuring her she'd take care of everything. They were sat in the front room of Mariah's house on Sunderland Street when she got up, asked for Mary Lou's handbag and went into the parlour. Mary Lou had an idea what Mariah was going in there for, they all knew about her stash.

When she emerged and gave the handbag back to Mary Lou, she told her not to worry about a thing. What was in her bag would take care of all she wanted. It was her gift, and as this was to be the first wedding of any of her grandchildren, she would not have it said by anyone that it was anything other than a big do.

Thanking her old granny, and without so much as peeking inside her handbag, Mary Lou kissed Mariah, before dashing off to meet Eddie at the Essoldo Picture Hall on the bottom of Westgate Road. The two met outside, and Mary Lou explained that she'd been to see her granny and that she'd received a gift from her to help with their wedding plans.

'How much?' Eddie asked.

'I don't know,' replied Mary Lou. 'I haven't had a look yet, and I'm not gonna pull it out here in the street,' she declared.

Once settled in their seats, the two could barely wait to have a look inside the handbag. Waiting 'til the house lights went down so no one could see what they were looking at, Mary Lou furtively undid the catch on the upright solid clutch bag and flipped open the lid. There inside, taking up almost every bit of space in the oval shaped bag, was stuffed one of the many rolls of notes that Mariah kept so neatly stacked under the towel in the bottom drawer of her parlour tallboy. Eddie took a sharp intake of breath, he'd not seen so much money in one go. Mary Lou was less shocked by the sizeable wad, she'd seen money all her life, and dozens of similar wads in her granny's parlour.

'How much is there?' he asked again.

'I don't know. Looks like a few quid though,' she answered nonchalantly.

'Looks like a right few quid!' he declared, taking it from the bag.

Under cover of the darkened cinema, they had a roll call. He started counting under his breath, and as Eddie reached £100 he was only a fraction of the way through the big white wedge of £5 notes.

'Two hundred, three hundred… fucking hell!' he exclaimed.

Mary Lou, however, was more concerned about him drawing attention to themselves than she was about the amount of cash he was counting.

'Mary, there's five hundred quid here,' he gasped in disbelief. 'My God. How much money has that woman got?'

It was a rhetorical question and one which nobody but Mariah knew the answer to.

'There's nearly enough money here to buy a house!'

He was shocked. 'Jesus Christ,' he muttered under his breath, utterly dumbfounded.

'Shhh,' whispered Mary Lou. 'Put it away before someone sees it. It's to pay for the wedding, and the film's starting. Shhh.'

After all, a monkey might have been a small fortune in 1953, but it was just a decent bung for the girl who took pound notes to school when she was a child.

From October 1952 to the summer of '53, Mariah had given away no less than £1500 to her two favourites, in birthday and wedding gifts.

Together with the annual Christmas distribution of £100 each to all of her children, and Mary Lou, which fell within that period, it took the old girl's generosity to two and a half grand in a little over six months. One thing was for sure, Mariah wouldn't give her last twenty-five hundred quid away in gifts. What wasn't certain, however, was just how much ready cash this shrewd old woman had in that bottom drawer. However much it was, or however much it became, would never be known, and sadly, would never be invested wisely.

The potential to put her family on the map in Newcastle was within Mariah's grasp, but circumstance, generosity, over cautiousness, and the curse of easy come, easy go, would come to haunt the Kelly clan in the years that followed, ensuring that their struggle to conquer the world would not be over for a long time yet.

GOING TO THE NEXT LEVEL

By the time Elizabeth II was getting used to the idea of being crowned Queen, Mariah had truly established herself as 'Queen of the Barrows' – the matriarchal figurehead of a family with a reputation that spread far beyond the streets of Newcastle.

Such was her influence in the fruit market at St Andrew's that she, at one time, had virtual control of the place they called the Banana Rooms. The Co-operative Stores on Newgate Street had a distribution warehouse there, just along from St Andrew's, from where they would send out produce to all of their stores and wholesale clients in the area. In the basement of the building was the huge store room where they kept their stock of bananas. Mariah, with her increased buying power, shrewd knowledge of the game, and persuasive charm, had managed to secure a deal with the head salesman there, and for as long as it lasted no traders other than the Co-op's own stores and clients could buy a banana from anyone but Mariah Kelly.

Loose bananas were a favourite line for the barrow boys and fruit shops. Mariah orchestrated a deal which meant every loose banana that came through the distribution warehouse went to her. Not only had she secured the rights to them, but she had the salesman straightened, on a bung, and he would make sure that every wooden box, the type that she had wrapped every one of her daughters in, was packed full by the salesman, and considerably overweight. The 28lb boxes would be filled with all of the Co-op's loose bananas, and there were mountains of them, all packed into boxes by hand, weighing more like 35 to 40lb.

The fact that she had it sewn up was good enough, but she was getting double bubble with the extra weight in every box, thanks to the salesman she had in her pocket. She was nobody's fool.

Now with eight living daughters and a son all married off, Mariah had no less than 21 grandchildren by the year 1952, and another 19 were to join within a few short years to follow. In the summer of the Coronation Year, Mary Lou was about to become the first of her grandchildren to get married. By that time the Sayers branch was complete, as were the Kelly and Patterson factions of the family.

Joss, although re-married, never produced any offspring. Chrissy and Bella had three between them; Bella was mother to Eileen, and Chrissy to Jo, plus the new Frankie Hewson Jr. Of the three of Mariah's kids born to Big Tom Cruddas, the oldest Peggy would have four girls, Muriel had yet to bear any children but would go on to produce no less than eight with Joe 'The Growler' Donnelly. Albert, at the age of 21, had not yet fathered any additions to the family, but would go on to have three with Elsie Elsender, later having four children with Jenny Muhammed, the daughter of a wealthy Asian businessman from the growing local community.

The husbands to Mariah's many daughters were all characters in their own right. Costermongers from the Mile End Road, showmen, hawkers, street traders, bookies and the talented saddler and carpenter who eventually turned his hand to a bit of weekend hawking, after getting a taste of family life. They were all thick with each other and would do bits of business together, work on the corner of Nelson Street, and spend time together drinking in The Carlisle bar, Parkers, The Marquis of Blandford, the Chancellors, and many other bars in the city; that was their manor. Another bar often frequented by the chaps was The Clock Inn at the top of Buckingham Street just along the road from the hallowed ground of St James' Park, the home of Newcastle United FC.

One night in The Clock, when the bar was full, and the drink was flowing, The Growler – Big Joe Donnelly – made a spectacular appearance. He'd been to collect a debt, which was one of his bullish talents, and just like in Jack and the Beanstalk he didn't come away with the money he was after. But rather than a handful of magic beans, The Growler had taken a Shetland pony as payment. Tickled by his acquisition of this little horse he decided to show it off to the boys. As it was night-time and no one was on the street, he headed for The Clock bar, knowing he would find most of the crew in there. He was a loud and imposing man, and when he walked into a room you certainly knew he was there, but sometimes wished he wasn't. When he burst through the doors of The Clock this night like Buffalo Bill, with his big size tens trailing the ground as he sat straddled across the back of the miniature horse, the entire place went into an uproar.

The traumatised pony tried to buck him off, kicking tables and stools all over the place in the process, sending drink and glass in every direction. He tried to calm the poor thing down as it jostled him around like a bucking bronco. The bar was on its feet as the pair bounced around the place like a rodeo gone wrong. If a clown were to have walked in behind them, it would've put the top hat on the whole episode.

So much for The Growler's grand entrance. His 'little pony' wasn't having any of it, and it finally displayed its feelings about the ridiculous spectacle by shitting all over the floor. Joe growled at the dear little beast and dragged it out the bar like a dog on a lead before kicking it up the arse. He certainly made a memorable appearance that night.

The men and women of this family led a colourful existence. They did their own thing and answered to no one, not even the law. They knew how to get money, and they knew how to spend it. Good days were always followed by good nights, often in The Clock or The Cuckoo just a couple of hundred yards away on Diana Street. The two bars got their names from the coal face of the former pit that ran beneath them at Gallowgate, called the Cuckoo-Clock coal face. Many men from this part of the world worked long hard shifts underground in the pits of Tyneside, or in dangerous shipyards tossing red-hot rivets around, navigating heavy machinery and red-hot furnaces trying to avoid injury, yet they would have far less to spend on good times than the men of this family, and far less time to spend it.

The boys were hard workers too though, most of them, but hard work in their world meant something slightly different, usually involving a lot less toil than that being done down a pit for 12 hours a day. They say crime doesn't pay, and that may well be true, but at least the hours were good. They had a different set of rules and a different way of life. Some of the things they did carried risk, but it wasn't the risk of injury or death each day at work. In their line of business, the threat of arrest and the potential loss of their liberty was the only thing at stake, but capture in their day usually involved being caught red-handed. It was like open season for many villains as CCTV, alarm systems and forensic detection were unheard of at the time, and the chaps were generally too smart to get caught in the act. The other danger of course was being grassed up for something, so working with your family meant you knew you were working with reliable people.

The very thought that any of your own would put you in for something was beyond their comprehension. They were staunch people, they stuck together, and they kept their mouths shut. They looked like what they were. Like Paddy always said, a sausage should never be judged by its skin, but these boys simply didn't look like working men. They were always suited and booted. They wore smart hats and expensive shoes. It was nothing to see them with a nice gold kettle on their wrist or a diamond ring on their finger. The nice bits of 'tom' that were worn by the men and women of the family were not bought or worn just for the flash, there was also a practical reasoning behind it.

People like them didn't put money away for rainy days. They didn't save up and keep their coppers for the weekend, they spent as they earned, so buying a nice diamond ring, a good kettle or an expensive piece of tom for the wife, or daughter, was their way of putting something aside. When the lean times came, which they always did, they would have that watch or piece of jewellery to cash in.

It's the same mentality that Travellers apply to buying Crown Derby china, Waterford crystal or even horses. Money invested into those sorts of assets is like money put away, just not in a bank. Buying flash cars, houses or other apparent displays of wealth, when you weren't in the system, could fetch unwanted attention from the law or the taxman. It's a lot harder for the powers that be to work out the value or the origin of a piece of jewellery, a set of dishes or even a horse, than it is to find out how much you'd paid for your car or your house.

Their wealth was kept under the radar, worn on their hands and their backs, or displayed in their cabinets. This was their rainy-day money, and it was not displayed under the noses of the authorities. Mariah would often be seen at Porritt's pawnbrokers on Newgate Street picking up brooches, rings, gold chains or any other bit of 'tom' that was handy money; knowing that she was not only treating her daughters, but effectively bunging them at the same time, safe in the knowledge that they'd have something to sell if times got hard.

Meanwhile, the chaps would be out, playing cards at the weekend and winning or losing the equivalent of a week's pay in just one hand, and they'd play like that all night, confident in the belief they could go out and get it back the next day, one way or another. Everyone in the West End knew them by now, and they knew everyone worth knowing. They had a growing reputation, one which would be taken to the next level by the new generation. Yet as much as the men of the family were respected, their women, the Kelly girls, got every bit as much respect, if not more. They were a force to be reckoned with in their own right, but now with men like theirs behind them, it would take a very brave soul to do or say anything to upset the girls.

The family were now scattered around the West End. The Hewsons lived on Elswick East Terrace. The Sayers and Kellys shared a house two minutes away on Blandford Street, as did Mary, Pow and the rest of the Patters; Joe, Pat, Michael and Terry. Bella and Joss lived just yards apart on Diana Street. The Donnellys lived around the corner in the Big Lamp area, Albert and Elsie lived close by, and Peggy moved furthest from the town into Ash Street in Benwell.

The family covered the West End of Newcastle, near the city centre for the most part, and when Mariah eventually moved to Buckingham Street, you could have virtually thrown a blanket over the whole lot of them.

Living so close to one another was important to the family. Their own were always around them. There was safety in numbers, and help was just a whistle up the back lane away. The house on Blandford Street, shared by the Sayers and the Kellys, was a hub the family gravitated towards. No less than 16 of this breed were split over two floors, Liza, Morry, Doodles, Sylvia, John, Peter and Albert occupied the ground floor. Young Mariah and Coronation shared the top deck with Buck, Vera, Georgie, Thomas, Marie and the twins, Frankie and Jimmy. The number of people under that roof on Blandford Street would swell at any given time as other family members would land there unannounced. It was a crowded house and a bit of a menagerie.

These were not quiet retiring people who kept themselves to themselves, and if they ever got into trouble, you could rest assured it wasn't for singing too loud in church. Shouting, bawling, effing and blinding, and endless raucous activity were the order of the day at the mad house on Blandford Street, and if either Liza or young Mariah had lived alongside different neighbours there would definitely have been murders on. But when the people you live on top of are your own, making a racket becomes less of a cause for complaint and more of an excuse to join in the fun. This being said, all of the family patronised their parish church, the beloved St Mary's Cathedral. Father Michael had since passed away and Mariah, although still unable to accept the Holy Sacrament, would still be seen there on a Sunday, with large numbers of her kin in tow.

Every one of her growing family was brought into the church under that roof. Christened, confirmed, first Holy Communion, and for those that made honest wives of their women rather than just jumping the broom, they were married from there. St Mary's was their family church and their sanctuary.

Living so close together, in more ways than one, can become claustrophobic, so when Mary and Pow were offered a three-storey house on Westgate Hill, they jumped at the chance. Mary approached her older sisters to see if either one of them fancied sharing the place with them. Young Mariah was the most likely candidate. She was a chip off the old block and so much like her mother in so many ways, not just her name. She had the bigger of the two families, the bigger of the two mouths, and the bigger of the two personalities.

Young Mariah carried more of the venom from the mad dog that bit them than her demurer sister Liza. Old Sally would tell Mariah, and all of her offspring, that somewhere down the line one of their family had been bitten by a mad dog. That's why they were all radge, a little bit crazy, off centre. Really it was just a fantastic excuse for their unorthodox behaviour.

Young Mariah also inherited some of her mother's stranger maternal instincts. Her home was seriously overcrowded and full of larger than life, and often mischievous characters. All of her kids were boisterous, even Vera, and when Marie arrived on the scene, followed soon after by the twins, Mariah decided that the place was just too small and hectic for them all, and she just couldn't be done with it. To ease the burden, Marie ended up spending much of her time with a neighbour by the name of Emma Holiday, so much time in fact that Marie almost lived with Emma for a couple of years, while Mariah worked her pitch on Fenkle Street, opposite Jackson the Tailors, with her older daughter Vera.

Things like this frequently happened in those days, it was no big deal. One of her twins, Jimmy, went to live with his granny on Buckingham Street. Old Mariah had a soft spot for the little fella as he was so small, bestowing him with the nickname Squeaky, and for a while his brother Frankie claimed not to have known Jimmy was his twin, swearing blind he was twins with his cousin Peter Sayers, due to their closeness growing up, and the fact they looked so much alike. When Jimmy, at a very young age, went to stay with his Granny Mariah, she had already taken in one of her daughter Muriel's girls, Terry Donnelly.

Terry didn't want to go and live in the East End with her mother and father. The Growler by then had moved the Donnellys to the end of the city he'd initially hailed from. Over time, Pat Patter went to live with Mary Lou and Eddie Lennie at Hill Court on Pitt Street, by which time Marie had also moved in with them for a while too.

At any given time, any one of the households inhabited by any of the clan could become a temporary residence for any one of their nomadic family, for one reason or another. Most likely the mad dog that bit them did so when they were sat around a stick fire on a camp somewhere in the bandit country of Carrickmacross, because even though the Gypsy blood they had may not have run thick through their veins, it came out plenty in their behaviour.

Young Mariah took up her sister's offer of the bigger place around the corner, as Liza and Morry were only too happy to have Blandford Street to themselves. That was until Morry got the opportunity to buy a house from Chuck Sheldon. Chuck was a friend of the family and the husband of a Travelling woman by the name of Agnes O'Neil. Agnes was typically travellerfied. Dark skinned, gold hoop earrings and a thick head of hair cascading down her back in long black ringlets, a real Black Face'n you might say. The big house Morry bought from Chuck was on Westgate Hill Terrace, and when the Sayers vacated Blandford Street to take up residence in the new house, Mariah took her mob back to the old place she had shared with Liza, leaving Mary and Pow rattling around the three-storey home just around the corner from Liza and Morry's new place. Morry was a shrewd operator, in some part no doubt, down to his Jewish heritage. Although he never practised his faith, he was often on the receiving end of a ribbing from the boys about the little bit of Yiddish in him.

The mix of blood and heritage that weaved through the family was from a cocktail of many different background: Irish,

Scottish, cockney, Jewish, Traveller, tinker, tailor, soldier and plenty of spies. Nothing went on that they didn't get to hear about, their eyes and ears were everywhere on the streets of the town.

The warehouse at Blackfriars was still on the go. It wasn't quite the centre of commerce that it had been during the rationing years when it was a virtual underground distribution centre, but a bit of stuff was still sold from there. Barrows were still rented from there, and it was a meeting place for the younger generation while growing up in the city.

Old Mariah had retired from working on the barrows, leaving that to her daughters and granddaughters. The men had their own pitches, and several other people were on the bandwagon by then. Dickie McLean, a family friend, had a warehouse just up from Mariah's from where he now rented out barrows and carts for hawkers and tatters, and although Mariah had enjoyed good times, and witnessed many changes, by the age of 65, she was undoubtedly beginning to slow down a little.

The woman had lived a colourful life, and although she had profited from it, it was not without hardship. She had seen the inside of a prison cell more times than most men would. She had raised ten children, with controversial methods, and had seen more than her fair share of trouble, if not with the law (police were a constant bane in her life), then with anybody that crossed her. The woman had endured great pain and tragedy, lost children and buried her firstborn. She had laid her parents Paddy and Old Sally to rest, along with the father of seven of her daughters, Billy Fleming. She had endured the whispers of the community and the loss of Catholic privileges over Big Tom, suffering the resulting disapproval of her family. She had born three further children during the change of life and had spent as much time on the streets of Newcastle as a point polis (police/copper), exposed to every possible element; and all of this was visibly etched on her weather-beaten face. She should have been comfortable by this stage, able to enjoy to the rest of her life in the safe knowledge that she had enough money to do so, but a name that held such significance in her life, would ultimately be her Achilles heel.

The Bazeley Line steamer ship Albert was where it all began, with Paddy and Sally hiding from the law, wheedling their way aboard, escaping from the old country in search of a better life on English soil. It was the Albert that brought them together and set the stage for Mariah's life journey. And it was to be Albert that would be instrumental in taking her right back to the start again, like a game of snakes and ladders played out on the cobbles.

The big event of 1953, besides the Queen's coronation, was Mary Lou's Rainbow Wedding. The handmade silk and lace wedding dress cost nearly as much as all the different coloured bridesmaid dresses put together, and they weren't cheap. Besides her Maid of Honour, Mary Newton, Mary Lou's best friend outside the family, all of her other bridesmaids were direct family; six of them blood to Mary Lou, her sister Jo, cousins Eileen, Pat, Sylvia, Vera and her cousin Moira, the daughter of one of Frankie Hewson's sisters from Gateshead. Eddie's sister June was the token bridesmaid from his side, while Albert Cruddas played the role of best man, at the request of Mariah, and since she was footing the bill for the whole affair, it was the least they could do to oblige her. He, or she, who pays the piper, they say, is the one who calls the tune.

St Mary's was full on the bright summer's day in July, the entire family turned out, and friends from all over the city and further afield came to celebrate the big day. No expense was spared on the reception in The Brighton Dance Hall on Westgate Road. Caterers supplied food continually throughout the day to the hundreds of guests, far too many to sit down for a meal, and these weren't really 'sit down on ceremony' kind of people. The men gathered with each other on one side of the room, and the women all sat together on the other, as if they were two different species.

The common tradition of long protracted speeches wasn't entirely their style either. Acknowledgement of how well Mary Lou and the bridesmaids looked by Albert, followed by the Father of the Bride's 'thank you to everyone for attending' was about the strength of it. More than enough food, drink at the free bar, business and eventually dancing and singing, were all of far more importance, and no time was going to be wasted on poncey speeches when they could all be enjoying themselves.

This era was a significant time in the history of the family. Just as rationing throughout the war years, and the heavily exploited black market had helped increase their earning potential and their notoriety, the influx of men into the Kelly family had given them a whole new dynamic. They were no longer just a remarkable group of self-preserving determined women, but almost as if chosen from a catalogue, the men the Kelly girls had selected for husbands, were all from the 'crooked section.' Big Tom, Frankie Hewson, Morry Sayers, Coronation Kelly, Pow Patterson, The Growler, they were all men of a certain ilk.

The sons and daughters they all brought into the family were born into a particular way of life. They lived in a world where the rules were different. Where being streetwise was far more important and valuable to them than a formal education. Where taking care of yourself was paramount. If you couldn't, you'd be trampled on.

There was a code they lived by, and it was a code that only certain people understood. They were real life 'wise guys', a term being introduced into British society by the motion picture industry and the James Cagney and Humphrey Bogart films of the day portraying gangster life in America. The young men of the family related to the anti-establishment attitude and the culture that went with it; it reflected their own lives and those of the people in their orbit. The old Ealing comedies of the time paid homage to the underworld lifestyle, and life for the men of the family began to imitate the art that was, in turn, imitating life as they knew it. Dressing well, speaking and holding yourself in a particular way, while living a life less ordinary, outside of accepted guidelines, was the theme of many of the cinema releases of the day, and what was being shown on the screen resonated with the young men of the family.

The world that Joe Public loved to come and see played out on the big screen was the world they lived in, by birthright. They knew they were different, they knew they were more like the people they were watching on the screen than the people they were sitting next to; only this wasn't an act, it was second nature and was all they knew. The world was beginning to understand the mentality of the 'outlaw' and the world was, and always had been, intrigued by it. Many people would enter this world. Some by default; loss of a job, some desperate circumstance, or desertion from the army, for example, would turn some straight people crooked for a time, but these people would come and go.

They would play at being a 'wise guy' just like George Raft or Edward G Robinson. They loved the idea of being part of something like the Lavender Hill Mob, but as the saying goes, everybody wants to be a gangster, until it's time to do gangster shit.

Newcomers to this world would buckle often under the threat of incarceration if nicked in the line of duty. They would lose their bottle if things got out of hand and swear a life away if it meant saving their own neck. If they encountered violence or the threat of jail, they would often revert to old and go back to working straight for a living.

This bunch, however, didn't know anything else. Their way of life was bred into them, and the new generation played the part better than most of the actors on the big screen. They were real life wise guys, third generation.

After all, what's bred in the bone…

A ROYAL COMMAND PERFORMANCE

By the time rock 'n' roll was starting to sweep the nation, Mariah's' family were sweeping Newcastle, as their numbers had swollen considerably.

Most of her 40 or so grandchildren had arrived on the scene, from Billy Buck, the oldest, right down to Frankie Hewson, the youngest at the time, while the next generation of great-grandkids were now starting to arrive. New husbands had joined the family, and even those who weren't cut from similar cloth soon became entranced by the lifestyle of this extraordinary family, and as history so often has a tendency to repeat itself, they all eventually succumbed to the appeal of being on the firm.

Doodles was a main player in the new generation of the family and was carving out a notorious reputation, not just as a fighter, but as a serious operator. He could handle himself, and he had three useful brothers by his side, plus an army of cousins, most of whom were happy to get involved in whatever Doodles might have had going down. For some, the barrows were enough. It was always an available option, and it was a good lifestyle. Little bits of this and that would not be a deterrent to many of them, but any serious villainy was the concern of just a handful of them.

For some, like Buck, Georgie and Thomas Kelly, Albert Sayers and a couple of the others, it would be for refusing to pay outstanding fines for street trading. Non-payment of blisters was a matter of principle, and a week or two banged up with one or two of your cousins was seen as a bit of a laugh, plus it provided them with an opportunity to meet faces from all over the country, as well as doing little harm to their reputation. It's just like normal society in many respects, all men are equal, but some are more equal than others. Crooked has many levels. Just because you work the street, buy a bit of hoist, or tuck someone up with a bit of tom, doesn't necessarily mean you'll screw a factory, hijack a truck or demand money with menaces, the latter only being done to people who tried to ‘play the game’ in their world and came unglued for falling foul of the rules.

Regular civilians were never on the receiving end of threats of violence, not unless of course they got above their station and disrespected any of the family.

Frankie Doodles had heart, he was a good pro boxer in his time; he was game and had no fear of anything or anybody. He was only a short man, serious looking, and a gentleman in many respects. Well-dressed, polite and extremely courteous around women. He was no stranger to tragedy, however. Frankie had two girls and two boys to his wife, Lilly. Sadly though, they lost little Carol early in her life, as a result of a tragic accident.

Surprisingly, all of Frankie’s kids went straight. His sons and daughters just never got involved in ‘family’ life. Lilly was a strong influence on them, and later in life even Doodles encouraged his kids to pursue a normal path, realising that jail, violence and sleeping with one eye open was not what he wanted for his children, and it certainly wasn’t what Lilly wanted. Then there was his younger brother John. He was fearless, reckless, and had no respect for the law.

John was always in trouble, it seemed to follow him like a black cloud but he dealt with it in his own way, it was an occupational hazard, just as being arrested for working the barrow had been for all of his family before him. But his brushes with the law were on a different level. His three sons John, Stephen and Michael, who all arrived some years later, would take those brushes to the very highest level, but that’s a whole different story.

Peter and Albert were more interested in working the street as young barrow boys. Sylvia was always by her mother’s side at Liza’s pitch on Percy Street, and although they still wouldn’t legalise pitches, the Watch Committee had conceded to the Kelly girls’ tenacity and determination, allowing them to earn an ‘honest’ living. Even they recognised how ridiculous it was to persecute these women for selling fruit and veg when there were so many other real crimes that required the laws attention.

Organised crime wasn't just prevalent in America at the time; in London there were plenty of hardmen making their way through the ranks. Jack Spot, Billy Hill and later Joe Pyle, the Richardsons, Krays, Frankie Fraser, Freddie Foreman all became names synonymous with British organised crime, and became known to some of the family over time. Doodles did a bit of bird with Frankie Fraser, who remained familiar with some members of the family 'til his death in 2014.

Newcastle, however, was an outpost of England. It was isolated in its location, almost a hundred miles north of Leeds, a city close to places like Manchester and Liverpool which in turn weren't too distant from Birmingham; all connected and interwoven in some way. Notorious families in these cities had competition and networks close at hand, just as London had rival families and firms vying for control and notoriety, carving up manors and territories, often with violent consequences.

But Newcastle was up north and on its own. Some soft southerners thought the 'town' was in Scotland, such was its distance from the other regions of civilised society in England. But the 'town' was the home of this family. It was their backyard, and they, along with a few other notable families, circulated on its streets. But this lot were not first generation. They had been around a long time. It was this family, their firm, that were born into this way of life. They were a breed apart, and they weren't about to let anyone from another city, or another family from the town, try to lay the law down on their manor.

They weren't organised criminals in the sensationalised terms used by the media. They were a notorious family, doing things in a certain way with an old-school approach. They had values, maybe not the same as some, but very honourable ones when it came to matters of a serious nature. They were clannish and stood side by side on any conflict with outsiders. But with so many in their ranks, and with little firms popping up, often including various members of the family, they would sometimes find conflict within their own.

After all, Newcastle wasn't Chicago, and the pound note they were all chasing was often the same one. Stepping on the toes of a family member would happen from time to time. It would get sorted, however, and although it may have caused a little bad blood, it never dismantled their standing as one family. Disorganised crime might have been a better description of their activities at the time, but the years would sort out the serious villains from the part-timers, and after all was said and done, they were family, and back then that's what was most important to them.

Buck and Georgie Kelly were proper barrow boys, George was a great street worker and plied his trade up and down the country, as did Albert Sayers; trading in Manchester and London as well as on the streets of Newcastle. They had great mentors in Morry and Old Frankie Hewson. Georgie and Albert were the like Del Boys and Arthur Daleys of their era, pitching up to work a line; they could charm the birds from the trees – and sometimes in a variety of accents, depending on where they were working. The Geordie dialect wouldn't always be music to the ears of a Manc or a cockney, so they lads would sometimes adopt an appropriate persona depending on what city they were working in; after all the punters needed to at least be able to understand them if they were to be talked into buying from them.

They were invited to London for the Queen's Coronation, at least that's what they told their kids. The reality was they went down to clean up on the streets of the capital, bursting with money-laden tourists and spectators in the summer of 1953. Frankie and Morry punted the cheap royal merchandise doing the rounds at that time. Working from a suitcase to crowds of eager punters was manna from heaven. They'd have hedges three or four deep and fiddle away all day, taking proper money and living it up in the West End in the evening, before hitting the pavement again the following day. Good times were had, whilst money and good friends were being made, with the boys gaining recognition as solid people in the street game all over the country. Determined to make a killing down in the Smoke, Frankie, Morry and co took a couple of tasty bottle merchants along for the ride, putting them to work in the huge crowds, an opportunity being one which was simply too good to miss.

If the chaps couldn't talk the money out of the punters with their patter and their Royal memorabilia, then the pickpockets would help themselves to it anyway. That was *their* game. The men worked the street with a bit of swag, while the dippers went about their business among the crowds of tourists and sightseers, paying the boys a cut of their take for being back up if they came unstuck; a small price to pay for being on the firm. Another move they carried out in London was 'grafting the smudge.' This involved one of the firm strolling up and down with a large, expensive looking camera around his neck offering to take photographs of the tourists outside Buckingham Palace or Trafalgar Square, or wherever they had decided to plot up. They'd charge the punters a shilling for a print, or one and six if they wanted an enlargement. The eager tourists would pay up and happily pose while the professional looking photographer took the happy snap. A numbered ticket would be given in exchange for payment, and they'd agree to collect their memento from a designated place nearby later in the day. It was a nice little earner. You could take 20 or 30 photographs, or smudges as they're called, in no time. It was nothing to get a tenner or a score in just a few hours. A working-class man might not get that a week in 1953. And it was all bunce, 100 per cent profit. No one ever collected their smudge; there was never a smudge taken, because there was never any film in the camera.

The little firm that went to the Coronation had a wonderful time down there, thanks to the Queen, but thank God they didn't get the job of taking the photos at Westminster Cathedral; the Queen would have no snaps to remind her of her special day!

In their absence, tales of the lads' escapades would be recounted in bars around town, no doubt being embellished a little on the way, enhancing their reputation as sharp operators and good earners. How anyone came by their money was less of a concern to the folks in their orbit than the fact that they could earn. Knowing the right people, not hurting anyone, and being respected were qualities of far greater importance.

Many families making their way in Newcastle at that time would often be in the company of Morry, Frankie and their clique. Scrap metal dealers, coal merchants, hauliers, builders; self-made men, legitimate businessmen who, like them, came from humble beginnings in the city. Many a good night was spent in company with the likes of the Grievesons, Ramages or Freddy and Charlie Shepherd, whose descendants later became owners of Newcastle United FC. This was a time when many people outside of the family were making a name for themselves in legitimate business; men who'd go on to become renowned for their success in the world of commerce.

The men of Mariah's clan didn't commit the time required to succeed with such legitimate methods, yet grew up, befriended, socialised and did business with such men. The family dealt in ready cash, black money, the kind the taxman knew nothing about, it was and always had been their way. The boys were known across all classes of society in Newcastle, from Prince to pauper, and knew how to carry themselves in any environment; building a network of friends, contacts and associates along the way.

The generation that would follow were raised to become adept at making friends with all the right people, the contacts needed to survive and prosper in the world they lived in. They were to become the generation that would take the family's reputation in Newcastle to yet another level. They were, as some people referred to them, the 'townies'. Other infamous family names emerged over time, some still of note in Newcastle today, but at that time, Mariah's breed and their extended network of loyal family and close friends were the firm from the town.

They may not have been referred to by one common family name, but everyone knew precisely who they were.

By the following year, 1954, rationing in Great Britain had finally come to an end, and this coincided with the arrival of Mariah's first great-grandchild.

He was the son of Mary Lou and Eddie. Tony Lennie, 'Legs' as he became known, was born on Armistice Day, the 11th of the 11th, on Elswick East Terrace in the city's West End. Tony would grow up, just like the rest of them, to be a young barrow boy for a time; it was a rite of passage in this family. If your first experience of it wasn't being packed in a banana box under the barrow, it was keeping toot as a child, then serving the punters as soon as you looked old enough.

But Legs had a wild streak, and his devil-may-care outlook would send him on a crooked path to yet another level in years to come.

The arrival of her first great-grandchild gave Mariah an excuse to spoil yet another of her family. She'd always had a soft spot for Mary Lou, so her first little one would no doubt receive some special attention. Mary Lou and Eddie had long spent Mariah's wedding gift of £500. Any change left over from the week-long celebration of their marriage was spent on expensive furnishings for their little home in Elswick. They got everything at cost price from W E Harker's where Eddie had been serving his time as a floor layer, a role which came to an end once Eddie got involved with the family, but not before he got the staff discount on all the furnishings for their little home.

The lifestyle of the men of the family was a pull for Eddie, being around them gave him access to things he'd never have seen at Harker's. He knew a few people of note himself, but now he was on the firm he would get to know many more. He became lifelong friends with an acquaintance of the Kellys, 'Lucky' Joe Lisle, who'd known Mariah for some time. He worked for a short while with Albert Cruddas, but Albert didn't really have much interest in work, being better at spending than earning, and spent a lot of money in later years in the 69 Club on Westgate Road, which Joe Lisle opened in the 1960s.

The temptation to join the firm was more than Eddie could resist. He went to work on the barrow, and spent most of his time socialising with the Kelly and Sayers boys and the rest of the team. They still had to make a living; the barrow game wasn't always guaranteed to bring the money in. The weather, a handy line at the fruit market, or a pitch on Nelson Street wasn't always a certainty, and if there wasn't any other 'graft' on the go, they would sometimes find themselves struggling.

Life for the family could either be a famine or a feast, and when it was a famine, they rarely had any money to fall back on. Nothing other than trinkets were ever put away for a rainy day. Their money was spent on good times and nice things when they had it. Easy come, easy go! Tomorrow was another day. So, when Mary Lou needed a new pram for the arrival of her first born, it was Mariah who stepped up to the plate yet again. The words of Eddie's mother were ringing in his ears. Mary Lou, so used to the finer things, had her heart set on a coach-built pram. Silver Cross was the must-have name for most people who could afford such things, but Mary Lou had seen a beautiful luxury model made by Osnaths of Warrington.

They weren't as well-known as Silver Cross, and in Mary Lou's opinion that made them more exclusive. Mariah didn't share her eldest granddaughter's enthusiasm for the designer accessory, declaring that you could buy a car for the money the pram cost and that she hadn't used a single 'chariot' for any of her ten children; if they weren't strapped to her, they were in a box under the barrow. But as usual, Mary Lou got her way, and from birth, little Tony Lennie was transported around town in style.

The first of this new generation was only a couple of years younger than some of his uncles and aunties. There seemed to be no generation gap, and as such, tradition and attitude differed very little from one generation to the next. They were all cut from the same chequered cloth, and very much in tune with what their family stood for.

Whatever path in life would be taken, whatever career choice was pursued, there was an underlying set of values, core beliefs, behaviours and rules at the heart of this family that would set them apart from others.

ROCK AROUND THE CLOCK

The 1950s were a time of transition in Britain. It was the dawn of a new era, and if the 60s are to be remembered in glorious technicolour, then memories of the 50s are, by contrast, still very much in black and white.

Tram cars still rattled through the streets, and most homes were still powered only by gas. Rationing continued until 1954, and even though the Second World War had finished almost a decade earlier, most things in life remained basic. Food, transport, home entertainment and communication were all still fairly primitive. Bars were the epicentre of every local community, even though the choice of ales and spirits was incredibly limited.

As far as post-war progress was concerned, we were miles behind our transatlantic cousins in every conceivable respect. Motion pictures from Hollywood, shown in cinemas up and down the country, gave the nation a hunger for Americana. Faster cars, flashier clothes, more exciting foods, heart-throbs, sex symbols, and of course rock ‘n’ roll.

In some respects, the 1950s were the best of times, with full employment, steady material progress and a sense of certainty and optimism about life. But the shadow of the war still hung over the nation. Wartime values were still very strong. Respectability, conformity, restraint and trust underpinned society at the start of the decade. Community was key and belonging to one was essential to many. The nation had been as one during the war, and was trying to hang on to that sense of solidarity, but the cracks were beginning to appear across the land.

The Kelly clan’s close community consisted of their own family, not just blood relatives or in-laws, but also included numerous trusted friends who were considered family, and treated as such. They would enjoy some degree of respect from people within their own circles, as a result of association with a family with a notable reputation based on respect rather than fear. The family had not yet taken that path, but sometimes a reputation must be lived up to, and that's when the road turns. Reputations had to be maintained, even enhanced, or else they ran the risk of being little more than a flash in the pan.

The family, like similar ones in cities up and down the country, were carving out a particular niche in life which would set them apart from everyday society. However, this didn't alienate them from their own community. On the contrary. They were respected within their community. They were not bullies or liberty takers, and certainly not 'low life' criminals like some of the less principled types in the area. They were respected, befriended and, in many cases, looked up to by many in their orbit. They were handy people to know, solid people to be involved with and generous to those in their circle, and none more so than Albert Cruddas.

As Mariah's only son, Albert led a charmed life. His mother's business acumen meant she'd grown wealthy, and Albert was well positioned to make the most of Mariah's cash-rich status. She would never let it be said that her only son was poorly dressed or living hand to mouth. Instead, Mariah would make sure Albert always had money in his pocket, even if he hadn't earned it himself.

He was always impeccably dressed, with a taste for the finer things in life. He had an eye for the women, and would catch their attention with his extravagant behaviour. There was always an entourage of hangers-on, only too happy to benefit from the carefree young spendthrift's generosity. It was nothing for him visit Jackson the Tailor on Clayton Street and have several suits made up in a single visit, often giving friends his barely used cast-offs. Albert's shirts were handmade at Harry Sergeant's at the top of Westgate Hill, and later by the dozen in Jermyn Street, London, having been impressed with Frankie Hewson's tailored shirts from there.

Albert was the one that always picked up the bar bill or paid all his cronies into the Dolly's (cinema) to watch the latest gangster flick playing. It's doubtful he ever used public transport or stood in a queue in his life, and the bars, clubs and dance halls of the time were where he felt most at ease, with all the hangers-on of course.

By the mid-1950s Mariah had given up working her pitch. Her arrangement with the Watch Committee prevented her from handing the reigns to one of her family. The girls were now running their own pitches, buying their own gear and taking care of their own growing families, so she no longer benefitted from their activities either. Now in her mid-60s, Mariah should have had more than enough to see her time out comfortably. She had been a generous mother, and Grandmother, if not a conventional one. However, despite being cash-rich she had no assets of worth, and the cash soon dries up when your only son is a high-ranking member of the easy come, easy go club.

Money doesn't last forever, and with an unreasonable amount of help, it didn't last nearly as long as it should have. It would be unfair to suggest that her son Albert squandered much of Mariah's money, but it would be fair to say that he helped knock a decent sized hole in it. From an early age he'd been able to wrap his mother around his little finger, and if Mariah wasn't forthcoming, he would help himself to whatever he wanted. The old piano in her parlour could testify to that.

Perhaps Mariah would've done things differently under other circumstances; had she still been a married woman rather than a widow, or had she not been living in sin with Big Tom. She could've been a woman of substance rather than just a woman with cash, but either way, Mariah Kelly was definitely a contradiction to the 'norm' for a woman of her time.

Women in the 1950s, married or otherwise, could not open a bank account, get a mortgage or obtain credit in their own name and joint accounts didn't exist. Even if they had, Mariah would never have allowed any man open access to the control of her money, never mind the tax man. That's why she never invested; even if she'd wanted to she couldn't get anything in her name, and she was far too cautious to put anything in another man's title. Mariah had grown up in a time when women were seen merely as homemakers, never the breadwinners, but she did not live that way. Raised by a strong mother at the time of the suffragette, Mariah saw herself in the same mould; fighting for the rights of the women in her family to earn the legal right to make a living.

She may have lived by a different set of rules, but she had a livelihood and a family to defend, and it was something she was prepared to fight for. She had been raised that way and she bred the same values into her children, to be passed on through the generations.

By contrast, men of that time were the kings of their own little hills. Society reinforced the idea that they should be waited on hand and foot by obedient, dependent wives, but Mariah bore nine daughters and only one son, and the thought of any one of her daughters depending on a man to feed them was simply out of the question. If they found a man that could keep them properly then all well and good, but they were taught to take care of themselves whatever the outcome. Sally had set the bar before the end of the 19th century, and the bloodline of strong independent women produced by her daughter were a contradiction to the female stereotype of the time in just about every sense. Women were supposed to be at home, looking after their men and their children, not out working like Mariah's girls were, and certainly not doing a job that a man could be doing.

It was little wonder that Sally, Mariah and her line of Kelly girls, became infamous around Newcastle during times of such sexual inequality. Mariah had raised a family that swam against the tide of tradition, daughters who would demand a certain type of man and live a certain kind of life. And that is precisely what happened.

The result was a family set apart from accepted social norms, defying the working-class stereotype of the time. A family who would leave their mark on the city Paddy and Sally had escaped to back in 1886, alone, unskilled and unaware that just seventy years later the roots of their family tree would have taken such a hold in Geordie soil. A hold, in some part, which would strengthen in time beyond anyone's imagination.

Food wasn't too great in the 50s, and that was putting it mildly. For most people fresh fruit and veg, fish, meat and poultry, were once a week treats, if they were lucky. Tinned meats, corned beef and spam were an everyday staple, often served up with rank bacon, rotten eggs, and tea with sour milk. Bread would usually be dry and mouldy, often dipped in fat dripping because the butter was on the turn. A fridge was a luxury most people weren't fortunate enough to own, and when Mariah moved from Sunderland Street to Buckingham Street she made sure she had one, as did some of her daughters, at least the ones that had electricity in their home. They weren't flash folk though, not by any standards. They were merely rough and ready people who were handling money on a daily basis.

Their money was for themselves, to spend on home comforts and their social lives. Package holidays weren't on the radar, so treating themselves here and there was no big deal, and if it wasn't for spending, then what use was it? You'd get no joy from being the wealthiest person in the graveyard! So the money came and went, and the family, like most at the time, spent many an evening in the public-house. The whole community seemed to live in the bars back then, and there would always be some of the team in one of the locals. They were great social company to be in, and they were good people to know. They weren't resented within their community for having a few quid, they were respected for it. They were hard workers, out there making money for themselves, unlike many of the corner standers in their manor who wouldn't get off their arse and do the same.

The chaps were likeable rogues, and the girls were colourful characters, but they were people you could turn to if you had a problem, financial or otherwise – and many did. They were the family that friends of the younger generation wanted to be around. Their homes were the places where a good cooked meal, or at least a cuppa and a sandwich would be on offer when any of the lads would turn up with a friend or an associate; one made with bread and best butter, usually with some home cured bacon and a nice fried egg, all fresh of course. The common poverty and hardship, under which many of their friends and most people around them lived, didn't seem to exist in their homes and as a result everyone loved to be invited into any one of them.

They were just like anyone else, however, with no airs or graces. The family were down to earth, yet somehow they were different. Something about them stood them apart from the rest. People gravitated toward them, became intoxicated by them, and if their friends were proven to be proper people, they sometimes became involved with them; and then you were on the firm.

By the mid-1950s, the generation that had grown up in the shadow of Frankie Hewson and Sarah, then later Chrissy, Morry and Liza, Pow and Mary, or Coronation and young Mariah, not only had a wealth of matriarchal women to look up to, but a collection of uncles and fathers that had shown them a different path and a way of life which had set them apart.

Buck, Doodles and Mary Lou were by now in their mid-20s and, in the case of the latter two, raising families of their own.

Buck remained a bachelor boy his entire life; there was only one Billy Buck, and there would never be another. He was a real character, with his slicked back, jet-black, collar-length ringlets, a suit and tie, overcoat and trademark muffler round his neck. He spent most days on the barrow and most evenings in the bar. He enjoyed a drink, and he'd never allow anyone to clear his empty bottles from the table during a session, just so he could keep count and be sure of just how much he'd had to drink. His opening gambit when you saw him was nearly always, 'Now then!' becoming his catchphrase, which later appeared as a floral tribute at his funeral.

Buck had a wicked sense of humour, a short temper and little time for foolish behaviour, much to the amusement of his many nephews. In later years growing up, they would come to know their family members' ways inside out, and much to his annoyance Buck's aversions and phobias toward certain things became fair game for their childish entertainment.

None of the family liked the word 'rat', preferring to use alternatives such as long-tail, long-chat, taily-boy, big-lads or anything else less unlucky and less offensive than the proper word for the vermin. If you so much as mentioned the unlucky word then the hysterical reaction, effing and blinding that would erupt from Buck like a volcano were well and truly worth the risk of tormenting him. But best be sure to get out of striking distance once his feet were back on the ground. In short, they used to work the shite out of him. Buck was a real one off though, and an uncle that seemed to be an old man nearly all of his life.

The two oldest lads and Mary Lou had several years on the rest of their generation, who were now all growing up in the shadow of their non-conforming parents. Their fathers had been 'active' during the war years, although not always in the line of duty, and out of Buck, Doodles and Albert Cruddas, it was Frankie Doodles who took some of the elders' less law-abiding activities to another level.

The family's young generation were, like everyone else of their age at the time, fascinated by the motion pictures portraying wise guys and crooks in the black and white movies of the day. The majority of regular cinema-goers would be swept along by the lives and actions played out on the silver screen; stories that were no more than a fantasy or escapism for the captivated civilised audience. But for the youth of this family, watching those gangster movies was almost like looking at the lives of their uncles and fathers, and a reflection of a lifestyle that seemed to resonate with them.

The street game and the barrows had always been a good and steady source of income for four generations of the family, but the 1950s brought about change, with the introduction of supermarkets and specialist fruit and vegetable stores like Bookless.

They were serving the smaller quantities of fresh produce directly to the public at prices they could afford, and they were clean, tidy and modern. This hadn't totally killed the game, but had definitely made it a bit harder. Although there would still be any number sly pitching around Nelson Street at any given time, Doodles knew there were easier and quicker ways to get money, provided you had the bottle for it. The strokes pulled by the older men, Frankie, Morry and co, were all well and good but they weren't exactly ambitious, and rarely resulted in a major tickle (financial reward). Doodles and the crowd he ran with, however, were taking far greater risks and far greater advantage of the lack of crime-solving tactics available to the law in those days. As was happening in every city in the land, villains were exploiting the lack of surveillance techniques and response capabilities available to the local constabulary.

Smash and grabs were commonplace in every city. Fingerprinting was about as good as it got by way of post-crime detection, nothing that a pair of turtles (rhyming slang for gloves) couldn't solve. Forensics and CCTV didn't exist, so unless you were caught bang to rights, the likelihood of getting nicked was fairly slim. Of course, there was the possibility of being identified by a public-spirited citizen or, even worse, grassed up by someone but otherwise it was a case of cops and robbers, and if you were working with good people, especially your own, then the chances of getting grassed or identified were even slimmer, especially if you had a reputation, and Doodles certainly had one of those.

A whole new generation of this family had started to arrive by the time the 1950s were coming to a close, and with all of Mariah's grandchildren now on the scene, it seemed like a new era was heralding the end of another. A time when the romance and innocence of working the barrow, dabbling in a bit of petty crime and the occasional caper as a side-line, were about to be replaced with more serious involvement in dealings of a criminal nature. The community mindset of a British society where people could genuinely leave their doors open gave way to a breed of criminal that seemed to emulate the outlaws of the past.

Villains who prayed on the burgeoning face of capitalism, stealing from the rich while respecting the poor, were often seen as the heroes of the day. Yet violent house burglaries, street robberies on harmless civilians, harassment of the elderly, and sexual crimes against women and children were all things virtually unheard of before the 1950s, However, gang culture was stealthily creeping in. Flick-knife carrying hoodlums hanging around on street corners and congregating in cafés were seen as a scourge on society, while crimes against the wealthy and upper classes were becoming the business of a specific type of criminal, the kind you saw in the movies.

News of robberies and heists from London, Manchester or Birmingham were reported in the press, and the villains of the piece were often applauded by the working class citizens of the UK, who seemed less than impressed with the state of post-war Britain, and more impressed by people who challenged the state. Times were changing, and the scent of Cultural Revolution was in the air. The opening of burger bars, the music, fashion and attitudes were all a far cry from the way things had been just after the war. Rebels without a cause were the idols of the time, glorified by James Dean in the movie of the same name which, in 1955, thrilled audiences in glorious technicolour. It was now cool to be anti-establishment, it was cool to be an outlaw, so long as you were an outlaw of the state and not of your own community.

And so it became cool to be part of a firm. It might have been as simple as rival Teddy Boy or Greaser gangs for most, but the younger members of this family were part of the coolest firm in the town, and Frankie Doodles was now leading the way.

Mariah's girls were, for the best part, raising families in between trading on their barrows, but, in an unexpected twist of fate, Joss acquired the tenancy for a bar that many of the family had used for years.

The Clock bar on Buckingham Street had become available, and since Joss had no children to look after, having been widowed by her first husband and then again, tragically, by her second husband Tommy Chapman, who had died suddenly from a heart attack, it seemed the bar might give her something to focus on. She knew all of the clientele and was related to half of them, so it didn't seem such a bad idea.

The Clock became the family's meeting place and centre of their social life for a while. It was their bar, on their doorstep, and it was now in their hands, but true to her name, it was Joss who was the boss. For the younger ones coming through, the 'new' Kellys, Sayers, Hewsons, Patters, Donnellys, as well as Bella and Joe Baird who had a little fruit shop just behind the bar, it was definitely a time to rock around The Clock. Growing up in a different world, like some kind of underworld they'd see in the movies and was in some ways being lived out by them to the soundtrack of the 50s, it really was a time of changing attitudes, not just for the family, but for the entire nation.

During this time, Mariah's family continued to grow with the addition of great-grandchildren. Tony Lennie was the first of the new generation, followed closely by Doodles' first son, Tommy Sayers. Doodles and Lilly went on to have a further two daughters and another second son Morris. Doodles' younger sister, Sylvia Sayers palled about with the Sheldon girls, family friends who'd sold Morry the house on Westgate Hill Terrace. The Sheldons were Travellers and would often take Sylvia with them to the fairs in Musselburgh, St Boswells, York, Doncaster and Appleby. It was at one such fair that she met Joe Reilly, a Gypsy boy from Scotland. Sylvia loved the travelling life, a throwback from Paddy Kelly's genes no doubt. She married Gypsy Joe, and they went on to have three boys and a girl.

Their brother, John Sayers' marriage to Yvonne produced three boys, John Henry, Stephen and Michael. Peter Sayers and his wife Rita had two boys and a girl, and the baby of the bunch, Albert Sayers, married Margaret and had only one daughter of the same name.

The offspring of young Mariah and Coronation Kelly added to the ever-growing family tree. Vera produced a 50s baby, Frankie, the first of five she had with Frank Shotton; a charming man and the centre of Vera's universe. Frank was from a West End family, and one of the boys. His older brothers George was already well-known villain. George Shotton was a larger than life individual, known to everyone as Blow. Some say that was a name given to him on account of the number of safes he'd blown up. Or maybe, like Pow, it was a hand-me-down from his Dad who'd went by the same nickname. Whatever the case, Blow was, like most people around the family, a real character.

Vera's brother Thomas, like their older brother Buck, never had family. Georgie Kelly married Joan; sadly they were destined to part, but not before producing their only child, Billy. Their sister Marie married young to a man from Blaydon and preferred to keep herself to herself, raising her three girls, sensibly, away from the maddening crowd. The twins, Frankie and Jimmy, added half a dozen to the family line between them; two girls and a boy to Frankie and his wife Anne, and two boys and a girl as a result of Jimmy's marriage to Valerie.

Three more great grand-children for Mariah appeared from the Patterson stable, with little ones being born to Pat, as well as to Michael and his partner. Their brother Terry inherited a step-daughter when he married his wife, Barbara.

Bella and Joe Baird's only daughter, Eileen, had three boys to Derek Wilson, an electrician from the West End. Chrissy and Frankie Hewson became grandparents, with two boys and a girl from Frankie jnr, and Jo's only daughter, Victoria.

Not forgetting Joss the Boss. Joss never had any children, and after her time running the Clock Bar and lived out the rest of her days on the other side of the counter with her new companion Jackie Black. He was another memorable character who would nip anyone he could for a drink, and often times a tenner 'just a little start money'. The drinks were rarely returned and neither was the start money, but Jackie would always give thanks to his benefactor for their generosity, promising to reciprocate their kindness in the not too distant future.

Mary Lou with Eddie Lennie went on to add a further two great grandkids for Mariah; a daughter and a second son following Tony, who was the eldest of this new generation.

Peggy, Muriel and Albert Cruddas, the three children Mariah had with Big Tom, were only slightly older than some of

Mariah's grandchildren, resulting in different generations growing up side by side. So, the kids produced by the Cruddas branch of the family were arriving on the scene at the same time as Mariah's great-grandchildren, making them biological aunties and uncles to members of their family that they were far younger than. Confusing if you didn't come from a big family, but relatively standard if you did.

Between the three of Big Tom and Mariah's kids came no less than 20 of Mariah's full quota of grandchildren, totaling 40 in all, at least that was considered to be the official number. As far as the number of great-grandchildren produced by the Cruddas branch of the family tree was concerned, they would swell the bloodline to well over 100. Not bad going considering the entire breed was spawned as a result of Paddy and Sally's chance encounter.

The free-loving era of the swinging 60s would see their numbers grow further, be it legitimate or otherwise, and by the time Mariah was an old woman, it seemed you couldn't walk down the street in Newcastle city centre without bumping into a cousin. With so many names to remember, the term 'cuz' was commonly used when greeting one of their own, and to this day whether it's cousins that are seen every day, or those further afield that are rarely seen, the term 'cuz' is always used as a term of endearment and a mark of belonging. But there were, and still are, many close trusted family friends, who would be acknowledged in the same way. If you were referred to as 'cuz', you were as good as family, and thereby treated as such.

But at the end of the day, as Paddy often said; 'We're all related through drink.'

INTERLUDE: TIME TO REFLECT

Maybe you've worked it out by now, but if you haven't, then allow me to explain: We are about to enter the swinging 60s, a decade of great change for the nation, and one of equal significance for the family. It was also the decade during which I came into the picture, along with my co-accused, Tony Sayers.

The story we have told you so far is a chronological account of our families colourful history once they reached Tyneside (as we understand it to be), thanks to invaluable input and detailed recollections from family members; family whose collective tales from their dramatic and unconventional past could fill a dozen books.

The accounts we will tell you from here on in, however, are the facts as we know them to be because, for the best part, we have lived through them and grown up around them.

We love our family, our history and the people in it. We are family orientated people, and although we set out on this journey to better illustrate who we are, and what we come from, as accurately as we can for the benefit of future generations, what we know to be true by witnessing the years yet to come, is just as shocking and more extreme than anything we have told you thus far, and we will tell you the rest of this story from our point of view.

It is commonly said that there is a book inside of everyone. That may well be true, but most people never write one. Now in my 50s, however, I realised more than ever that this story had to be written. I say that merely because the story you have read so far is a story that will be lost on many of our descendants. Worryingly, it is already a history lost on many of Paddy and Sally's increasingly long line of offspring. For the majority of the millennial generation, family history is of little importance. Life for them is all about what's happening in the moment, using super-fast technology and social media. Life in real time is all they want to know about. What their friends are up to and what's happening anywhere in the world, at any time, to anyone, is all that matters. Yet knowing where you come from is something we feel everyone should be aware of.

We recognised that the rich and colourful history of our family was one which should be remembered and recorded for our future generations, before it is lost forever. Some members of 'our generation' of the family, however, have already created their own legacy, much of which is documented in thousands of press column inches, newsreel coverage, social media platforms and referenced in several books. Regrettably much of this has been distorted and blown out of all proportion, resulting not only in a one-sided view, but in creating a stigma and a reputation which has been both a blessing and a curse to many of us.

We all grew up in a period where the street life was still very much alive and part of the fabric of our family. A life which set the stage for the way many of us would turn out to live our own. Raised in a culture of self-preservation and non-conformity was not unusual to any of us, it was all we knew, it was simply our way of life. Me and Tony, however, recognised, as did all of us born onto our generation that, from a very early age, our lives were not entirely normal. We say that in the best possible way, as neither of us would swap the lives, the upbringing or the education we've had. It has made us who we are; 'Old School', when in reality we have always been 'Old School', even before the day we left school.

Like angels with dirty faces, we would be seen in our numbers running around the city centre of Newcastle, just as our elders had. It was our playground, although playing wasn't always what we were doing there.

We would be seen on the streets throughout the 70s and into the 80s, keeping toot for our dads, grandads or uncles on the barrows, or while they were pitching from a suitcase. Eventually, even as youngsters, we would be seen going to work ourselves. They were great times, growing up on the street.

Every year, on the run-up to Christmas, one of our parents or grandparents would supply us with our stock of wrapping paper, and we would hit the cobbles like the dead-end kids. I remember we used to sell five sheets of the proper glossy gear for 20p, or ten sheets of the crap thin gear for the same money.

Funnily enough, even the manufacturers knew the cheap paper was crap, the name of it was printed on the wrapper of every ream, K-WRAP. You couldn't make it up.

I can recall one time when there were five of us pitched up along Clayton Street between the Grainger Market and Lipton's supermarket, formerly The Green Market, which was later developed as part of Eldon Square shopping centre. It was around 1979, we were probably between the ages of 13 to 15; part of the 60s baby boom when loads of our mob arrived within a few years of each other. I was stood next to my uncles, Frankie Kelly and Billy Buck, by their pitch near The Clock bar (a different one) at the junction of Nun Street and Clayton Street, just up from where my Granny Sarah had her pitch almost 60 years earlier.

Our cousin, young Frankie Kelly, was on the same side of the street as me, about a hundred yards along outside Lipton's, and our Philip (Sylvia and Gypsy Joes son) was at the far end by the Fish Bar. Tony (Sayers) was on the opposite side of the street, working in the entrance to the Grainger Market, next to Paul's Fashions, and a bit further along, his brother, Peter was working the second entrance by the side of the Market Tavern, where my grandad Frankie Hewson was probably sat knocking out a bit of tom; that bar was like his office at that time. Anyway, it was late afternoon, daylight was fading, decorations were all up, and the Christmas lights were on. I was at one end looking down Nun Street and along Clayton Street toward the junction with Newgate Street, watching for the law. Our Philip was doing the same at the other end, at the top of Nelson Street, while the other three were scattered either side of the street between us; we thought we had it boxed off.

I clocked a horney (police officer) coming our way from Newgate Street, and gave out our whistle, the same one our lot have used forever, and still use today. I packed my arm full of

K-WRAP into my holdall and took off in the direction of the Market Tavern. On the way I chatted our Frankie Kelly and he, in turn, marked our Philip's card to 'hedge up'. He chatted Tony, and we all headed towards Peter. Our families had fruit shops in the Grainger Market at the time, so once inside, we could put our gear in one of the shops and give it five minutes before we went back to work.

As we all converged on Peter, with our bags full of swag, we were aware that the copper was on us, following swiftly in our direction.

If we'd have been captured, we'd be nicked. Even if we only got a caution because of our age they would most definitely confiscate our gear, and you didn't want that as you'd have to stand the cost of the gear that had been laid on to you. Even if it had been laid on by your family, *especially* since it was laid on by your family, business is business. As we got right on top of Peter, whistling and chatting him to 'hedge up' the whole time, he simply chose to blank us, keeping his nut down and fiddling away with about half a dozen punters waiting to buy paper from him.

We marched past him shouting 'Lively cuz!! It's on top,' but he wouldn't hedge up. As we got past him and into the relative safety of the market, picking up his bag of stock in case the copper claimed it, the bastard turned up and collared Peter. K-WRAP and shrapnel (loose change) scattered across the floor as he was dragged away by the scruff of the neck. He had a face like a smacked arse as he looked back over his shoulder and saw us all in kinks.

We were pissing ourselves laughing as he was frog-marched off along Clayton Street with his arm up his back and his feet trailing the ground. As the Christmas lights flickered Peter was dragged away hooting and hollering to the sound of Jingle Bells playing in the background. Happy Days, and funny now to look back on. Even funnier at the time to be fair.

The reality was, like all our family before us, we were breaking the law. Equally the law knew who we were, they'd been doing this to our family for nearly 100 years before we came on the scene, and they were still doing it now, because we were still at it.

Sadly, however, we were the last generation of our family to experience those days. Nostalgically romantic times, when instead of spending our weekends watching Saturday morning TV, we'd be out working the streets.

School holidays were spent pulling barrows through the Grainger Market, taking rubbish away from our dads' shops, keeping toot, or taking loads of empty wooden tomato trays round to the Co-op or Laws on Stowell Street. We'd get 5p a-piece for tomato trays at Laws. Other kids would get the same when they took their pop bottles back to the corner shop and maybe get half a quid a week off them. We were taking a hundred tomato trays a day to Stowell Street and picking up a fiver on top of our wages for working the shops or the barrows.

It was a wonderful period, halcyon days of a time gone by, and fortunately for us, we caught the tail end of it. Sadly, however, it is a way of life no longer available to the likes of us. We had been born into a life learning streetwise ways from childhood; understanding the value of a pound, and how to go out and get one. While our school pals were doing paper rounds for 30 bob a week (£1.50), we were getting six or seven quid a day wages for working in the shop, maybe a fiver for keeping toot on the barrows. By the time we cashed our trays in we could have as much as a score in our pockets over a weekend. We were being baptised into the life, it was our tradition and our culture.

It was a life that showed us how to carry ourselves, how to handle and look after ourselves. It was the best school in the world in many ways, and the work didn't even feel like work, most of the time. The dark early starts at the fruit market in winter, which by then had relocated to the Team Valley trading estate in Gateshead, didn't seem like a hardship because we knew as soon as we got there we'd see half a dozen of our cousins, and the day's adventures would start for us before most people were even out of bed.

We were having the best of times, frisk from the crack of dawn, and we were picking up wages in the process. And in the summer, from May through to September, strawberry season, the smell of the fruit market is something we will never forget.

The scent of fresh strawberries, peaches, bananas, grapes, oranges and millions of flowers would fill the air as salesmen shouted across the warehouse floors, slapping hands and striking deals with our dads. We knew everyone in the place. It was a wonderful experience for any young lad, and we were fortunate enough to have been in the thick of it.

Those days stood us in good stead and have taught us many things, the only dodge was we were slowly and unwittingly becoming initiated into the 'easy come, easy go' club, and there wasn't a thing we could do about it.

WELCOME TO LITTLE VEGAS

For all the gloom and doom of the 1950s, the swinging 60s seemed to arrive in glorious Technicolour. In just ten short years, London had transformed from a bleak, conservative city only just beginning to forget the troubles of the Second World War, into the vibrant capital of the free world, full of hope and promise. It was the epicentre of all excitement; the city where anything and everything was possible. This optimistic and free-spirited attitude spread like wildfire throughout every major city in the country, and even Newcastle jumped on board the 60s love train. In contrast to the rebellious attitude shift of the 1950s, the era of free love, sex, drugs and rock 'n' roll was finally upon us.

Newcastle is always a little behind the capital, but always catches up, eventually, and much of what was available in London's West End – the good and the bad – soon made its way to Tyneside. The club scene was booming and the dance halls of the previous decade, once filled with teeny boppers jiving the night away to Bill Hayley and the Comets, were replaced with glamorous casinos and stylish nightclubs swinging to the sounds of the Mersey Beat, The Rat Pack and The Animals. By the mid-60s, Newcastle was gaining a reputation for having the country's best nightlife, outside of London.

There were around a dozen nightclubs in the city centre with top acts appearing almost every night of the week. The likes of Cilla Black, Tom Jones and Jerry Dorsey, who later changed his name to Engelbert Humperdinck, were regular headliners, to name just a few. The late great Bob Monkhouse actually owned a club in Newcastle called Change Is, and with such buzzing hot spots as Emmersons, The Cavendish, Club A'Gogo, Billy Bottos, The Bird Cage, The 69 Club and La Dolce Vita, it was little wonder that London gangsters were keen to get in on the action. But even before the Kray twins arrived on Tyneside, which they did on more than one occasion, there were already faces on the scene, making a killing in the town they called Little Vegas.

Mariah's operation had reduced considerably by the start of the decade. She was now in her seventies and had long since been a regular on the streets. Her daughters, thanks to the intervention of the Watch Committee, had thankfully been able to ply their trade without disruption for several years and had been doing so independently of their mother. Their men would also turn out, usually on Nelson Street, and do their best to nick a few quid on a pitch before the old bill made an appearance. Fortunately for them, that wasn't every day, unless the SPG were on one.

The law, to be fair, had bigger fish to fry. Crime was on the rise, and little firms were making themselves busy around the North East. More chaps from the family, along with associates within their circle, were more frequently turning their hands to a bit of villainy; after all, they had a social life to pay for.

Their run-ins with the police became far more frequent in the 1960s, and they certainly became more intense. The older generation, Old Hewson, Morry and co had all found themselves on the wrong side of the law over the years, and the younger ones like Doodles and his brother John, had now begun to make real names for themselves in the Underworld on Tyneside.

A fair number of the menfolk of the family had done a bit of time for one thing or another while they were making their bones. It's probably the reason why they got so badly mistreated by the law if they ever got nicked for working on the barrow.

If the SPG decided to have a purge, as they often did, they would turn out in force, and anyone sly pitching would be nicked in graphic fashion. It would be nothing for a Black Mariah to turn up at the bottom of Nelson Street, and for half a dozen gavas to jump out with truncheons at the ready to arrest everyone working on that corner.

All the barrow boys, even those not in the family, would be seized, wrestled with and handcuffed before being slung into the back of the police van and carted off to Pilgrim Street, often getting a few digs from the coppers en route. The tactics were heavy-handed for such an offence and served only to create even greater resentment between the family and the authorities. The police knew, however, that they were not just nicking barrow boys when they lifted a member of our family, they were simply taking the opportunity to dispense a little rough justice of their own on a group of individuals that were now becoming a painful thorn in their side.

Big money was being ploughed into the swinging nightlife of Newcastle, and those who had the readies to invest in it were positioned to set themselves up for life.

Mariah sadly failed to seize the opportunity. Circumstance, attitude, generosity and a playboy son had put paid to that. The men who'd married into her family were certainly not suitable candidates for the gaming and liquor licenses required to run a club or a casino, but that's not to suggest that they didn't have a presence on the scene at the time; they most certainly did, and it would come to light in horrific style in 1963, the same year that La Dolce Vita opened its doors on the site of Mariah Kelly's old warehouse.

Mariah had all but given up the ghost by then, leaving the day to day running of her dwindling operation to her son Albert. So, when Morry heard about the Levy brothers, who were of Jewish descent, expressing an interest in opening a new nightclub on the site of the warehouse, he utilised his own family background to secure a sizeable payment for his mother-in-law, paving the way for Newcastle's latest nightspot, La Dolce Vita. Mazel Tov!

It was no more than a drink in the scheme of things really; comparable to the kind of money Mariah gave her son for his 21st birthday some ten years earlier when she was financially better off. But a grand is a grand, and given that Mariah didn't own the warehouse, it was viewed to be a fair payment from the Levy brothers, two men of the world who understood the way things worked with people of respect on the pavement.

The men of the clan were warmly welcomed at all of the nightspots around town, receiving special attention whenever they went out, which was almost every night. No queuing up like the regular punters, complimentary drinks on arrival and the best seats in the house. They were friends with all of the club owners, who were happy to have them in their establishments, not just because they were good spenders but because they could keep the peace should any trouble start to brew.

Doodles had a reputation as a hardman, as did several others around the town, but what Doodles had over the others was a family of likeminded capable men and associates, who collectively made up their firm, and messing with their firm was not something many people dared to do.

Everything was changing. The mood was good, the music was even better, and the fashion was straight off the catwalk. Movie-goers' fascination with the murky criminal underworld continued to be fed throughout the 60s, with classics like *The Frightened City, Murder Inc, The Italian Job* and *Young Dillinger*.

I recall my father telling me about the night he went to La Dolce Vita with my mother, Uncle John Sayers and Aunt Yvonne. They'd arrived late in the evening of January 4th 1967, and the place was in full swing even though it was midweek, such was the appeal of The Dolce and other clubs like it.

The Dolce's manager, Johnny Cuff, knew my dad from his days in the carpet trade. Johnny made a beeline for my dad and Uncle John as they scanned the busy room looking for a table, peering through the blanket of smoke hanging, as if by magic, just feet above the happy revellers intoxicated by alcohol and the cocktail of sweet-smelling perfume, musky cologne and the cloud of a hundred cigarettes. The only empty table in the club was one permanently reserved for Angus Sibbet. It was the best table in the house, and six nights a week it would sit empty until he turned up. He wouldn't always show up, nevertheless, his table was always reserved and ready for him in case he landed. On this particular occasion, he was in the club and just about to leave. Johnny Cuff explained to my dad that he could sort out Angus' table for them, knowing that he wouldn't be returning.

Angus exchanged pleasantries with my dad and Uncle John, as Johnny showed them to the table and duly returned with a bottle of bubbly courtesy of Mr Sibbet, who was now heading off to The Bird Cage on Stowell Street.

That was the last time Angus Sibbet was seen alive by my father. The following morning, less than 20 miles away in South Hetton, miner Tom Leak was making his way home from night shift when he spotted a badly parked, damaged Jaguar Mark X by Pesspool railway bridge. Reportedly, Leak saw a man lying across the back seat, and assuming the occupant was asleep he opened the door and shook the man's leg to wake him, with the intention of telling him that he couldn't stay parked there. Realising the man was dead, he hailed three passing colleagues returning home from the mine, and they called the police.

Angus Sibbet had been shot three times at point-blank range in a shocking crime that would go down in underworld history as the 'One Armed Bandit Murder'. The classic British gangster flick, *Get Carter,* starring Michael Caine was based around these events, and showed Tyneside just how close to home gangland violence was to that of London's, once you scratched the surface.

Angus Sibbet had been a money collector for a company run by the Luvaglio brothers, all Faces in Newcastle during the '60s. Their company provided much of the North East with fruit machines, or one-armed bandits as they were called, representing a very lucrative business.

This case, however, was one of the most notorious killings in the North East to date, and the first real gangland killing, sparking fears that organised crime was gaining a foothold in the region. The Luvaglio's Italian surname sparked the scare-mongering headline in the local press 'The Mafia are coming'.

Two men were charged with the murder, and both have always protested their innocence. Dennis Stafford, allegedly claiming that the murder was committed by a Scottish gangster, while Michael Luvaglio suggested it was part of a failed attempt by the Krays to muscle into the Newcastle club scene. The two, however, were convicted for the killing of Sibbet, and subsequently sentenced to life in prison.

For as much as everyday folk were enjoying the decade of free love, there was a far more sinister side to the era, one that elevated a certain kind of criminal to both local and national notoriety. For them it was a world where men were men, and women were either at home raising the kids, or out on the tiles with their 'fellas', roles often filled by more than one woman.

These were heady times, the country was growing up, and so were we. Products of the baby boom generation, it was a world we only caught a glimpse of before our teenage years.

For us personally, it was a time that changed the perception of our family and established them firmly in the ranks of the infamous and notorious.

HELL, FIRE AND DAMNATION

With the onset of the 1960's the new generation, our generation, was once again seamlessly overlapping with the previous one.

Frankie Doodles by now in his late twenties, was in his prime, sharp-dressed, well-connected and earning. He may still have been a barrow boy, but he was now also a bad boy with a growing reputation, and an army of like-minded cousins, friends and associates ready to back him up. Like Doodles, his brothers John, Peter and Albert, his cousins Billy Buck, Georgie, Thomas and the twins Frankie and Jimmy Kelly, and those married in like my Dad and Frank Shotton, were all very much the men about town.

Almost every one of them was born into the street life, and those who joined the family were baptised into it and classed as their own if they chose to become part of the firm. Grafting the barrow, for all the lads, was their staple diet to begin with, but variety, they say, is the spice of life and these chaps were ready to go through the menu.

It may have been the decade that would come to define the flavour of British culture, but it was also a period which would define many of our clan. Towards the end of the 1950s, my Dad (Eddie Lennie) and Frankie Shotton had immersed themselves in the 'family life'. The entire team of lads would work together and socialise together; a crew, or some might say a gang, if you were to compare them to the firms that were running around the capital, or the streets of New York.

But this was Newcastle, not London and certainly not the mob-riddled streets of the Big Apple, just a crazy little place near the border of Scotland. The folk of Newcastle built ships and mined coal. They worked hard and played hard. The men were raw boned labourers who loved a drink and a good old fight, usually in that order. It was rough, tough, cold, and miles away from anywhere. Very few people at the time ventured up that way, let alone stayed, unless they had some connection with the area. Even throughout history, Newcastle has been seen as the last civilised outpost in England, before reaching the wild, rugged badlands of Scotland. Even Hadrian and his Roman army couldn't get much further north and resorted to building a wall across the country in his name to keep out the mad Scotsmen that resided just up the road.

Even the Windrush Generation which had swept into the country a little over a decade earlier, held reservations about coming so far north. It was too fucking cold.

People just didn't want to come here and settle unless they had to; a mindset not lost on the captains of organised crime. It was just too far away to look after. The residents were unpredictable, and the streets simply couldn't be controlled, unless you lived there and had a presence. The 60s, however, saw the most significant influx of ethnic minorities to the region; leading to the Italian, Chinese and Indian restaurant trade taking root in the city centre. This influx of new business added to the notorious club scene and vibrant nightlife, and soon the town began to attract attention from some of the country's infamous criminal faces of the time, hoping to help themselves to the some of the rich pickings up north that they'd heard about on the grapevine.

Their plans, however, didn't work out quite the way they might have hoped. In order to control Newcastle's streets they would need to relocate completely, and that was never going to happen. It was simply too remote, plus it already had its own little firms; one in particular that had been around for a while now and had the respect of the people on the ground. There were also one or two of its own homegrown families from rough and ready backgrounds, all producing large numbers of young men prepared to take on the world and make a name for themselves on the streets of Tyneside.

Many of the Tams had settled in Newcastle, they were from Scottish Travelling stock and were scattered all over the West End. Elswick's Big Trevor Harrison was fathering boys left and right, while Margi Findlay, an old family friend who'd grown up alongside Mariah, had a rake of young sons and nephews all capable of throwing their weight about. Not to mention the Conroys, whose father Big Lenny was a bit of a hardman, and was also producing a swathe of young bulls in his name.

Even within our own ranks, The Growler had brought a handful of Donnelly men into the mix during these years. All of these lads from different families would cross paths in the years to come. Yet in the free-loving years of the 60s, the majority got along with each other, most of the time.

Growing up as kids together on the streets of the West End, with similar outlooks, anti-establishment attitudes, and the urge to be the new kids on the block, they were 'making their bones' as they say, and people were beginning to know who these families were. And because, unlike Mariah, they were all producing boys, people referred to them by their inherent family name, something that had not applied to us up to that stage. Our pioneering generation had been made up of women – strong, self-preserving independent women – but, obviously, the surname of the men they married was still the one which would be carried down the lines.

Had Mariah produced ten boys instead of nine girls and Albert, then the Kelly family name, or Fleming by birth, would have been carried on, and would have been the name applied to the entire family as a group, but, as we know, that was not the case.

However, all of that was about to change in the spring of 1963. The decade itself didn't get off to the best of starts for the family. After the relative calm of the 1950s, with little loss of life within the ageing clan, and the generation of Mariah's grandchildren emerging onto the nightlife scene, the swinging 60s was about to turn everything on its head.

The country was in the grip of winter at the time, one of the coldest on record. It was what's known in the trade as 'kipper season' – the quiet period following the festive season – so-called, some say because when things were tight, a kipper was all you could afford to buy for tea.

All was quiet on the western front as far as the barrows were concerned. Bad weather, a lack of available gear in the market, and everyone feeling the pinch of Christmas overspending was not a good combination for nicking a few quid on a pitch.

If the men weren't out with the barrow, then they would have to be out doing something else. They might hawk a bit of stuff if they could find a line, something to go to work with; suit lengths were always good graft, or maybe go at the 'prop', which was basically going out on the knocker trying to take some roofing or property repair work, which some of the boys did from time to time, but nothing was easy when it was kipper. This being the case, they would resort to looking elsewhere for a few quid, and often that meant taking a risk or two. You must remember if they didn't work, they didn't earn, and if they didn't earn then they didn't eat; there were no salaried men on this firm, and poverty was never an option.

During the latter part of the 1950s and early 60s, most of the chaps had been in and out of trouble. Small custodial sentences had been served on just about every one of them, for anything from obstruction (working the street) to warehouse breaking, theft and violence related offences. Getting into scrapes with other young men was as easy as falling out of bed in those days, as little gangs were commonplace during that era, spurred on by the motion picture industry and the changing attitudes of the younger generation of the country. Even straight goers would knock about in little cliques in the evening or of a weekend, and occasionally the young chaps of our family would find themselves in rolling around the floor with any number of rough young fellas who thought they could have a row.

A row with our lot, however, would usually turn out a bit naughtier than most of their opponents might have expected, and what would start off as a disagreement between one or two people could often turn into a full on tear-up. There may have been no bad intentions at the beginning, but our lads had to make sure they left any battle victorious. Reputations can be ruined in an instant, no matter how long they have taken to build, and with

Frankie Hewson in uniform, circa 1939

Sally with grandchildren (L-R) Frankie, Sarah, Liza.
Circa 1919

Billy Fleming during the Great War,
with his war horse Kitty

Jimmy 'Big Tom' Cruddas leaning against the cart, with an unnamed grafter.
Outside Mariah's Blackfriars warehouse 1930s

The only existing photo of Sarah Hewson as an adult, circa 1939

The Double Wedding.
Back (L-R) Frankie Hewson, Chrissy, Jo Baird, Bella
Front (L-R) Sylvia Sayers, Joe Patterson, Vera Kelly and Joe's nephew Henry 'Henna' Baird

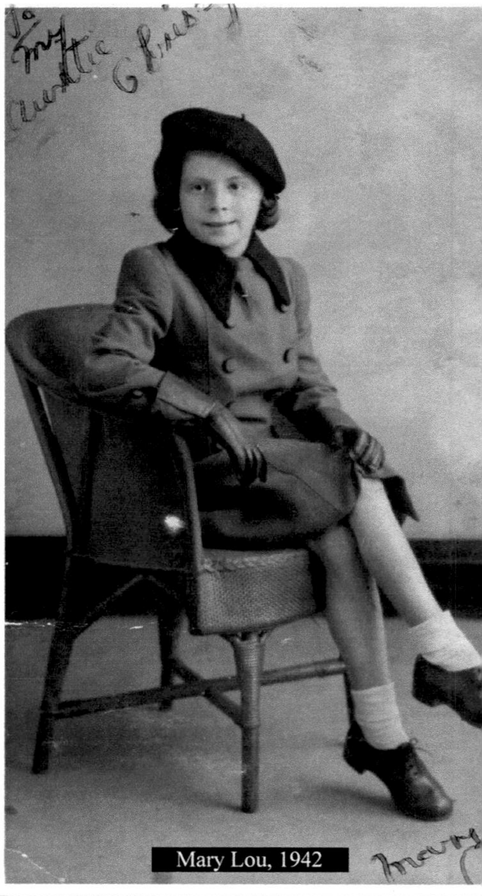

Mary Lou, 1942

Back (L-R) Mary Lou, Billy Buck, Albert Cruddas, Frankie Doodles.
Front (L-R) Young Mariah, Joss, Liza, Bella, Peggy and Chrissy, circa 1946

-R) Alex and Irene Levy, Jean Dryden, Lizzy Henderson, Liza Sayers, Esther Sayers, Tilly Sayers, Peggy, Bella, Young Mariah, Joss, Jinny Sayers, Lizzy Chapman, Nelly Drummond

Back (L-R) Pat Patterson, Sylvia Sayers, Beattie Forden's ughter, Marie Kelly, Jo Hewson, Terry Patterson, Tommy Kelly, Frank Hewson Jnr, Eileen Baird, Vera Kelly.
Front (L-R) Albert Sayers, Jimmy Kelly, Frankie Kelly, Thomas Kelly, John Sayers, Peter Sayers

Mariah, at the double wedding of Bella and Chrissy, with Peggy to her right, 1947

young John Brian Sayers and Eddie Lennie Sr, late 1950s

Mariah with her first great-grandchild, Tony 'Legs' Lennie, circa 1955

(L-R) John Sayers Sr, Eddie Lennie Sr, Mary Lou, Yvonne Sayers, Marie Kelly

Billy Buck (left) with Morry Saye and his new daughter-in-law Yvon outside the family home on Westg Hill Terrace, early 1960s

(L-R) Sheila O'Donnell, Yvonne Sayers, Anne Kelly, Rita Sayers, Mary Lou, 1960s

(L-R) George 'Blow' Shotton, former heavyweight world champion Joe 'The Brown Bomber' Louis, Frankie Doodles, Jimmy Calvert, Sid Graham

(L-R) Muriel Donnelly, Joe Lisle, unknown, Georgie Kelly, Georg 'Blow' Shotton (below), Dinky Slater (Shotton's sister), Billy Buc behind Albert Cruddas

Old Frankie Hewson with Counsellor Bennie Abrahams on Nelson Street, 1970s

Singer Tom Jones getting in on the act with Eddie Lennie, Jo Hewson and Mary Lou

e Battle Of Percy Street

EVEN of eight men involved in the "Battle of Percy Street" were jailed at ewcastle Assizes today. The men, all om Newcastle, were sentenced on charges nging from wounding to causing an affray.

Three were given 15 months each—labourer hn Sayers (23), of York Street; his brother, -year-old ex-profes- nal boxer, Frank yers, of Brunel Ter- ce; and labourer ank Shotton (27), of andford Terrace.

Four others were each ntenced to six months.

They were John Jeffrey 3), labourer, of Glouces- Road; Kenneth Ander- n (25), labourer, of Albion ad; Ronald Tait (31), employed, of Markey ll; and Ralph Holmes 9), unemployed, of Hill urt.

The eighth man, Frank elly (19), street trader, of andford Street, was sen- nced to three months in a tention centre.

Two men found not guilty sterday of causing an fray and discharged were eorge Shotton (39), car ealer, of Thorpe Street, d Thomas Bowman (26), nemployed, of Parker reet, both of Newcastle.

Local newspapers covering the battle of Percy Street

Mariah trading on the street with daughter Liza at her Percy Street pitch, 1971

Albert Sayers working the Big Balloon on Hampstead Heath in the 1970s

Eddie Lennie gets a stare down from The Greatest,before Ali's fight against Larry Holmes in Vegas, 1980

Peter Sayers Sr mixing it up with Rocky Graziano

Edward Jr as a youngster with (L-R) 'Jinky' Jimmy Smith, Tommy Gibb, Frank Clarke, John Tudor, legendary sports writer John Gibson at Roy's Two Rooms

Eddie Lennie Sr and Peter Sayers at Albert's wedding, 197

(L-R) Peter Sayers Sr, Jimmy Kelly, Joe Riley Jr, Eddie Lennie Sr, Jimmy Sayers, Frankie Kelly Sr, Cockney Jack Ashton, Joe Riley Sr, John Sayers Sr, Jack Kindley, Bobby 'Curly' McGreivy, Billy Buck, Georgie Kelly, Billy Kelly

(L-R) Peter Sayers Jr, Tony, Edward on Uncle Albert's wedding day, 1977

Celebrating the legalisation of their trade;
(L-R) Michael Patterson, Jimmy Holmes, Frankie Kelly Jr, Frankie Kelly Sr, Billy Buck, Harry Drummond, Albert Sayers

The last man standing. Albert Sayers and wife Margaret at his barrow, a Newcastle City landmark

Traders' 'royal' tribute

HUNDREDS of street traders paid tribute to the undisputed Barrow Queen of Newcastle.

Maria Kelly, who died last month aged 80, was one of the city's most popular and familiar figures.

She ran a fruit and vegetable stall on Clayton Street until her retirement five years ago.

During her life she fought tooth and nail for the legalisation of pitches in the city, and once was jailed for breaking the law.

Maria was one of the original family of barrow traders who have been selling fruit and veg around the streets of Newcastle for 150 years.

Her nephew Albert Sayers is now the spokesman for the Barrow Traders of Newcastle.

After the service at St Mary's Church, traders formed a procession through the streets of the city on their way to Elswick cemetery where Maria was buried.

● **GRAND LADY** — Maria Kelly

Legs and Blow, laying low in Tenerife

(L-R) Tony, Uncle Albert and Edward, 2018

other families flexing their muscles in the town, coming out second best in any scrap was never good propaganda.

One such incident with a group of lads in Whitley Bay ended up in North Shields magistrate's court with half a dozen of the chaps up on violent disorder charges. It was recorded as the longest sitting ever held in the building, as every one of our mob professed their innocence for 14 hours solid.

My old man, Frankie and Blow Shotton, together with the Sayers and the Kelly boys were all active around that time, and would often pair up with one or two of the team or put a little firm together for a bit of graft. Sometimes they went out looking for it, maybe get a card mark, or it was opportunist thieving. It would be easy to judge them, and many people will, but they had to put food on their tables. They were unskilled, and uneducated in the most part, although my dad was a time-served floor layer, a trade he eventually put to use before the end of the decade.

But they were all living life by a different set of rules. They had a survival instinct that came with their way of life, one shared by many like-minded people all over the country who don't conform to a system which pigeonholes them, preparing the lower or working classes for a life of hard labour, earning a wage on which they could barely exist. An existence where a lifetime of effort, hard work and dedication to your employer will never see you living the kind of life the boss does. It's what most people do, and that's fine, it makes the world go round. But if that's not the life for you and you lack the education, skill set or opportunity to improve your status, then you'd do whatever you consider necessary in order to survive.

As long as that didn't involve a certain kind of crime. There is a code, an honour among thieves – or at least there used to be – and that code was all about respect. Crimes that were considered low life, crimes against those in your own community, your own people, those struggling to survive, were for the dregs of the class system that exists in the underworld. No one wanted to be known as a slag or a slink. You wanted to be seen on the pavement as a loveable rogue, a dandy highwayman, not a sly, stroke pulling toerag; that was contrary to everything men of respect believed in.

The risk of fines was always a problem to factor into the barrow game. But it went further than that. A fine might only have be a fiver back then, but when you got five in one day, you were looking at a pony. They might have earned a tenner or a score a day on the barrow, but they now had a pony's worth of blisters up their arse, and the penalty for non-payment of fines was jail.

If the barrow trade was your game, then what were you to do, go out again the next day and run the same risk, or go out the next day and get a job? Clearly, that's what the law was hoping. But if you had no trade, couldn't read or write properly, or if you had form, then it simply wasn't as easy as that. Were they to starve; let their kids go without? Endure a hand-to-mouth existence, living off the state and unable to provide for their wives and children? Circumstance dictated their actions, and if their actions were questionable, then so be it. Survival was paramount.

Freddie Foreman, one of Britain's most feared and respected hardmen, once stated, 'There is no greater crime a man can commit than to allow his family to live in poverty.'

These were proud men. They may not have been educated, but they were certainly not stupid. They knew how to get a shilling, and if the authorities wouldn't allow them to get one straight then they had no choice but to continue plying their trade, or turn their hand to something less legal to clear their outstanding fines. Ultimately, they became the victims; victims of circumstance. If they had the chance of a tickle elsewhere, they would take it. If they got nicked in the process, then so be it; they were probably going to jail anyway if they couldn't find the money for their mounting fines for street trading.

It became a vicious circle. They were at odds with the law, and the law hounded them. But in spite of this, the 1960s were coming to life, there was an air of optimism sweeping the country, and it had arrived in Newcastle. This was not lost on the younger men in the family, many of them now with children of their own. The period would have huge implications for all of them and would serve to diversify many of their activities, but not before tragedy, bloodshed and jail had been served up in large portions.

It was in the depth of winter 1963, a time when Doodles and the fellas were around town most nights in any one of the many nightclubs in the city. Their hours weren't exactly nine-to-five, and being out and about at night was just as critical to keeping your finger on the pulse of what was happening on the street. Contacts would be made in the clubs, cards might be marked, and opportunities would be presented. Nothing was going to fall into your lap sitting in the house.

Every house had open coal fires back then. Many homes were still powered just by gas, and having an indoor toilet was considered flash. Hygiene, health and safety issues were not the legislative concern of today's Nanny State, however if they had been, maybe some of the heartbreak that was in store, might possibly have been avoided.

Frankie Doodles had three kids by 1963, Carol being the youngest, aged just five. In January that year, in a freak household accident, Carol tragically became the victim of such an accepted lack in health and safety standards.

While warming herself near the open fire in their home on Brunel Terrace in Elswick, fresh out of the bath with her clean flannelette nightdress on, little Carol was faultlessly hit by a spark, the kind often spat out by real fires. Without going into the finer details of that tragic night, by the time her mother Lilly heard the screams from her daughter downstairs in the front room, it was too late. The nightie was in flames. Poor Carol sadly never survived the devastating effects of that horrific night, and the young soul of the dear departed child was laid to rest before winter was out.

Needless to say, this had a huge impact on the family, later contributing to troubles between Doodles and his wife, Lilly.

Frankie had always been quite an intense character. A serious man, with a serious approach. Many of the other men in the family may have favoured frisk, high-jinx and cross-kidding whenever they were together, and although Doodles was not void of a sense of humour, he was one of the oldest of his generation, and led by example. He mourned in private and maintained his reputable profile in spite of his dreadful loss. His upbringing was such that tragedy and hardship were not considered something that should bring you to your knees.

If it doesn't kill you, it makes you stronger. Mariah's daughters had learned that lesson first hand when she left them and Billy Fleming for Big Tom. They had worked through that difficult time with dignity and fortitude, and those self-preserving traits formed the backbone of our family, instilled into each new generation that came along. But sometimes the blows just keep on coming. Just like in the ring, when you're on the ropes, you have to cover up and ride with the punches. You take your punishment, and if you have the heart and strength to weather the onslaught, you can come back fighting. It's an analogy that applies as much now as it did then.

Doodles was a boxer and knew how to soak up punishment but, still reeling from the blow of losing his baby girl, he found himself on the ropes again within a matter of weeks, following an event that would break his heart even further. A tragic incident, and one which he was lucky to walk away from, even if it didn't feel like it at the time.

By 1963 Joe Lisle had opened the 69 Club on Westgate Road, next to where the bowling alley now stands. 'Lucky Joe' as he was known, had worked his way up successfully from the days of running around hawking and taking Albert Cruddas under his wing. He'd been in the motor trade and had opened a car pitch on Bath Lane, and another in Gallowgate, right where many of the family resided. He was a smart and shrewd operator and had amassed enough 'straight' wealth to take advantage of the lucrative club scene that was sweeping the city.

The 69 Club was frequented by all the boys. They would be in there several nights a week, dining, drinking or at the gaming tables. They were always well looked after by Joe, but they were also good spenders, and kept troublemakers out of the place. Several of them were in there on Friday the 22nd of March, just weeks after Carol's tragic death. Doodles, his younger brother John, their cousin Joe 'Patter' Patterson, Aunt Bella's husband Joe Baird and their good friend Jimmy Nichol were all out for the night and had started their evening in Lucky Joe's club. Even Joe Patter's dad, Pow, was with them, an honorary member of the firm for that evening.

Sadly, back in those days drink driving was commonplace. The laws to protect people from the dangers of driving under the influence were yet to be passed, and people didn't always take the sensible route where booze and motors were concerned.

Jumping in their motor, a black Humber Super Snipe, in search of their next port of call, the chaps headed off from the 69 Club. Joe Patter was driving, and Doodles was riding shotgun with Joe's old man Pow sat between them on the bench seat. Their good friend Jimmy Nichol sat behind, with Joe Baird in the middle of the back seat between him and John Sayers. For some reason Doodles just didn't fancy it, and bearing in mind it was only a matter of weeks since the loss of Carol, he decided to call it a night. Resisting the tried persuasion from the rest of the team, Doodles stuck to his guns, and they dropped him off at his home in Brunel Terrace.

When he got out the motor, John jumped out from the back and claimed the front seat where his brother had been sitting. Jimmy Nichol also jumped out and went around to the other side of the motor to have a word with Frankie about something before they parted company. With Frankie now heading through his front door, Jimmy Nichol climbed back into the rear of the car, using the opposite door to the one he'd just got out of. Budging Joe Baird along, Jimmy now occupied the seat directly behind Joe Patter, the driver. They took off down Brunel Terrace and turned left along Scotswood Road towards Marlborough

Crescent, no doubt discussing where to go next, when suddenly their night took a dramatic turn and was brought to a shockingly gruesome end.

Whether it was down to too much alcohol, a lack of concentration due to the conversation in the car or, as the press suggested, the fact that the rear wheel had a nail in it we'll never really know, but the car hit a bus head-on as they neared the junction with Westmorland Road, and two of the occupants in that motor never lived to tell the tale.

Joe Patter, Mary and Pow's eldest, was critically injured, suffering hideous injuries from the collision. He bravely fought for his life for a further ten days, sadly passing away on the 2nd of March , aged just 25.

Pow and John, who had been sitting in Doodles' seat in the front, were both hospitalised along with Joe Patter and Jimmy. Pow escaped with only cuts and bruises, but suffered unimaginable pain at the tragic loss of his firstborn as a result of the accident. Incredibly, Joe Baird walked away from the crash with minor injuries, having been moved from his seat by Jimmy Nichol just moments earlier when they dropped Doodles at home; the cruel twist of fate cutting short Jimmy's life, who also died following the accident.

Fate had played a hand in many of the decisions that affected the outcome of the car's passengers that night. Some would thank their lucky stars for the way things transpired, but others had made split-second decisions which would alter the course of their lives, and bring about the end of others.

Within weeks of the family grieving the tragic death of little Carol, they were now mourning the loss of another of their own, Joe Patterson, The Golden Boy as his mother called him, handsome and smart with his cheeky smile and a glint in his eye.

Spookily, in a conversation at Carol's funeral, Joe Patter and his close friend Jimmy Nichol had been overheard commenting on the tragic accident and the loss of one so young. 'When it's my time to go, I'm taking you with me' Joe said, jokingly.

Jimmy turned and said the same thing back to his pal Joe. Nobody could have foreseen that within a matter of weeks the two good friends would indeed meet their fate, side by side.

The year had hardly begun and already, the blows were raining down heavily on the family. A fire had wiped out the life of an innocent child and damnation, although they didn't know it, was just around the corner. Tragedy visited for a second time in quick succession when Joe's motor hit that bus head-on. Before the dust had even settled on the crash and while John was recovering from his injuries, all hell was about to break loose on the city's streets, and by the end of April, many of the firm would be facing jail time.

Doodles was in the wake of the worst time of his life, on the one hand questioning his faith, and on the other thanking the Blessed Lord that he wasn't in the car on that fateful night. It wasn't even spring yet, and the events of 1963 were far from over. Doodles was doing all he could to keep his anger, guilt, frustration and grief at bay. Three funerals in as many months as the year had seen, and all of them painfully too close to home. It was a sad, dark time. He'd frequently miss the odd night out with the boys, but would always put in an appearance when it was necessary to do so, or when his services were called upon.

His good friend and family member, Blow Shotton, enjoyed working relations with the Luvaglios, often being asked to enlist Doodles and another close associate, Kenny 'Panda' Anderson, when needed. Being out on the club scene was still part and parcel of their activities but on the odd occasion, Doodles would have a night off if he didn't have to be out. It was on one such night, when his brother John was having a drink in The Dolce, that the trigger was pulled on a series of events which would test the family's mettle once and for all, seeing their names hit the headlines; elevating their infamy to yet another level.

In the restroom of the club, John bumped into Davey Findlay; a familiar face of the time who, along with his brothers, was known to the family. Davey's Aunt Margi was an old friend of Mariah's, and it was Billy Findlay who had introduced my mam, Mary Lou, to my father. The Findlays were no mugs; all handy lads from the West End, keen to make a name for themselves. Their family and ours had previously co-existed, in fact, had gotten along, both before and ever since the drama of what was about to unfold as a result of the testosterone-fuelled encounter that night.

Davey Findlay was a known face in around Newcastle and had a reputation as a bit of a loose cannon. His interest in the music industry led to friendships in London and he'd often be seen mixing with the artists and celebrities who'd appear in the clubs around Newcastle, sometimes working his way into their entourage when they were in town. He was an avid music lover and a bit of an impresario. A raconteur some might say, and others might say he was a would-be gangster.

It's been rumoured that he was instrumental in bringing the Kray twins to Newcastle; whether there is any truth in that was known only to them, but he was seen in their company on at least one of their visits and would no doubt have loved the idea that he was behind any takeover they may have had in mind, but more of that later.

Along with a couple of friends, Davey entered the gents' toilets at the club to find John Sayers, still on sticks following the accident just a few weeks earlier. There had been some disagreement at the time, a bubbling of bad blood between the two men.

Words were exchanged in the toilet of the Dolce that night and, in short, John ended up on the wrong side of a hiding from Davey and his accomplices, a questionable act given the fact that John was still on sticks and outnumbered three to one. Despite both families getting along until then, bad blood was now coming to the boil and there was no way John or any of our family would allow the liberty that had been taken to go unaddressed.

Both parties will tell you different versions of how events unfolded after that night. Suffice to say, in the weeks that followed, tensions between the two firms reached boiling point, eventually reaching an unholy head of steam on the city centre streets of Newcastle, played out with all the horror of a Quentin Tarantino style bloodbath.

Straighteners had been arranged, then rearranged after the Dolce episode with John Sayers and Davey Findlay. Other family members had been dragged into the name-calling and the threats, and before they all knew it, battle plans were being drawn up. This was no longer going to be a straightener between John and Davey, it had escalated far beyond that. It was now a war between the Findlays and the Sayers, one which would be fought out publicly and violently on the streets of Newcastle in a bloody episode which would become known as 'The Battle of Percy Street', at least that was the headline in the press. We've always referred to it as the Percy Street Massacre.

Contrary to the statements provided by Davey Findlay, and documented in the press, both firms had agreed to meet in town on Friday the 26th of April, 1963. Both teams would be mob-handed and intent on putting the other firm well and truly in their place, by any means necessary. As we understand it, there were around 20 men from each faction on their chosen battleground in the middle of town: Percy Street, more or less where Liza stood every day with her barrow. But Liza would be saved the trauma of witnessing what unfolded as it was evening time, and the troops were preparing for war. The variety of weapons recovered by police during the encounter suggests that very few prisoners would be taken that night, and the intent with which the weapons were used would indicate that lives could easily have been taken, on both sides.

Like gladiators of old, the warring troops entered the fray with tools aplenty, even a ferocious Alsatian dog was led into battle by the Findlays, only to be almost decapitated with an axe in the barbaric clash that ensued. Another axe was lodged in the head of Billy Findlay, the man who'd introduced my parents, and was only noticed by the police officers arriving on the scene as Billy stumbled onto Percy Street covered in blood to the waist and upon shaking his head, dislodging the axe that had been plunged in to it. Doodles took a hit in the jaw with a hammer, which broke the entire side of his face, and Davey Findlay had been chopped up and battered to within an inch of his life.

Blades, axes, hammers, chains, spanners, metal and rubber piping and even an African spear, were all found at the scene from which many of the waring firms had scattered when the law arrived. Chief Inspector Tom Clifford's account of the scene he and his colleagues encountered is openly graphic, and documented in several excerpts in the *Evening Chronicle*, although his understanding of the events is somewhat less believable than the reality.

The 20 or so men that fled the scene were made up of rival gang members, not the sole legion of men accompanying John and Doodles, as suggested in the press by Mr Clifford. Clearly, it made sense for Davey Findlay to intimate that they were all part of the 'Sayers firm', the name by which this bunch of wild young men would, for a long time, be referred to.

Only four of the Findlay mob remained on the pavement when the law arrived, with at least twice as many of the Sayers firm standing their ground and getting nicked. Such was the level of violence that had been served up, that the police immediately looked at Davey and his two or three pals as the victims of a sustained and vicious attack. In Davey's defence, what was he to tell them? Only four of them had been nicked, so he certainly wasn't about to say to them that his mob were 20-handed as well. If he had done, they would have all been up on the same serious charges.

All in all, ten men were nicked for the events of that night, all from the Sayers side; several of them family, the others being close and loyal associates. It has been said that if the law had arrived and captured ten of the other mob and found just four of our lot, with claret all over them and axes hanging out their nuts, then maybe it would have been the Findlays in the dock answering charges of affray, actual bodily harm and intent to cause grievous bodily harm, but that would have been reliant on our mob providing testimony. Something that they simply would not, and do not do.

For all the bad blood, and all the bloodshed, and after sufficient time had passed, the Findlays and our family managed to remain friendly, as they had done prior to the 'Battle of Percy Street'. Time heals many ills, even axe wounds to the head, and that watershed uprising which spawned a collective name for the firm was seen in the fullness of time, by those involved, as nothing more than a flexing of muscles; young guns, high on 60s life, puffing their chests out with points to prove and reputations to uphold. To be fair, the Findlays are good people, they were before, and have been since that fateful night, and no grudges have been held.

It's life. Maybe not to everyone, but it's life as it was in their world. Having said that, it wasn't a case of shaking hands after the event, far from it. Eight of our lot were convicted of their charges, several receiving custodial sentences amounting to almost seven years in total. Their time served was time to reflect, to contain anger, and to consider their less than ordinary lifestyles.

But it wasn't all gloom and doom. The 60s were just picking up speed. The Beatles were about to become the biggest music sensation on the planet, and England were only two summers away from winning the World Cup. What a time to be alive… even if you were locked up.

Heartbreak for the family, however, was far from over, and only weeks after being released, Doodles and John were hit by yet another catastrophic loss. Their father, role model, and head of their family, Morry Sayers, passed away suddenly at the age of 57; just a week or so before Christmas 1964, following a fatal cerebral haemorrhage. This wasn't just another body blow for the family, it was more like a low blow after the bell. Frankie Doodles, now head of the family, had to step up to the mark for everyone around him, regardless of what may have been going on in his own life.

Morry's passing greatly upset Mariah, she'd always had a soft spot for him ever since the day the young cockney chancer landed at her warehouse. Needless to say, his death devastated Liza and their daughter Sylvia, and had a profound impact on the youngest of the family, Albert, while Peter had to cope with the loss from behind bars, having received half a stretch not long before his father passed away. In an inconsolable state, Peter was only able to spend an hour at the funeral, to pay his respects and grieve in the bosom of his family, before being whisked away unceremoniously back to Winson Green Prison in Birmingham to complete his six-month sentence. This angered his brother John terribly and fuelled his hatred for the law even further.

All of this was going on in Mariah's 77th year. She hadn't had the easiest of lives, and it certainly wasn't easing up in her old age. Loss of those she loved had plagued her life. She had lost two unborn sons, buried her husband, Billy Fleming, father to seven of her daughters. She'd mourned the loss of her firstborn child Sarah, grandson Joe Patter and great-granddaughter Carol, and now the husband of her oldest remaining daughters, Morry, had joined that sorrowful list.

Burying your child is something that no parent should ever have to do, let alone a grandchild and a great-grandchild. Mariah had suffered the punishment of having some of her Catholic privileges restricted as a result of her relationship with Big Tom, and endured the indignity surrounding that entire scandal some 40 years earlier, not to mention the internal controversy over two of her daughters both marrying the same man. She had fought for her family's right to stand on the streets of the city without prosecution and served time in Victorian prison conditions during her campaign for legalisation. What was left of her dwindling business was being frittered away by her son Albert, who simply didn't offer the time or have the inclination required to maintain his interest or any ongoing success. He finished up with a small fruit shop on Pink Lane with his pal and family friend Ray Mouzon; it was called 'Sally's', in homage to his Granny.

Mariah's family were under the cosh from all angles, and the younger ones of Mary Lou's generation were doing little to bring calm to a turbulent sea. Although it was only halfway through the 60s, there had been more than enough to deal with to last Mariah the entire decade.

Light was on the horizon by 1965 though, with some happiness filtering through the various branches of the family with the arrival of new great-grandchildren. From 1964 to 1966 there must have been a new addition just about every month, with about ten of us boys alone arriving within an 18-month period. Happier things to focus on for a change, with the prospect of new offspring coming into the fold, rather than the sadness and loss suffered in the first half of the decade.

Mariah had endured much heartache and controversy over the years, and the 60s had provided little respite, yet sadly there was a lot more to come before the decade was over.

DO ONE, RON!

By 1965, the year we appeared on the scene, the city of Newcastle was attracting socialites and celebrities from far and wide, such was its reputation as a hotspot of the 60s swinging club scene.

Outside London, Newcastle was 'the' place for artists to be seen performing. Lucky punters could see their favourite stars just a few feet away from them, while dining at a table in a smoke-filled nightclub not unlike the lounge rooms of the Las Vegas strip, or the clubs of Soho in London's West End. Newcastle's grafting pecks and straight goers would happily queue to see the likes of Tom Jones or Shirley Bassey; feeling like royalty if they managed to get a good table or a booth. But being a 'face' around town meant you'd be ushered in, looked after and given the best seats in the house.

On any given night you might find several of the family and their associates in one of the clubs, all dressed to the nines and looking every inch the 'box of toys' (boys). Thanks to the events on Percy Street in the spring of '63, it didn't matter if it was Eddie Lennie, out with Blow Shotton or Georgie Kelly and a couple of pals, they would all be referred to as being part of the 'Sayers firm'. The Battle of Percy Street was between the Findlays and the Sayers and, as a result, all those known to be on one side or the other were thereafter recognised as being part of that firm. Our firm, made up mostly of family bearing different surnames, would, for some time after that event, be recognised as the Sayers firm.

John, Doodles, Frankie Shotton and Frankie Kelly were jailed, along with associates Kenny 'Panda' Anderson, John Jeffreys, Tommy Bowman and Ralphy Holmes following Percy Street. The jail they got served less as a punishment to the chaps that were involved, helping to do more for their reputation than anything else, even for those who got away. If anyone wasn't aware beforehand, it was well documented after 1963 that the Sayers firm was not one to be taken lightly. So, when there was talk of the Krays coming to Newcastle to see what all the fuss was about, in the town they called Little Vegas, it was little surprise to anyone that their visit was short lived.

There are several accounts of what happened when the Krays came to town. It is true that they visited Newcastle on more than one occasion between 1963 and '64 and were seen in the company of Davey Findlay. Whatever went down when they were here, it is true to say that they didn't stay and weren't made welcome, in certain quarters.

The talk in London was of this crazy swinging town up near Scotland, where there was over a dozen well-known nightclubs with restaurants and gaming tables, all scattered around a tiny little city centre. This was precisely the kind of fertile ground that the gangs of London were reaping such great rewards from. What then could be easier than taking a trip up north, laying down the law, and getting their thieving fingers into a few of our homemade pies?

During one visit the Krays hit the town with Joe Louis, the former heavyweight champion of the world. Joe loved the nightlife and the adoring young women that went with it, but he was just there for the flash. He had no illicit interest in Tyneside and its underworld activities, he was just happy to be paraded around and treated like royalty wherever he showed up, especially as a guest of the country's two most infamous gangsters.

They say the Krays brought Joe Louis to the UK as a favour to the American mob, at the request of Crazy Joe Gallo from New York. They had similarly organised a 'gangster tour' for American singer Billy Daniels at the mob's request. Joe Louis was broke at the time, having been shafted by the IRS and spent what was left on wine, women and song. With virtually nothing left to show for his days as 'The Brown Bomber' and Heavyweight Champion of the World, Joe's tour of England as a guest of the Kray twins was like some kind of testimonial for the great fighter and helped put a few quid on the champ's hip. But getting their own way in Newcastle was not to be one of the Krays' many documented criminal achievements.

The truth is, the Krays had heard tell of the swinging nightclub scene in Newcastle and wanted to get in on the action. The reality was, even though the town was 'on wheels' as they say, it certainly wasn't London, not least of all because of the wealth divide. The sums of money being spent in the clubs and gambled at the tables in Newcastle was chump change compared to what was changing hands in the capital. Had that not been the case then things might have turned out differently, but that is something we will never know. Our family and other nightclub regulars had plenty of cash and no problems spending it, but the majority of Newcastle's revellers were once-a-week merchants; doing what they could to scrape by on a working wage, they just didn't have the disposable income of the tourists, high rollers or city slickers of London's West End. The Newcastle punters simply weren't spending like those down south, mainly because they didn't have it to spend. It just wasn't enough to make the Krays decide to make a move; or any other outfit with ideas of getting a grip of Newcastle, especially in the face of obvious resistance to their presence.

It would be unfair to comment on every visit the Krays made to Newcastle due to the lack of credible accounts, however, one particular event that can be recounted with absolute accuracy is the time when one of them visited the 69 Club.

Many people have given accounts of what happened when Reggie Kray and one of his heavies, a big Irish fella, Pat Connelly, landed at Joe Lisle's place. Some accounts are documented in the press and discussed online in interviews and the like, and many simply claim to have been there when they turned up, probably hoping to gain a bit of kudos from saying they were there when the Krays came to town. But whatever the reason, and whatever the case, most of the people who really know what happened that night are unfortunately no longer with us, and one of them was my dad, Eddie Lennie Sr.

My old man had been friends with Joe Lisle for many years, and they remained close friends for life. So close was their bond that I referred to him as Uncle Joe until he passed away, and his son Jonathan still refers to my mother as Auntie Mary. My dad, Joe, and Johnny Heenan, whose ancestor fought Tom Sayers back in the 1800s, were the best of friends, remaining close throughout their lives, holidaying together and travelling to Vegas on numerous occasions to see the likes of Ali, Frazer and all the great legends of heavyweight boxing's heydays of the 70s and 80s. Johnny Heenan was an ex-pro footballer turned entertainer and raconteur. He was MC at many of the clubs in the town during the 60s, a charming man who continued to perform almost up until his passing in 2011. I recall, a beautiful bouquet of white lilies arrived at Johnny's funeral with a hand-written note of condolence from Dame Shirley Bassey. Johnny was well got by everyone, and besides his short career as a footballer and his much longer career as a stylish entertainer, Johnny was also a great grafter. He worked the 'run out' on many gaffs (markets) and cities around the country. The 'run out' or 'ram' as we call it, is a mock auction, an old scam carried out often on the seaside promenades of places like Scarborough, Skegness and Great Yarmouth, or in squat shops on busy high streets up and down the country. It's a half-crooked game and one not seen so much these days, but it still pops up here and there, pandering to the greed of a new and unsuspecting generation of bargain hunters that haven't been drawn into the 'run out' before.

Johnny, however, on the night in question, was doing a spot at Botto's club in Byker. Johnny was a lovely singer and delivered all the old standards with the style and panache of a seasoned professional. He perfected his craft and learned from the best; Sinatra, Dean Martin, Perry Como and the like. He once managed to blag my dad, Joe Lisle and himself a front row table at the Flamingo in Las Vegas to see the great Frank Sinatra. They were in town to see a fight and just had to seize the opportunity of seeing Ol' Blue Eyes in the flesh. Johnny put on his best showbiz accent and fannied (sweet-talked) to the security on the door, telling them he was from the BBC in London and they were over there making a documentary on Mr Sinatra.

'If you could just let Mr Sinatra know that Mr Heenan is in the house. We met at the Palladium back in 1950 when I was with the Royal Philharmonic. There's a good man.'

Sweet as a nut, they were ushered in and five minutes later were seated at the best table in the house, even getting a nod and a wink from the great man himself. As Johnny would often tell me, confidence will open more doors for you than anything in this world.

Back to Botto's. Johnny was performing in Billy's club when they received a visit from Reggie Kray and a couple of their firm, with Davey Findlay also in tow. We cannot comment on what transpired at Botto's and whether or not they had any success in putting the bite on him; but aware that they had been in and had left the club heading for Joe's gaff, Johnny immediately made the call to the 69 Club to mark his old pal's card.

The 69 was surprisingly quiet on the night. None of the chaps were in, which was a rarity. Only my dad, Joe Lisle and another pal, Big Jack May – a well-known bookmaker and friend of the family – were in having a quiet drink together. Johnny spoke to Joe and, following the call, told Jack and Eddie that the Reggie Kray was en route to the club to see him. They'd been to Botto's to put the squeeze on, and now they were heading in his direction.

Joe was understandably concerned. He was a respected businessman and club owner and by no means a villain, but he was nobody's fool. He kept a revolver in the safe of his office, and uncertain as to how events would unravel thought it best that he armed himself with his tool. 'If they want to start getting naughty and waving things about, then I've got one to wave about as well,' he said. Fair play Mr Lisle.

Joe, Eddie and Jack retreated to the office at the end of the passage on the ground floor. Not knowing what to expect, but not anticipating a friendly drink. The three sat anxiously awaiting the arrival of their unwanted visitors, and heard a knock at the office door. It was opened by one of Joe's bunny girls. Joe was the first club in town to employ 'bunny girls', the type with white ears and fluffy bob tail costumes, made famous by the Playboy brand. She announced that there were some men at the door of the club, wanting to see Joe. He left the office with Jack and my dad and walked into the lobby of the club, in full sight of the public, with the gun neatly tucked in down the back of his waistband. Reggie, the big Irishman and Davey Findlay had muscled their way past the reception and met Joe, Big Jack and my dad in the passage.

Whether or not Davey was party to the Krays' intention, or whether he was merely playing host to them while they were in town, only he can know, but he was with them when they entered Joe's club. Surely enough, they were there to put the squeeze on Joe. But he wasn't having any of it. He never offered them a drink and kept them standing in the lobby where they could all be seen, before imparting his advice.

'I'm afraid I can't ask you to stay,' he told them. 'There's a strict members policy in this club and, as none of you are members – and you're barred by the way –,' referring to Findlay, 'the staff on reception have probably already pressed the alarm button that links the club to Arthur's Hill Police Station. It's only fifty yards from here.'

Even if there was no such button to press, it was a smart move on Joe's behalf. Reggie told Joe that he was disappointed that they had not been made welcome at his club and that he would not forget Mr Lisle for his inhospitable rebuke. Joe calmly replied that he would not forget them either, suggesting they leave before the response from the alarm. Handshakes were replaced by steely glares and no pleasantries were exchanged, before Reg and his cohorts turned around and left the club, climbing back into the big black motor that was waiting for them. They took off down Westgate Hill heading towards the city centre. Reggie, most likely unimpressed with the reception he'd received in some of the clubs up here, decided to call it a day on Newcastle, and they headed for home very soon after that.

They weren't railroaded out of town, there was no shootout, it was neither glamorous nor violent and certainly not how it has been recounted by many people over the years. The Kray twins left Newcastle to take care of itself. It may be an account that conflicts with many people's versions, even some who claim to have been there and are mentioned so far in this book. However, when the Krays came to the 69 Club, only my old man, Joe Lisle and Big Jack May were there to greet them. No firm to back them up, no bats, no beatings and no bungs were given, either during or after the event, and nothing was exchanged in anger, other than a few hard stares. Just half a dozen men in the lobby of a nightclub, with at least one gun between them, but probably more.

We will never know that for sure, but it is said that the twins never left home without their tools; however, the only thing put inside anybody that night was a stiff drink, after Reggie vacated the premises. Joe had just dealt with some serious people, and needed to calm his nerves, as neither he, my dad nor Jack May knew at that point what the outcome might be.

Fortunately, there wasn't one, at least not one that would result in reprisals from the twins, much to Joe's relief no doubt. As it turned out, the Krays visited Newcastle a couple of other times around then. Ronnie made an appearance with Joe Louis at La Dolce Vita, guests of the Levy Brothers who owned the club which stood on the site of Mariah's warehouse. The champ, they say, became so drunk on the night that he had to be taken home sprawled across the back seat of the Kray firm's motor.

They were reportedly stopped by a police vehicle on Grey Street after flying across the junction from Dean Street. The officer stated that two very smart gentlemen got out of the car and explained that they had to get the former world champion back to his hotel in Jesmond. Doubtful of their excuse for driving too fast, the officer looked through the back window to see The

Brown Bomber out for the count. Starstruck by this finding, the officer duly escorted the vehicle back to Jesmond, with blue lights flashing all the way. The two fellas in the car must have been pissing themselves laughing, having blue lights escort them for a change, instead of chasing them. It was only later, when the bobby saw pictures of the Krays on TV and in the press, when they were on trial for the murders of Jack 'The Hat' McVitie and George Cornell, that he realised one of the smart young men in the car with Joe Louis that night was Ronnie Kray; the same young man who had spoken to, and given all due respect to him when he'd stopped them on Grey Street.

It's a nice little story, and true by all accounts, yet it underlines what the Krays must have thought about their time spent in Newcastle. They were not made welcome in certain quarters, they were certainly not feared, and they were not impressed with the place. It also seemed that the place was equally unimpressed with them, even the Old Bill didn't know who they were.

So, Newcastle was left to its own devices by the captains of organised crime, and any void on its streets would have to be filled by firms who lived there, leaving the Luvaglios and Dennis Stafford to run their one-armed bandit business unchallenged. But that didn't run as smoothly as they might have hoped.

The same year that saw the 'Battle of Percy Street' take place also brought the 'Great Train Robbery' to the nation's attention, and the public were equally appalled and enthralled by the daily news reports of the masked gang who'd carried out the daring heist. Three of that firm were sent to Durham jail in the August of '64, crossing paths with some of our family during their time there. It is always advisable to make contact with other faces in jail, especially those that are well known in the jail's location, and Durham was our local shovel (nick).

The Krays and the Richardsons were at war on the streets of London. Mods and rockers had running battles on the sea fronts of Brighton, and the country was again challenging authority on a national scale.

YOU'VE GOT TO DO WHAT YOU'VE GOT TO DO

On the home front, some of Mariah's younger grandchildren like Frankie Hewson, Pat, Michael and Terry Patterson, Joe Donnelly and Muriel were out with their mams, dads, aunties or uncles working the barrow, along with some of the older great-grandchildren, like my brother Tony Lennie.

The game was steady away, at least for the girls who'd been reprieved by the Watch Committee, but for all the sly pitchers working the barrow it was becoming increasingly difficult. Fines would often outweigh the rewards, not to mention the inconvenience of getting locked up. But our family still turned out. We were grafters; it's what we knew, it's what we did, and without many alternative options, it was what we continued to do, in spite of uniformed resistance.

You must remember, our family members were not academic people. Some were barely literate, having to get their sons or nephews to write out their price cards for the barrow. The shit we used to put on them sometimes was nobody's business; 'dirty stinking plums', 'soggy strawberries', 'peaches on the turn', ' rotten tomatoes'…any old bollocks! Yes, even bollocks; hairy ones, ripe and ready to eat! They were written just for a laugh because it was known that the aunties and uncles lacked the formal education to be able to read them.

Our world may have been different because of our breeding, however, maybe if the authorities had taken a more liberal view of what we did, and allowed us to work the street legitimately, then possibly much of what transpired outside of the barrows may never have come about. This, however, was not the case. The family was persecuted and prosecuted to the point where they might have starved if they didn't continue to turn out or look elsewhere in order to survive. The fact that some of the chaps did look elsewhere for money only served to further frustrate the authorities, meaning they clamped down even harder on sly pitching. It made little sense in hindsight, but it certainly intensified the distrust and animosity that existed between our family and the powers that be in Newcastle. They looked at us with contempt, both generally and in relation to much of what was going on in the city on a criminal level. It's fair to say we, in turn, could have lain the blame at their door for putting us in a position where a few of us had to do work outside the law in order to provide for our families.

For four generations we had been penalised for trying to earn an honest living with the barrows yet were constantly pushed further into the shadows of society, which resulted in harsher penalties for less legal activities. There was little love lost between our family and the 'law', and it was to become a relationship that would deteriorate and spiral into something of a witch hunt against some members of the family in the years ahead.

The generation of Mariah's grandchildren were now in full swing, busy producing the next generation of great-grandkids, - our generation. But just like Bob Dylan said, 'the times, they were a changing.' So, what would become of this new line of descendants, Mariah's great-grandchildren, born into a family of street traders and hawkers? Was there to be a living available for us on the street? Were we going to be driven further underground? Were we going to win the right to trade legally? Or, was this to be the generation that would break the mould? Would we all stick in at school and become doctors, dentists, lawyers or civil servants? Well, we can only tell you from our point of view.

Our dads, grandads and uncles were our role models. We grew up surrounded by so many of them, grafters, tricksters, wise guys, every one of them. Sharply-dressed, quick-witted, colourful, charming and totally unconventional, and whether they imparted their knowledge upon us, or we just watched how they went on, we learned the ways of our world from them.

We went to various schools, usually those already attended by some of our older relatives, whose attendance was not so usual. Many of our elders were often in the nick or had been for one reason or another. When they weren't inside, we would be helping them on the barrow or out hawking with them in our spare time. We were picking up wages while our school pals were studying for their 11-plus. We'd be taken down to the Pavilion on Westgate Road on the back of a flat-backed wagon with our cousins to watch the latest movie, and we'd all try and jib in to save the shilling entry fee so we could spend it on ice cream or sweets. We spoke differently, we saw things differently and we acted differently to other kids, because that is what was bred into us and was inherent in our personalities.

We were a product of a particular way of life. A way of life that will resonate with some, but one that will be alien to many. We saw actors on the screen that were just like our dads, grandads and uncles, and we were the last generation to get a feel for life on the streets. We were our own little clan. Cousins, half-cousins, similar aged aunties and uncles, all with the same street mentality and upbringing. We had no chance. Our future was already mapped out. We were the last of the old school, but the first of the new breed.

The public's attitude toward crime during the 60s was one the judicial system struggled to comprehend. The press coverage reporting the 'daring-do' of the Great Train Robbers, and the later scandalisation of the Kray twins' trial, did little to alienate outlaws from the general population, let alone damage the perception already held within everyday society. Much to the annoyance of the courts, the judges and the thin blue line, the portrayal of their exploits seemed to resonate with the psyche of the British public at the time. To be fair, had one of the train robbers not clobbered the driver with a metal pipe, then there is plenty to suggest that they would have been unanimously hailed as heroes by the working class.

Even the killings of Jack 'The Hat' McVitie and George Cornell were considered as an occupational hazard for people of the underworld, and failed to revile the nation, who were largely more interested in the lifestyle and attitudes of the East End villains rather than the bad things they did to each other.

To be honest, it seemed like everybody was on a different wave length to the law-makers, and lots more people were 'at it', one way or another. In our town we grew up amongst it, in a world where virtually none of our family had a proper job, although they worked long and hard at times, out hawking or grafting fairs and markets, unable to rely solely on the barrows.

However, this was a time when shops and warehouses were rarely alarmed, and CCTV was no more than a twinkle in a camera's lens. Young men from all walks of life were trying their luck at a bit of villainy, even straight-going grafting pecks. Smash and grabs were common place, warehouse and shop breaking, jump-ups and wage snatches were the standard bill of fare for most would-be villains of the day, most likely to get away with their bit of toil unless they were caught in the act. The deterrents simply weren't there to stop them before they carried out their actions, and unless the law had your fingerprints and you left your dabs all over the place, you'd probably get away with a little bit of nonsense. So, the judicial system, in their infinite wisdom, used the unjustifiable sentences of the Great Train Robbers and the Kray twins to set an example, a bench mark that would act as a crime deterrent to any would-be gangster.

However, these 'examples' did little to restore many of the general public's faith in the judicial system, and served only to highlight just how personally the government could take their attitude toward crime and punishment, especially where money was concerned. The heavy sentences were supposed to be a warning to everyone, but they simply fuelled the belief that the authorities were bullies, just as bad, if not worse, than those they were locking up for a 30-stretch a piece. It did not go unnoticed that while they were dishing out 30 years like it was half a stretch, they were giving 18-months or two and three years to perverts and nonces. They had to look no further than prominent politicians and would-be prime ministers of the day in order to see that far more debauched activity, much of it with criminal intent, was going on within their own number, but that was different.

They didn't need money, they were the people in control of the stuff. They preferred perverse gratification, the kind that the underworld reviled, but God help any poor bastard that tried to steal any of their money, that was simply not tolerated.

Before the decade came to a close, just about all of our fathers, grandads and uncles had been locked up and served sentences for anything from resisting arrest, to warehouse breaking, shop robbery, theft, violence, inducing police officers and charges of fraud for suspected long firming. Intimidation of witnesses and jury nobbling were even thrown into the mix, not to mention the Percy Street carry on.

It was hard to pick up the *Evening Chronicle* for a while without seeing one of our family in there for all the wrong reasons. Again, not something that helps the next generation on their way to 'Straightsville'. The press, however, were doing a fantastic job of enhancing the family's reputation, not just within our own tight-knit community, but throughout the region and beyond. Meanwhile, many of the land's most famous villains of the time did spells in Durham jail. Its location, miles away from the south, made it more difficult to access, therefore harder for the families of the convicted to visit, and it had a reputation as one of the toughest jails in the land.

Needless to say, when any of the high-profile faces would end up there, they would be sure to dig out one of our lot if they happened to be in Durham at the same time. Even if none of our team was locked up when they landed there, word would get to someone in our family from down the road, and they'd ask that we made sure their associates were looked after while they were on the Durham landings. Even without any of our mob doing bird at the same time, there'd always be someone on the inside who could be relied upon to make their friends welcome in Durham. This type of favour is one that is always acknowledged and puts you in good stead within the prison population and the criminal fraternity. Favours can always be called in, and even if they are not, they are never forgotten amongst men of honour.

There were two worlds dealing with the changes taking place in the country during the 60s. They lived side by side, but on directly opposite sides of the thin blue line. The system wanted to stem the wave of support and a 'devil-may-care' attitude towards crime, which was simmering away among the general population. The country as a whole was becoming more and more disillusioned with the upper-class approach to dealing with crime and punishment. However, the era was one that brought the entire country together in revulsion to a particular type of crime that was beginning to rear its ugly head.

It seemed the days of being able to leave your door open with kids playing in the street 'til all hours were something that might become a forgotten privilege of a time gone by. The Moors Murders of 1963 to '65 shook the nation to its core. It didn't matter what side of the fence you were on, the general population were repulsed and appalled by the depraved acts of those two evil bastards. Sentencing for the likes of them could not be harsh enough, and that was, for once, a universal mindset. It didn't matter if you were a magistrate or a safe-blower, everyone agreed that those two animals should have been left to the families of the dear innocent children whose lives they had so hideously taken.

People around the country were terrified to let their kids out of their sight as details of their evil deeds unfolded. Crimes of this nature were rarely reported, probably as they didn't happen so much back then, but now they were being written about and talked about with uniform contempt all across the land. This was something that genuinely warranted the most severe punishment, and the entire country hoped that the system would recognise this. And they did, but their punishment was no greater than that dished out to certain villains for lesser crimes. Something was wrong with that principle, and the population knew it.

The heinous acts carried out on the West Yorkshire Moors during those years became an issue of even greater concern in

Newcastle by the end of the decade. During 1969, a 10-year-old girl called Mary Bell, from the West End of Newcastle, was found guilty on two counts of murder of a couple of three and four-year-old boys. The evil of the moors, like the murky mist that sits on Saddleworth, had silently spread north, and it was now on our doorstep. The two young boys were from the Scotswood area. The city and the region were in shock, not least of all because their killer was only a child herself. These crimes heralded another shift in attitude, and in a knee-jerk reaction, innocence was lost almost overnight.

Children were now potential victims and it seemed nothing was sacred anymore. Communities closed rank, and people looked out for themselves before they considered their neighbours. Communities needed protecting, and faith in the system was waning even further. If a family felt threatened, they needed someone to turn to, a door they could knock on, a friend and protector in times of need. And although the system fails to recognise such a need within a close-knit community, it is something that existed in inner city environments back then.

Today we look back on such a thing with nostalgia, as it is a structure that no longer exists in our society. For all the wrong that certain people might do in the eyes of the law, the same people can hold a vital position within a tight-knit community. Just ask anyone from the old East End of London and they will tell you that their streets were safer when the Kray twins were on them. Others, of course, will tell you that the twins were animals, bullies and coldblooded killers, yet for all their misgivings, they never took the life of a child and they looked out for their own, be it family, friend or neighbour.

Some people are born into a family of professionals, sportsmen or soldiers or whatever, and nine times out of ten they will go on to produce more of the same. Our family was no different. Except we were none of the aforementioned. We were street traders, hawkers born and bred, living in a city that tried to prevent us from doing what we did. We followed in the footsteps of our predecessors and learned the ways of our world from them. We were no less moral than the next man, in fact we conducted ourselves with more respect than many people from backgrounds with far greater opportunity and privilege. We kept ourselves, looked after ourselves and those around us, and like it or not, people like that are becoming a thing of the past. Old school values are becoming a romantically nostalgic concept, God help us all!

There are bad guys, and then there are bad people. Our family may have done many things that some might not have; but they did what they had to, and knew very well what things should never be done.

The 1960s had been a time of great change, great loss and great expectation for the family, as it was also a decade when dozens more of us appeared on the scene. Growing up a stone's throw from each other and feeling the warmth of family wrapped around us at all times, we lived in each other's pockets as an extended family, and learned very quickly that the first people you can trust are your own. Your first friends are your cousins, and by and large they stay that way for life.

But this is not a fairy tale and it doesn't have a happy ending, at least not in the traditional sense. There were fall outs from time to time, that's only natural. However, sometimes the blood runs cold, and with so many of us running around town in search of the same pound note, minor rows could quite easily become feuds, and family feuds are the very worst kind. Lines are often drawn and neutral parties can become easily compromised by any rift within their own. There had been controversy with earlier generations, not least of all when Mariah left Billy Fleming for Big Tom Cruddas, or when Frankie Hewson married my granny's sister. Thankfully, however, these episodes had blown over without too much damage to the fabric of the family. Mariah, however, was now in her 70s and her many offspring and were of a different generation.

Her grandchildren had grown up during the Second World War and the years that followed, a time when things were good across the board for all of them, thanks to the black market, and family at that time was all that mattered. The rest had grown up during the changing times of the 1950s when rebellion was in the air and attitudes were different. And now in the 1960s with its free love, sex, drugs and rock 'n' roll, all of which had an impact on everyone; attitudes and values were changing once again.

But just like the inevitable changing attitudes which occur over time, our united family front would unavoidably be tested to the full in the years ahead; internal differences, disagreements and rivalry would sadly undermine much of the real strength that was bred into us, to always look out for your own. Luckily it wasn't to happen for a while yet, and our youth and early adulthood as a strong and close-knit family was an incredible environment in which to grow up.

All of that growing up was done in the West End, in a maze of nearby streets to the west of St James' Park, within the sound of the Gallowgate roar, something that many say is the definition of a true Geordie. More than being proud Geordies, however, we were proud of being from our family and proud of our heritage. It wasn't where we came from that defined us, it was what we were.

Blandford Street, Blenheim Street, Buckingham Street, Diana Street, Westgate Hill Terrace, York Street, Pitt Street… you could have thrown a blanket over the lot us. It was our neighbourhood, our manor, and those streets, and the streets of the city centre, were where our family had learned to survive, to duck and dive, and to find a shilling. Uneducated in the traditional sense, but street smart, wide, tricky, game people. Our dads had done anything and everything in order to provide for us. They were barrow boys predominantly, but not all. They dodged arrest or prosecution to work a pitch and bring home an honest living. That's what the barrows could provide. Being a street trader or peddler is one of the oldest professions known to man, that and being a brass of course.

Since the early days of civilisation, street vendors were at the very heart of all communities. There were builders of course, carpenters, servants and the like, but traders and merchants were the business people of the working classes, and people like them would sell their wares and trade their goods on the streets of every nation on the planet, throughout every age since time immemorial. We were purveyors of an old and noble tradition, yet we were hampered and persecuted by the authorities for exercising our heritage on the streets of Newcastle. Yet we were determined as a family to pursue our inalienable right to be bona fide street traders. If only that had been permitted sooner, then the outcome of the family and so many of their lives may have turned out very differently.

The law's reluctance to accept our costermonger activities, and the circumstances that our family faced as a result, were not earth-shattering by any stretch of the imagination, yet they were enough to alter the course of many lives. We were too many, and too rooted to our home town now to simply up sticks and move to another city that would tolerate our historic methods of earning a living. If that were to have been done then it should have happened four generations earlier when there was only Paddy, Sally and their children, Mariah and Frank.

But they had set out their stall in every sense, and Sally was determined to become recognised and legitimised in the city they had chosen to call home.

Mariah continued the fight, and it was a fight that was now in its 70th year. They were resilient women, passionate about what they did, they believed in what they did, and were determined to fight for their cause. That baton had been handed on to every generation that followed Sally, just like the education that was handed down to every one of us, but 70 years after Sally first pulled her cart onto Newgate Street in 1887, and even with the limited reprieve offered up by the Watch Committee, we were no closer to becoming fully legalised than we were back then.

The only thing that the passage of time had really served to do in that respect, was to cause a sense of animosity, a disregard and create a bitter relationship between our family and the authorities in the city.

It would be naïve to suggest that some of the family turned to crime simply because they weren't permitted to stand with a barrow, and we would never imply that to be the case. But as you may have gathered, many other factors played a part in that process. Menial, manual and unskilled work was never going to be a preferred choice for them, and that's all that would have been available to people from their background. They knew they could get a good living on the street, they knew the fruit game and enjoyed what they did, especially without having to answer to anyone, and that spoiled them.

They dealt in cash on a daily basis, outside of the system so to speak, and as a result had less fear of operating outside of it in other ways. They spent as they earned and failed to become part of the 'system', but times were most definitely changing, which meant that once again, attitudes would have to.

Much of the villainy that went on within the family during the 1960s is documented in numerous column inches of the local press. For some of the chaps, the barrows and the street were enough, despite the fines. However, for some, a little bit of nonsense was something they made a conscious decision to do because of circumstance, or sometimes simply because they wanted to. One thing is for sure, however, for some it was time to look at where they were going with their lives. People like my father, Doodles and Albert Cruddas all had children and families to raise.

Being in and out of the nick, and sometimes not knowing where the next earn was coming from, was not what they wanted to be doing in their late 30s with three or four kids on their top lip. The system was becoming increasingly difficult to avoid, if success was to be achieved, yet legalisation for the barrowboys of Newcastle seemed to be as far off as ever.

My dad had been married into the family for the best part of 20 years and now had a wife and family, living in a maisonette in Hill Court on Pitt Street. It had been a happy home, the party venue for many of the family, and a home that was shared by some of them from time to time during the 1960s. But he had a bit of an eye opener when he was handed a nine-month sentence for dangerous driving while resisting arrest and assaulting a police officer; thankfully avoiding the threatened charge of attempted murder for driving with the officer stood on the footplate of the motor, claiming my dad tried to dislodge him with right hander before crashing the car. It was significantly reduced to a much lesser offence, but the short sentence did give him a bit of a wake-up call. What happened while he was inside, however, really made him take stock of his situation.

Whilst inside, the running of the house was left to my mam, who had my brother, Tony 'Legs', my sister Michelle and me to take care of. One day, with Tony and Michelle in school, My mother left me at home for ten minutes with a young girl by the name of Yvonne Patton, a friend of mam's sister Jo. During that time Yvonne, in her infinite wisdom, decided to try and stand me up on the windowsill in the front room, with the intent of getting me to jump into her arms. I was only around 12 months old at the time. The window was one of the old-style ones with a latch and an arm with holes in that you set at various lengths on a prong fixed to the sill to keep the window ajar.

Unfortunately, little Edward didn't respond correctly to the command to 'jump' into the open arms of Yvonne, and instead fell backwards, out of the window, and onto the ground three floors below. God was on my side that day, as I miraculously landed on a triangle of grass between the pavement and the path leading to the flats. A foot either way and you wouldn't be reading this book, or at least I wouldn't be writing it. My mother recalls returning from the shop to see a crowd outside the flats, and approached with curiosity, never in her wildest dreams thinking they were gathered around her little baby boy, who'd just fallen 30 feet, almost to his death. Luckily, I escaped with nothing more than concussion – the original bouncing baby.

I didn't see Yvonne Patton again after that day until about 15 years ago, she'd moved to Brighton as a teenager (nothing to do with the accident). Knowing full well who she was, I jokingly told her that I didn't recognise her, before lying down on the floor to look up at her and saying, '*Now* I recognise you!' She was a little freaked out, but I thought it was funny. Maybe you had to be there? In any case, it was something that made my old man think long and hard about getting away from there and away from the town, in order to straighten himself out once he was back on the pavement.

Hill Court proved to be a memorable residence for the family, and was home to any number of them at that time. It was right next to Newcastle Breweries and just up the street from the Magpie, a supporter's drinking hole that stood opposite the football ground at the bottom of Pitt Street. The Blue Star Club was a little further up the street, as was the Lord Hill pub, clearly visible from the same window I fell out of, and one at which my parents pissed themselves laughing at one night when they heard and saw three or four familiar faces from the manor screwing the place to chore (steal) a load of snout (cigarettes/tobacco) and drink.

Buck used to use the Blue Star Club a lot. He'd often be in there if he had a sharp finish on the barrow, supping his bottles of Mackeson Stout and keeping count of them, as he always did, and making himself busy with many of the lorry drivers that used to get in there. He got to find out a lot about what was getting shipped around the region.

Hill Court was a happy place for the best part, an open house, and a party house. For a period, it was a favourite place to end a night out, and many a good time was had there. Many nights I remember wake up to the sound of music and laughter downstairs, and for as young as I was when we left there I still have fond, if somewhat vague, memories of the place. However, by the time my dad got out the nick, he'd decided it was time to grow up and straighten out. He was in his mid-30s by then, and fortunately the opportunity was soon presented to him in the form of one George Luke.

George had been a professional footballer in his youth, turning out for Newcastle during the Joe Harvey years, and was introduced to my father by Johnny Cuff, the manager of La Dolce Vita. They became good friends, opening up a carpet pitch together on Blenheim Street. It was a partnership that lasted about ten years and later took them to premises in Forest Hall, where Carpet Crafts House became an established and highly reputable business. The business still trades today under the name of Forest Hall Carpets, ran by George Luke's sons Hilton and Tony at the time of writing.

This was my dad's ticket out of a way of life that was becoming perilously dangerous. Jailtime was being dished out, scrapes were getting closer and he wasn't getting any younger; he also had a wife and three kids wrapped around him. The opportunity to earn an honest living running a proper business with a legitimate and perfectly straight partner, who was as clean as a whistle with lots of friends from the world of football ready to spend a lot of money with him, was simply too good an offer to turn down. It was the chance to move our family into a new-build home outside the city in a brand new estate somewhere else. To take Tony under his wing, away from the temptations of the town and put him through his paces to become a time-served floor layer, a trade he could always fall back on, and one which could provide him with a decent honest living. It was a father's opportunity to try and better himself and his family, and to stay out of trouble.

So, before the 1970s arrived in its platform shoes and glam rocking glory, we moved from Hill Court, from Pitt Street, the town and the interwoven web of the wider family. Only time would tell whether the right move had been made, and whether or not being a few miles from the rest of our breed would make any difference to the outcome of the children whose future my father was trying to safeguard.

For many others in the family of a similar age to him, no such opportunity had yet presented itself, so for them it was life as usual on the streets of the town. With the likes of our Tony's dad Peter Sayers and his brother Albert, Thomas Kelly and the twins Frankie and Jimmy, Frankie Shotton and young Frankie

Hewson, as well as the Patter brothers Michael and Terry, not to mention the Donnellys, there were more than enough young barrow boys, and girls, in the family to crowd around the corner of Nelson Street, and more than enough cousins to do a bit of work with.

We may only have moved three or four miles away from Hill Court, the town and the family, but West Denton felt like it was a hundred miles from home. You had to get a different coloured bus from the town busses just to get there, it was that far away! You'd have to go past newly built motorways and wide open fields with real life cows in them, it was amazing! It's no more than a ten-minute drive from West Denton into the city these days, it's just on the outskirts of the town now really, but 50 years ago it felt like you were on a proper day out if you were going to the place. As a result of the move I saw less of my cousins for a period of years, but it didn't keep us apart for too long.

The carpet business was good and with the nice new house (out in the country) came nice motors and nice holidays abroad, as early as 1969 even one to Miami for my mam, dad, Joe Lisle and his wife. It seemed like my dad had made the right move. He was getting a few quid straight, mixing with the footballers in Roy's 2 Rooms, and enjoying the fruits of his labour. The carpet shop was in the town so he still saw all the chaps regularly, socialising with them from time to time. They were all still ducking and diving, or making a few quid on the barrow or, in Doodles and John's case, nicking a few quid, literally.

All of the chaps of that generation were growing up by then, yet the rest of the decade was still littered with jail sentences for many of them after Percy Street, as well as various other incidents. It seemed the 1960s was filled with events that scarred, saddened and tested the family to the extreme. However, one sad event ironically brought about a positive change for Mariah.

Mrs Cruddas, Big Tom's legal wife of many years eventually passed away, which finally left the door open for Mariah and Big

Tom to sanctify their union, and so she officially became Mrs Mariah Kelly Cruddas, following a private church service at St Mary's.

Big Tom had to be baptised in the Catholic faith in order to marry Mariah, just as my father and one or two others had done in order to marry into the family, so there were two somewhat happier ceremonies before the end of the decade. Tony's dad, Peter Sayers acted as Godfather to Big Tom, while their only son Albert Cruddas acted as best man for the wedding ceremony, which was a symbolic act of morality as much as anything else, due to the fact that Big Tom was not a well man, and the end of the decade, just as the 60s had started, finished with yet more heartbreak for the Old Queen of the Barrows.

Mariah Kelly was officially Mrs Cruddas for less than a year before she became a widow for the second time in her long and eventful life. James 'Big Tom' Cruddas passed away on 11th of February 1970, aged 72.

GOD SAVE THE QUEEN

Sadly, the end of the decade didn't herald the end of heartbreak for the family.

Following the loss of her new husband, 1970 was to deliver even more sorrow for Mariah and her family. The young, gregarious and charming Frank Shotton, husband to young Mariah Kelly's daughter Vera, had his life prematurely cut short in the July of the same year by cancer, at the age of just 34, leaving behind five children and a young widow.

For all the new blood that came into the family during the 1960s, some of the more influential and memorable characters were no longer around. Mariah however, was still the matriarch, her rapier wit, wisdom and turn of phrase was now legendary, and to this day are often recounted and regularly used by many of her descendants. This great old woman, Queen of the Barrows, had earned her place in the history of Newcastle's streets, as well as the hearts of her family; a family that was all around her, and who loved and revered her. A family that were who they were thanks to the way she had taught them to function in the world.

One thing, however, had eluded Mariah, and that was the legalisation of her family's street trading activities. As unpredictable as working on the barrows was, it was still something that many of the family did for a regular living. It was not just a means to an end, or a way to get a shilling, as it was for many of the newcomers now on the streets alongside members of our family. For us, it was tradition.

Our family had been on the streets for almost five generations, while many others had dipped in and out over the years. Some had stuck it out for a couple of decades alongside us, but the one family that had been there as long as anyone could remember was ours. Mariah had fought for most of her life to have her family's costermonger activities legalised, and at one time even seen off would be extortionists in order to protect her interests. Some years earlier, before Big Tom was on the scene and prior to her daughters getting were married, a young chancer by the name of Darkie Armstrong had teamed up with a local tearaway, Jimmy Somerville.

They somehow thought they could put the squeeze on Mariah, taxing her for protection of her barrows. It was a bold move to say the least, and between the two of them, it fell to Darkie to make the approach. Mariah was still at her home on Sunderland Street when he came knocking at the door. The would-be gangster explained his fabulous idea as Mariah listened intently to the young fool. She knew the lad from around the town, and knew he wasn't a real jumpy-jack and so assumed someone must have been pulling his strings.

'Alright, son. Just wait here,' she said, as she left him on her doorstep. 'Your granny's got something for you.'

Darkie must have thought she was going to stand for it as he waited patiently outside Mariah's front door.

She returned within a minute, opened the door and covered the silly clown with the contents of a pepper pot. Proceeding to chase him off in no uncertain terms, Mariah shoved him on his arse, slamming the door in the face of the blinded Darkie, who was coughing his guts out and rolling around in a cloud of pepper. When the dust cleared, he must've thought better of it, as Darkie never darkened her door again.

Soon after that, my Granny Sarah married Frankie Hewson, he knew Darkie, and following an apology for his reckless behaviour the matter was never discussed again. Darkie ultimately became a well-known tatter, scraping a living with a yoke (horse and cart) on the streets of Tyneside until his old age. But Mariah was in her 80s by now, and the baton for legalisation would have to be taken up by someone else within the family. My grandfather Old Frankie Hewson, was still working the barrow with his son Frank Jr and my brother Tony, but was now in his mid-60s. Georgie Kelly and Billy Buck were both proper barrow boys too, as were young Albert and Peter Sayers, not to mention the Patters - brothers Michael, Terry and sister Pat.

Just like young Joe 'Dapper' Donnelly and his sister Muriel, who were also regulars on the street, every one of them had generations of heritage in the game, and one of them at least would have to continue the crusade.

Albert Sayers was another of Mariah's favourites; never afraid to make flesh of some of her breed and fowl of others, it was just Mariah's way. She loved them all, and now there were almost too many to count, but she loved some more than others, and that was that. Albert, however, seemed to be the standout candidate to continue the campaign for legalisation.

He was eloquent, semi-literate, and smart enough to sit down with the authorities and present a credible argument, one which would hopefully fulfil Mariah's legacy. Even though he'd been raised on the street and in the boxing ring, with his older brother Doodles, he didn't benefit from any real formal education. But Albert looked the part, could talk the part and most likely would get the part. The question was, would the authorities even be prepared to sit down with Albert? In light of the growing resentment between our family and the powers that be, especially since some of the family had taken their illicit activities into other areas, it seemed unlikely; and even if they did sit down and listen, would they be prepared do anything about it? Albert was convinced that if he went about things in a certain way then maybe they would. It wasn't going to happen overnight, after all, we'd been banging on about pitches for decades now, and even though the Watch Committee had given some of Mariah's girls a break, that was as far as it had gone. Albert was convinced, however, that he could change things, and the challenge for him was to make sure that change took place while his granny was still around to see it happen.

Meanwhile, it was business as usual: go to work, get a few quid and finish sharp, without a fine if you were lucky. Get nicked and go back to work to pay the fine, if you were unlucky.

This had gone on for so many years now that it was no little more than an occupational hazard. Even some of the Old Bill were now far less bothered about it than they had been when they were rookie bobbies on the beat. The decent warrant officers would often visit some of the lads and tell them to get their fingers out, make a payment before things got out of hand and finished up in court, where they would ultimately get locked up. Some of the coppers had been on the pavement for as long as we'd stood the barrows, and they were as fed up with the dance as the family were, but they had a job to do; after all, the law had to be upheld.

The young rookies looking to make their stripes, however, didn't look at things quite the same way, and would think nothing of making an example of some of the chaps whenever they had the opportunity, confiscating gear and dragging them off the street if fines were still outstanding. This would result in a court appearance the next day, and if outstanding fines were not paid, then a proportionate amount of time behind bars would be the consequence.

Albert Sayers and Georgie Kelly were street traders through and through, and both spent short spells in jail for refusing to pay fines. Not because they couldn't afford to pay, but because they refused to; it was a matter of principle, just the way it had been for their parents and grandparents before them.

Georgie and Albert would work in other cities from time to time, cities where enforcement for street trading wasn't nearly so hot, and where they knew they might have a touch. They also learned very quickly that the less conspicuous you were, the less chance you had of getting nicked, so picking up a line like the Rubik's Cube, the Big Balloon or the Squirble (a fluffy caterpillar-type toy on 'invisible' thread, which made it appear to move unaided, became the perfect tools to go to work with.

Lines like these which came along in the 1970s and 80s were a godsend, a great way to work the street without the need for a suitcase and box, never mind all the fuss of a barrow full of gear; and if you mastered the art of the toy (the Squirble, not the Rubik's Cube, you had to be a proper tricky trousers to do that!) and delivered a pitch while showing the punters how it's done, then you'd cracked it. Once you reached the 'bat' it was payday, simply serving stock from a holdall, in and out, short and sweet as a nut! And if the Old Bill did come your way, then it was simply a case of putting the toy in your pocket, picking up your bag and blending in with the crowd. Job done, punters served, no nicking, no blister. Happy Days!

Albert and Georgie would work the new craze toys of the day on the streets of Newcastle during the 1970s, and us youngsters would watch them go to work while we kept toot, in awe of their ability with the line, and their seamless sales spiel. They had learned their trade from the likes of my grandad and Morry, resembling them in their delivery and style, mixed with their own individual charm. They looked every inch the type of character you'd love to listen to selling something on the street. Georgie Kelly was just like Arthur Daley, a real old spiv type character, complete with Trilby hat, suit, collar and tie, and top coat to finish off the ensemble.

Albert looked more like a young Michael Caine, dressed in the more modern suits of the day, always with a collar and tie, a nice groin (ring) on his finger, gold bracelet on one wrist and a good kettle on the other, topped off with a smart pair of gold-rimmed bins. He even sported the original Del Boy-style sheepskin coat on occasion. Both of them were genuine characters, long before *Only Fools and Horses* or *Minder* were ever on our screens. They were proper wide-boys, and both of those two famous TV characters that we have all grown up with could have quite easily been inspired by Georgie and Albert. Instead, however, these two had become the torch bearers of the street trading game within our family.

They influenced many of us within the family who followed in their footsteps. Another John Sayers, for example, would also often be seen on the cobbles around that time, working a bit of 'tom' or anything else that might turn a bob or two. Unlike his name-sake who'd chosen a far more precarious path, Skinny John, as he was known, knew how to pull a pitch and twirl a hedge. He was the daughter of one of Morry's sisters, who having declined to use the surname of her children's father, her several off-spring bore the name Sayers, and Skinny John would often be seen going to work form a brief-case whilst his brother Georgie kept toot.

They were all pleasure to watch and a delight to learn from. When we were keeping toot for them, we weren't just doing our job, we were getting an education. Learning how to pull a pitch, how to get the hedge on your side, how to build up the excitement and ramp up the value, before leading the punters to the all-important 'bat'. Then 'BANG!!' once the punter heard the price, and one of them dropped in, the rest would usually race to follow suit. They boys would always go to work with a 'rick in', sometimes two or three of them.

A 'rick in' is someone on the firm who would mingle into the hedge posing as a punter. They would be the first one to pull up the money once the 'bat' had been delivered. The purpose of the 'rick in' was to kick start the rest of the punters into buying. Once they'd seen someone else having a go they were far more likely to take a punt themselves.

No one likes to be the first person to buy in this situation, there's often uncertainty and they don't want to be seen as a complete mark for jumping straight in for fear of getting conned. So the 'rick in' takes the dairy off them and starts the ball rolling, once they drop in the rest will surely follow, like lambs to the slaughter, and bingo! You're twirling the hedge (converting the punters) and having a pitch.

There was good money in lines like these when they came along, but they weren't always there. The barrows were always there to fall back on, but that game wasn't getting any easier, what with self-service greengrocer shops like Bookless and supermarkets popping up all over, offering vast varieties of fresh produce at keen prices, not to mention the other people in the town who were now regulars on the streets with their own barrows; Tommy Quinn, Jimmy Holmes, and the Drummond twins Harry and Jimmy, who were both related to our family by marriage. Their mother, Lilly, was a sister of Morry Sayers.

They all knew, just like our family had done for generations, that there was a good living to be had on the barrows, and an even better one if they could be allowed to do so without the cost of mounting fines.

The fruit market moved to Gateshead on the Team Valley Trading Estate by then. Our family was still well known in the market as all of the old wholesalers from St Andrew's were now relocated there. Unlike the days when Mariah would monopolise the game, supplying the barrow, pitch and stock for a small cut of the profits, it was now every man for themselves. At the market different members of the family would all see each other on the warehouse floors in the early hours of the morning trying to secure a good line, for handy money, to go to work with. They were all in search of the best deals, and all chasing the same pound note back on the streets once they hit the town.

It was no longer organised and evenly spread amongst us, it was a free for all, toes would often be stepped on in the race to get the best line at the keenest price, and hopefully be favourite to secure the best pitch when they got back to the Newcastle. There was no longer a figurehead running the show. Mariah had retired, and her son Albert had little interest in continuing in her vein. Albert was now married to Jenny, with four kids of his own to contend with, along with the three he had to his first wife. All of Mariah's daughters were getting on in years, and the young chaps were more than capable of taking care of themselves, and that's precisely what they did. Taking care of yourself by definition means taking less care of anyone else, so if you stepped on the toes of one of your own at the market in pursuit of the best line of the day, in order to put food on the table for your own family, then so be it.

The sad reality was that we were becoming disenfranchised as a working family and, with outsiders now in on the act, it really was every man for himself. It even got to the point where there were verbal disagreements on the street about where you chose to pitch up for the day, normally depending on how soon you secured your line at the market and got back to the town to claim the best pitch on the corner of Nelson Street. The 'front', as it had become known by then, was always the desired location. It was very central, close to Northumberland Street, but not quite as warm for getting nicked.

Many of the other usual pitches were temporarily unworkable at the time due to the massive amount of regeneration which was going on in the city centre. A pitch one of them may have worked for years might be completely boarded around to protect passersby from the scaffolding and debris, as old shops were being pulled down to make way for new developments like Eldon Square.

The face of the town was undergoing a major reconstruction and, so it seemed, was the face of our family.

Albert Sayers, however, had different ideas. He felt he could regain the streets for our family and present a credible argument to the new regime at the local council, one which would eventually give us the right to trade legally. Unfortunately, his idea was not universally accepted by everyone in our ranks, some feared a pecking order might be dictated by the council and that some of the newer barrow boys might be favoured over members of our family if pitches were given out. Albert was determined, however, realising that unity would be the ace card if we were ever to get our own way.

Unfortunately, loyalties were becoming divided and, with the newcomers in agreement with Albert about his way forward and certain family members suspecting agendas might not be as they seemed, the formulation of the Newcastle Barrow Boys Association was not something everyone was in favour of. As far as Albert was concerned, it was the only way forward. Having a unified and diplomatic voice was the way to bring about the very thing our family had been calling for ever since the end of the 19th century.

The thought among some of the family was that people like Holmesy, Tommy Quinn, Bobby Balmer, Ray Mouzon and the

Drummonds would swallow up pitches that could otherwise be worked by other members of our family, if indeed the council were to decide that pitch allocation was the way forward. There was no way, or so they thought, that the council were going to give our lot preferential treatment. If anything, the law might encourage the council to put some of our lot to the back of the queue just to spite us.

For some, this was too much of a risk to run, especially if the number of potential pitches were to be limited. Sometimes you're better with the devil you know, and the way it had always been seemed preferable to some, and a whole lot better than being overlooked for a pitch, to see a few outsiders jumping on the bandwagon and being gifted something we'd been striving after for generations.

Despite the infighting and the squabbling, it was, it seemed, the only option available. The alternative was to run the risk of a potential blanket-ban on all pitches in the city centre, post-regeneration, and that would have been the end of barrows in the town forever, Watch Committee or not. Half a loaf, they say, is better than none, and with that attitude in mind Albert planted the seed about forming the association and providing the voice needed in order to come away from a generations of struggle and prosecution with something worthwhile to show for it.

At this point, my old man was no longer concerned with the barrows. We had in a new house on a modern estate with a new life, and he was getting a good honest living from the carpet business. Doodles was still a well-known face in the town and getting money his own way, while John had become a bit of a marked man due to his prolific activities and endless scrapes with the law. Once you become gazetted (known to the police) it's difficult to go anywhere without being hassled. Even a night out with the wife and friends could result in a spontaneous car chase, just to avoid John getting a tug from any eager copper who'd spotted him behind the wheel of a motor. It seemed there was always a warrant out for his arrest.

Uncle John became a target in the town, and he led the law a merry dance whenever he could. He had developed an even greater contempt for them than most of his peers. Don't get us wrong, none of our chaps liked them, but John despised them. They blamed him for the atrocities that unfolded on Percy Street, and pinched him for several other things over the years. He would openly fight with them and had no respect for authority. They'd refused to allow his younger brother Peter little more than an hour to attend their dad's funeral; he was doing half a stretch at the time. They'd locked up his mother, her sisters, his granny and even his great-granny, treating them all like common criminals, just for trying to make an honest living.

In John's opinion, the police were worse than him because they were bullies, hiding behind a veil of 'law and order' which simply entitled them to take as many liberties as they chose to, and no one likes liberty takers. The system was of no consequence to John. It did not apply to him, and he had no desire to become part of it, instead taking pleasure in bucking it at every opportunity.

The upshot of such behaviour, of course, is that you make a rod for your own back. Taking on the system is futile. They have the manpower, the money, and the resources to bury anyone they choose. There is no bigger firm. But John didn't give a fuck, not for them, and not for anyone else. He was a rebel in every sense, and his hatred for authority was the catalyst for a lifetime of turbulence that would become the environment in which his boys grew up, and one which would have a lasting influence on them and their relationship with law and order.

For all we had moved to what seemed like the country at the time, my brother 'Legs', would still gravitate toward the town. He'd grown up there, it was in his blood. Although he obliged our dad and became a time-served floor layer before he was 21, it wasn't something he had any desire to do for a living. He would be in the town at every opportunity, on the barrow with our granddad and his son, Frank Hewson Jr. His uncles would be out on Nelson Street alongside them, and his cousins would all be there giving a hand just like he was. It was the 'life.' It's what we did, and regardless of what other options were made available, the 'life' was a pretty good one.

What could be better? On the pavement, in the fresh air, hawking your wares alongside half a dozen of your family, all getting a few quid at the same time. It was like a magnet to him, as it was to all of us.

When all is said and done, we lived in a city inhabited by hundreds of thousands of people, but there were only a handful of barrow boys, and we made up the majority of them. Just as it always had done, life on the barrows and on the street exposed them to many things, and whatever fringe benefits didn't come their way on the pitch would surely come their way in the boozer, or the snooker halls, somewhere Legs would often finish up after work.

The Royal Court at the top of the Bigg Market had been a well-used club for years. My old man played there throughout his misspent youth, but it was old-fashioned, dated and full of old men, so as soon as the Chalk & Cheese opened up down the bottom of the Bigg Market all the younger lads gravitated towards there instead. It was a seedy little downstairs club with about eight or nine tables, and it seemed like every villain in the town used it at one time or another.

To someone like Legs it was a social club, a place to hear what was going on with the rest of the chaps who got in there. It was a den of iniquity really, and a breeding ground for would-be villains, gambling away their ill-gotten gains or plotting and scheming their next bit of work. Legs knew all the chaps in there, many of them West Enders, who'd grown up in the streets around us, and it was only a matter of time before he got himself involved with a little firm and ventured into a life of crime. He would see some of his pals rolling up in there, having been to toil somewhere down the road creeping shops, or whatever, and they would be poked-up (holding money). Legs might have just put a shift in on the barrow, after being at the fruit market early doors, and maybe had a score or 30 quid in his pocket for his corner.

His pals, however, were playing cards and betting 30 quid a hand, or playing crash for a tenner a man. His money might have been quick, ready money, but it wasn't anything compared to what his pals were getting 'at the other'. Before long he'd rolled himself in with a couple of the boys, and they would be at it two or three times a week, spending the rest of their time in the Chalk & Cheese. They might head off to North Yorkshire, or up the Scotch side, looking for a bit of toil, and if they had a touch they'd be back in the club with a few hundred quid between them, or two or three times as much if they had real tickle. Naturally, our dad wasn't too happy, but what could he do?

Tony had served his time as our dad had wanted him to do. He had a trade, but he hated the job, being on his hands and knees all day in some poxy house where the punter didn't even make you a cup of tea, and fluff from the carpet getting up his nose all day just wasn't his idea of a life.

He'd been exposed to the easy come easy go antics of his older family members, and was a full-blown convert to that way of life, even before he started to get his fingers dirty. I was only a child at the time, about ten or eleven, Legs was 11 years older than me. Although I didn't know what my brother was doing, I had an idea he wasn't fitting carpets. He and my dad were at loggerheads constantly about him not showing any interest in the game, yet Tony would always have a few quid on the hip. He would turn up at home with bags of designer clothes from Marcus Price, Cecil Gee or Trelawney's.

I never asked any questions. All I saw was my big handsome, curly-haired brother, looking a million dollars and having the time of his life; a proper Jack the Lad. Legs, however, came slightly unglued around the mid-70s when he ended up on remand for a violent assault charge, for which he was acquitted, much to the relief of my mam and dad. It was a case of mistaken identity, and he was taking it on his toes (taking the blame) for his pal who had previous for violence and would have certainly got a lump of bird over the matter. Fortunately, Legs served no sentence as a result of that episode, and his staunch behaviour in the face of possible jail time didn't do his reputation any harm either.

He was going down the very path that our dad had gone down, one he'd moved our family away from in order to prevent Tony from doing so, but it had little effect: 'What's in ya, comes out of ya'. So, with his new found standing as a man of honour, someone who could be relied upon under questioning, as well as having a little jail time under his belt, all be it only remand in Durham, Legs was emerging as quite the boy by the time I reached my teenage years.

I ended up spending much of my youth out in the sticks of West Denton, at least that's what it felt like. My visits to the town were occasional, I was just a child, and we lived what seemed to be miles away, so I could hardly just walk in to town like I could have if we'd still been on Pitt Street. But there'd be weekends at cousins, and visits to their granny's – my Aunt Liza, who still lived in the big house on Westgate Hill Terrace. That house was the family's open house and the centre of the universe during our youth. There were also some great times spent on the camp up at Bedlington near Morpeth, which was genuinely out in the sticks, about 14 miles from the town, where our cousins Joe, Frankie, Philip and Lisa lived, in a couple of trailers with their mam and dad, Aunt Sylvia and Uncle Joe.

That was a camp we were often on as a young children, and one both me and Tony Sayers ended up stopping on for many spells later in our lives. The pull toward family was strong, they were our first friends and best friends. As a family, we all spoke the same language and thought the same way. We looked out for each other, and we worked the shite out of each other too.

The Gypsy crew would land at their Granny Liza's every weekend, and there'd often be half a dozen or more of us kids sleeping over. Tony and the rest of them did this all the time, as they were on the doorstep, but for me it was less frequent and I loved it.

Because the Riley's lived out the way, in pitman's country near Ashington, and travelled occasionally, plus their dad was a Travelling man out of Glasgow, they all had a different twang to the rest of us from the town, and it was one we all soon learned to mimic. We often recall the lickings our Philip got from Granny Liza for messing her about, shouting 'Granny come 'ere a minute will ya,!' We'd all be in the same bedroom sharing two double beds and every time she got to the bottom of the stairs, she'd bounce back up to the bedroom shouting, 'Somebody's gonna get it tonight!' calling him all the ginger bastards, before bursting in the room and laying into him for being such a fucking pest. Poor Philip hadn't opened his mouth, it was us taking him off, and he'd be protesting his innocence claiming it was us shouting for her, in between getting bats from his granny.

'I know your voice, son. I might be daft, but I'm not stupid,' she'd tell him. 'And stop trying to get your cousins into trouble, grass!'

Well, that was it. We'd be pissing ourselves under the blankets, while getting one or two sly bats off her. She knew what we were up to, so she made sure we all got a sly dig for good measure.

They were great times when we were all together, and happy memories. We recall vividly the heavy blankets with a satin quilted top cover, and the bed warmer; talk about a fire hazard. It consisted of an electric light bulb in a fitting, fixed to a frame, inside of a metal cage. It would be switched on, lit up, and placed under the blankets for an hour to warm the bed before we got in, an accident waiting to happen when you think about it, but this was still long before the days of health and safety rules that our lives are governed by these days. There was always home cooked food on the go, and just like her mother before her, Granny Liza would bake religiously, and the old place always smelled of freshly baked bread. Westgate Hill Terrace was a fantastic place, and a hark back to the good old days when our granddads would congregate there, discuss business, have deals and divvy up, except now it was our fathers and uncles that were doing the same.

Even though Westgate Hill Terrace was the focal point for everyone, you could always find any one of us young ones staying at one of our cousins on a weekend, or even longer during the school holidays. It would be nothing for one of your cousins to come and stay over on a Saturday night, after a day's work in the town, and still be at your home a week or two later. Just as in the old days, we lived in each other's pockets. It made us close, tight, and very clannish, just like we had always been through the generations. These were some of the traits that were bred into all of us, regardless of where we were living, be it in the city centre, out of town or up at the camp.

We had an indoctrination that was universal among us, yet we were starting to see other things and other ways too. We had our street life in the town in common, and we were able to revisit our Traveller heritage up at the camp, and even though the family's dynamic was changing with the times, the mad dog had already bitten and the damage had already been done a long time ago. An element of which had followed my family to West Denton in the shape of my brother Tony.

Legs had started to move up the ranks after his time on remand for protecting a friend, and although he went back to the barrows for a short while following that episode, it was only a matter of time before he succumbed to the lure of bigger prizes and even easier money. He would be stood on a pitch when one of his cronies would roll up and tell him about a touch they'd just had. Or, even worse on one occasion, when a bit of a face and active villain at the time, Dicky Ford, bouled down Northumberland Street looking a million dollars in an old Rolls Royce he'd bought himself. He pulled up by Legs, and they had a bit of craic through the window of Dicky's Roller, and all of a sudden selling a pound of bananas simply didn't have the same appeal for Legs anymore.

With little firms keen to roll him into nits of work, it was hard for him to resist. While he was weighing out pounds of apples for pennies, his pals were driving up and down in flash motors, with pockets full of dough. So, inevitably, he got involved and there was little anyone could do about it. He was a grown man in his early 20s and, other than the trouble he brought on himself, he'd never brought any real trouble to our parents' door. Heartache yes, but nothing naughty like drugs or van-loads of Old Bill, at least not yet. Our dad had been there and done the same himself, and as much as he didn't want it for his son, he was certainly not going to disown him for the way he was going, that would have been the height of hypocrisy. Obviously, he tried to discourage him, but just as history repeats itself, so do people. The apple rarely falls far from the tree.

One teatime, Legs arrived home wearing a beautiful camel hair coat and carrying three or four big red Trelawney's bags full of the very best of tuggies. Trelawney's was the best menswear shop in town, all the chaps used the place, and they were big spenders, especially after a good tickle. I remember following him excitedly upstairs, admiring the beautiful coat, thinking he looked like a movie star. Upstairs in the bedroom, he showed me all his new clothes, Van Gils suits, Wexman trousers, Swiss cotton shirts, Italian hand-stitched shoes and cashmere sweaters. Then he asked me to close my eyes. Was a surprise coming? Absolutely! A whack around the chops with what felt like a bag full paperwork. It was as well, but not the kind of paperwork you find on an office desk.

'What the fuck's that?' He'd nearly taken the side of my face off.

'You've just been hit in the lips with twenty-five hundred quid, son.'

I asked no questions. I knew it wasn't from carpet fitting, or grafting the barrow. I also knew it wasn't from working for the post office either, at least not in an official capacity.

This is what I was soaking up as an impressionable young boy.

On the one hand, I was ducking and diving around the town with my cousins, keeping toot on the streets for family or pushing barrows full of rubbish through the Grainger Market shouting ‘mind ya legs’ to the crowds of shoppers. Then, on the other hand, my brother was at it, Jack the Lad, my role model, and looking like somebody I wanted to be, dressed to kill with a pocket full of readies, a nice little motor, and loads of birds on the go. It was a heady combination, and a world away from what my school pals were seeing and doing.

What we young’uns must have looked like! Bits of kids with flat caps on, pulling barrows, whistling and shouting at people as we barged our way through the Grainger Market alleys, across Clayton Street and through the tunnel next to the Fish Bar taking us underneath Eldon Square and round the back of the Green Market to the rubbish skips.

We knew the town, some parts that most people never got to see, and even as kids we knew them like the back of our hands.

The smack around the chops became a ‘thing’ during those years, increasing in value every time, and whenever I was sat down by Legs and told to close my eyes, I knew what was coming. Two, three, four large, and before we left West Denton in 1978, I must have got at least one smack in the lips with a cockle (cock and hen; ten). It was also a measure of how much Tony was at it.

Legs ended up in HMP Thorp Arch and Rudgate, near Wetherby for a stretch before we moved nearer to the town in the late 70s. We shifted into a big bungalow on the West Road, just half a dozen bus stops from Westgate Hill Terrace and the heart of the family. The 18-month jail sentence for Tony was upsetting for our mam, naturally, but it sounded like a great giggle for him and his pals. Thorpe Arch was a semi-open nick back then, and there were a few faces from the town in there at the same time, like Terry ‘Scone’ Rigney and Michael ‘The Mouse’ Carr.

Visits with us were spent with Tony telling stories about the amount of frisk they were all having in there. They had the run of the place, with cash changing and tobacco rackets. They even popped out for half a lager on one occasion, or so he said. Legs was a wild card, and The Mouse was cut from the very same cloth. Michael Carr became a close friend of the family and someone we always remember with smiles on our faces. He was a real character, a street trader among other things, and he brought loads of lines to the town streets during the 1970s and 80s, including the 'chocolate mouse', which is where he got his name 'The Mouse'. He even opened up a string of swag shops in the North East at one point, with Peter Anderson, opening stores in Newcastle and Sunderland, both of which I had pitches in one Christmas time, engraving pens and selling Christmas cards and paper.

I'm jump the story a bit, but my granddad had come across a parcel of about two thousand matte black, brushed gold, and silver Parker-style ballpoint pens, all individually boxed, complete with an electric engraving machine. I remember talking Legs and one of the boys he was knocking about with, Derek Tams, into buying the parcel to do something with. I was about 15 or 16 at the time, and they both knew I could go to work with a bit of gear like that. Even at that age I had the gift of the gab, as they say.

I suggested speaking to The Mouse about getting a pitch in one of his shops and busting up with them if they bought the parcel. They were more interested in cashing the gear up and just wanted to flip it. I paid them about £750 or something for the lot. My sister's boyfriend Jimmy Moore, or Roger as I've always called him, in homage to the late great 007, came to my rescue and loaned me the money to buy them out of the machine and all the pens. Roger was a dealing man from the East End, his family were, like ours, hawking people and shop owners. He was a motor dealer mainly and very pally with The Mouse, so the two pitches in the 'Super Stores' were secured.

I had a good Christmas that year, thank you very much, and I got a real taste for business after running those two pitches.

So, yet another decade of change was marching on, so far without any further loss of life to anyone in the family.

Although I did get a fright when I was about ten years old, when my mother told me my dad had been taken to hospital after suffering a heart attack. I was a young bot and thought heart attacks killed people, and the thought of losing my dad frightened the life out of me. Fortunately, he recovered, and during his recovery decided that he was going to part company with George Luke and the carpet business. He wasn't well enough to stay on the tools, and the prospect of sitting all day in the shop in Forest Hall didn't appeal to him. That's when we started to move back into the town.

My dad bought a fruit shop in the Grainger Market with his proceeds from the sale of his half of the carpet business. By this time, Tony's dad, Uncle Peter, had taken a big pitch in there just a year or so earlier, around 1976.

Uncle Peter had been grafting the barrow on the 'Front' for a few years and had a feeling that the current regeneration of the city centre was going to kill the trade. The likelihood of him getting his own pitch as part of the Barrow Boy Association was fairly slim, not least of all as he had a bit of form and felt the Old Bill would definitely put the spoke in for him.

A reliable contact within the Civic Centre marked Peter's card about the possibility of a pitch in the Grainger Market. Shops in there were like gold dust back then, as the place was still enjoying its heyday. Peter jumped at the chance. He knew, just like my old man did when he was Peter's age, that it was time to take stock. Like him, Peter now had three kids wrapped around him, had done a bit of time, and avoided a lot more by the skin of his teeth and a helping of good fortune. So, keen to get straightened out and into the system, P. Sayers & Sons opened up in alley two of the Grainger Market, and a year later my dad bought the Magic Roundabout; a circular shop in the glass covered section that was alley number one.

Within a year our family had moved down to the West Road, and Peter had bought a nice house on Bentinck Road, just around the corner from Arthur's Hill nick and the old 69 Club, which had long since closed its doors.

Uncle John had also acquired premises, a scrap yard in the West End, with Trevor Harrison. Later teaming up with Uncle Peter, Doodles and Ward Smith, a broad red-headed Scotsman who had married my mothers' sister, Jo. They took a big demolition yard, just a bit further along Skinnerburn Road, by the River Tyne towards Scotswood.

The yard was a great place and another playground for us to run riot in. On top of everything else that we saw going on around us growing up, we now had our own go-cart track on the banks of the Tyne, where we would tear arse around the place in any old banger that had a bit of juice in and started off the button. There were about ten of us lads all born within a year or two of each other, little men, dodging around the town getting a wage, or driving bangers around our uncle's yard, while our school pals were either corner standing or watching *Swap Shop* on a Saturday morning.

At home we'd be bagging up change from the shop or the barrow and helping our dads cash up, or even hearing them divvying up with their associates, depending on whose house you were in. It was intoxicating and exciting, and we were seeing the world from a completely different perspective.

After his marriage in 1977, Albert Sayers turned his attention to the Newcastle Barrow Boys Association and made a concerted effort to ensure there was still a living to be got on our streets once the city's redevelopment was complete.

In a considered approach to the issue, and with Mariah's consent, 'The Queen of the Barrows' made a final appearance on the streets she had worked for nearly 80 years. It was a photo opportunity and good publicity for the cause. Albert managed to get an article in the press acknowledging Mariah's struggle and fight for legalisation over the decades, and in doing so planted the seeds for his approach to the authorities. The move was one that had to be made. In hindsight, however, had things been likely to remain as they were, even with the arrests, then maybe sleeping dogs might have been best left to lie.

After all, no one was starving. The 1970s had been a good decade for the generation of our family now making their bones on the street. 'The front' was still producing good business for any number of barrows that would pitch up there, and they were all shifting plenty of gear. Usually working two-handed on a barrow, it would be nothing for both men to get themselves £40 or £50 a day, and have the boards clear by mid-afternoon. Not bad when an average man might only take home £70 for a whole week's wages. Even the odd pinch or two wouldn't knock too much of a hole in your take, and you could always turn out the next day and repeat what you'd done the day before to get it back. However, every now and again there would be a purge, and the law would make an example of somebody on the barrows.

One event which really made Albert think that all pitching might be abolished outright was when Seppy Stuart, a barrow boy from Byker in the East End, set about a police sergeant on Nelson Street in broad daylight in front of the watching public. He and his brother would often turn out with a barrow, and apparently, it was quite a serious assault on the officer, one for which Seppy was arrested, charged and jailed, and for a short period of time it naused the job up for everyone.

Nobody could turn out on 'the front' that summer without it coming on top immediately, and the situation became very tense as no one got a shilling for months.

Albert went looking for a few quid further afield. Leeds, Manchester, London, anywhere he could get a slip in with a line and go to work. I remember being in London with my mam and dad visiting publican friends who had The One Tun on Saffron Hill in Hatton Garden, the capital's diamond and jewellery quarter. It was 1977, the year of the Queen's Silver Jubilee, and London was buzzing with tourists as the streets were preparing for the Queen's procession. We got to see Her Majesty on Fleet Street and, following the procession as we neared St Paul's Cathedral, we heard a familiar voice coming from within a crowd of people. Before I could squeeze my way to the front, I knew it was Uncle Albert. No words were spoken, only a wink, as I winked back and waited for him to get to the bat. Even at a young age, I knew Albert would have a 'rick in' working with him, but another one wouldn't hurt. As soon as he delivered the bat for whatever Jubilee souvenir it was they were grafting, my hand was up, and my money was out. Only when the pitch was finished did we eventually acknowledge each other.

It was great to be down there and see Uncle Albert going to work in the heart of the capital, in the middle of such a celebration, no doubt reminiscent of the days when Albert's dad Morry and my granddad went down to graft the Coronation a quarter of a century earlier, taking money on the pavement, and a generation later our family were back down there doing the same thing again. God Save the Queen.

Just like Albert had modelled himself on his dad and uncle, I had decided that he wanted to be just like Albert, far more than I wanted to be like my own brother, or in the carpet or fruit game like my dad. I loved the street, and knew how to work it from an early age and, not surprisingly, I returned to London as a young man in the early 90s, working Oxford Street for six months with a good friend named Dennis, a half-Traveller and a prolific grafter out of Doncaster. We would work the MOT with kettles, tom and funkum. That means working a system called Money on Top (MOT), with watches, jewellery and perfume. We had it off for six months before Dennis opened the Run Out shop on Oxford Street.

A big, flash, lairy Jewish fella out of London, Victor Meisel, was on the firm with us as top man, on the hammer, running the sale once I'd had pulled the pitch. A lovely fella, who it turned out had worked with Uncle Albert some 20 years earlier. Just like in the real world, the one we live in is very small.

During the 70s, however, the country was plunged in and out of darkness many times. Large-scale blackouts became a common occurrence as the government struggled to conserve electricity, as industrial action by coal miners meant power generation was severely restricted. The Three-Day Week for commercial electricity users was introduced, and TV channels were restricted from broadcasting after 10.30 at night during the crisis. It was a hark back to more primitive times as households were often lit by candles for long periods when the power cut out. In fact, candles were a line often worked on the street during the frequent blackouts. It was a time of both the good, and the not so good, and will be remembered with mixed emotion by many people, as was the year 1977 for our family.

Albert Sayers married his sweetheart Margaret in December in a ceremony at St Mary's Cathedral. A clutch of new arrivals had appeared in the family stable, as almost all of our parents' generation had by now produced the majority of 'our generation', our numbers now becoming almost too many to count. Mariah Kelly had more to look at now than she could ever have imagined. She would struggle to remember the names of some of them, there were so many, arriving in rapid succession. She was also now in her 90th year and still lived in the house at the top of Buckingham Street which she had shared with Big Tom, and any number of her offspring over the years. Her health was deteriorating, however, and it seemed that her matriarchal era was about to come to an end.

Visits to the house on Buckingham Street, or Bucka as we called it, would often be confined to her bedroom when she was unwell. The old-fashioned room with a carved wooden bed, heavy blankets and satin top quilt, floral wallpaper with the obligatory crucifix above her headboard, a picture of the Pope on the opposite wall and a statue of the Virgin Mary on her dressing table was a sight none of us will never forget. Nor will we forget how her home no longer smelled of freshly baked bread, now replaced by the smell of snuff and medication in her bedroom.

There was still some activity in the house whenever anyone visited, but it was sombre activity. It was as if members of the family who we didn't see every day were often putting in appearances. The conversations were quieter, and the mood was one of impending sadness. Could it be that this great old woman, this matriarch of a breed so big and so bold, was finally coming to the end of her time? She wasn't just our granny, she was our 'Great Granny', in every sense. She was a unique figure, a woman of substance, a role model, a mother, a tyrant, a sweetheart, as hard as nails and as soft as clarts. She was careful yet generous, she could be spiteful yet caring. She was an enigma, a character like no other, and we all knew her ways so well. Such a blessing.

Some people don't even know their granny's name, never mind have an affinity with their great-granny, the kind that we were lucky enough to have had. Seven years had passed since Big Tom died, and from the same house he was buried we witnessed the biggest funeral our family had seen up to that point.

In the days that preceded the event, it felt like the world had stopped spinning. No barrows were out, and it felt there was no life in the air, and for that time up to the funeral, it seemed like someone had just switched the power off, like we'd had our own personal blackout. Every member of the entire family was in a daze, yet somehow, during such abstract sorrow and chaos, a dozen black funeral cars, horse-drawn carts and flat-backed wagons ordained with hundreds of floral tributes, turned up on Buckingham Street for a traditional costermonger's funeral.

The street was packed, as a flow of family came in and out of the house, while neighbours and friends stood ten-deep on the pavement to pay their respects. Her coffin left the old house to much wailing and crying. The funeral cortège snaked its way into the town, followed by dozens of motors as it took a route through the streets of the city centre that had been Mariah's stamping ground for almost a century. From our seats in the back of a funeral cars, people could be seen stopping at the roadside looking on in amazement as the procession for our queen crawled slowly by them. Traffic police were stationed at junctions to prevent the cortège being disrupted as we passed every pitch that had been worked by Mariah and her girls over the decades. The barrows were all out and draped in black with white crucifixes, and some of the bystanders and shopkeepers were in tears as they watched this great old lady pass them by for her final time. It was a surreal moment, filled with both sorrow and pride. The drive through the town following the ceremony to a packed St Mary's Cathedral seemed to take forever.

If two or three hundred people followed the procession from Buckingham Street, there must have been twice as many waiting at St Mary's, and by the time we reached Elswick Cemetery there must have been two hundred more. It was a send-off deserving of Mariah Kelly Cruddas, 1887-1977. 'The Queen of the Barrows' was dead, and God couldn't save her.

RIP, Granny.

The passing of Mariah Kelly was indeed the end of an era. One in which an entire breed had been spawned that now had a considerable reputation on the streets of Newcastle.

Not just as hard-working street traders and barrow boys, but also as a family of loyal and reliable people within their community, and one not to be trifled with, unless of course, you wanted to go to war with all of them. The era of the family headed by Mariah and her daughters was now the concern of a crew of felonious young men born of nefarious stock. A lifetime of survival on the perimeters of acceptable society was driving the clan further and further underground.

Skirting around the law all your life to earn an 'honest' living was not the kind of lifestyle that attracted most people, and as a result, all of Mariah's daughters by and large, had married men cut from similar cloth. Their children, as a result, were raised in an environment where survival was paramount and contempt for the law was the norm, not just within their own household, but across the entire family. Growing up in a world where our parents, grandparents and even great grandparents had received custodial sentences, living in homes where the police might come to our doors with a warrant any one of them, was something that would serve only to intensify any thoughts of distrust or ill feelings we might have harboured for figures of authority.

This is by no means used as an excuse for unlawful behaviour, it is merely an explanation. Where we are born and what we are born into are major influencing factors often determining the lives we are likely to lead. It takes all sorts to make the world go round and breaking or bending the rules to suit your own needs is something that is done in every walk of life and in every profession. From nicking a few envelopes from the office to knocking off an hour early without telling the boss; petty misdemeanours maybe, it's evidence of dishonesty all the same, and everyone is guilty of some small lapse of judgement at some point.

The law is broken millions of times a day by a million otherwise straight people. Even more worryingly, there is not one industry, service or profession that is immune to it, and not one that hasn't suffered the shame of corruption or abuse, of either power, position or people.

Doctors, nurses, priests, judges, civil servants, police officers, movie moguls, pop stars, TV personalities, footballers, athletes, charity workers… the list is endless, and littered with corruption. Unfortunately, offenders with careers in any of the professions above tend to carry out crimes that are not usually motivated by money. Take a look at those professions. Money isn't generally what they desire or what they need. Their crimes are usually targeted against individuals, vulnerable, naïve, impressionable, innocent people. Their motivation being one the common man finds hard to comprehend, often because their crimes are heinously depraved, and that is frightening.

The common man, however, is not in this discreet, perverse and highly dishonourable club, disguised by acceptability. So when these types get caught with their fingers in the till, or their trousers down, then it is up to the 'not-so-honourable' law makers to decide how they should be treated and how they should be punished. An equally worrying thought. We make this comment only because we have been raised in an environment where criminality was all around us, in the West End of Newcastle, and often within the ranks of our own family, however, it was a type of crime that rarely overflowed into the civilian population.

We might have been raised with rogues and villains, but they were ultimately honourable people, unlike the abusers of power, people that have the luxury of being able to hide behind a veil of respectability, and the good fortune of being judged by their own. Proper people don't kill you for kicks, interfere with your kids or tamper with your women. They're not megalomaniacs on power-crazed collision courses with disaster, spurred on by their need for fame or a desire to feed their perversions, nor are they the seedy types you'd cross the street to avoid. We were rough and ready people who would do you a favour before we'd do you a wrong turn. Motivated by only by the need for money, survival and a desire to better themselves against the odds. Not a cliché, a fact!

Despite all that had passed, however, and despite the decades of death, scandal, heartache and persecution, the 1980s was to be a decade like none that had gone before. Our family was to be tried and tested on every conceivable level. The West End was on the brink of becoming the Wild West End. Power struggles, armed robberies, gang warfare and murder would become the hallmarks of the 1980s and 90s; and thanks in some part to the relationship between our breed and the authorities, the family found themselves in the very thick of it all. Thank God Mariah wasn't around to see it.

But thank God she had instilled a depth of character and a fighting constitution into her family. One which would give them the strength to come through whatever adversity came their way, long after she was gone, and one hundred years after Paddy and Sally had decided to make the streets of Newcastle their home.

SWINGS AND ROUNDABOUTS

Mariah had outlived several of her offspring, and had lived through times of incredible change during her remarkable 90 years.

From the Victorian days of the late 19th century when her parents arrived in the city on a horse and cart, she'd lived through two World Wars, witnessed the arrival of the motor car, electrical power, telecommunications, moon landings and even the infancy of computer technology. Thankfully however, many of her old-fashioned ways were instilled in her daughters and passed on through the family. Even though her era had come to an end, she lived on in many forms, but time was now catching up with her daughters too.

During the 1980s, we lost many of the generation that followed Mariah. My Granny Sarah had passed away some 40 years previously, but by the end of the decade many of the old characters in our family were all but consigned to memory. It really was a case of out with the old and in with the new.

For all the light-fingered skullduggery that had gone on down the years, the cat and mouse with the law and the barrows, the little bits of villainy, the little bits of jail, and even the violent escapades of the 60s, it all seemed quite harmless by comparison to the events of the 80s. Gone were the days of our chaps being referred to in the press as 'scoundrels', receiving six or nine months 'hard labour' for getting caught in the act of some unscrupulous misdemeanour.

Jail was about to be dished out in quantities that were almost unthinkable, and the law, with the aid of the press, would ensure no such waggish terms, would ever be used again when referring to the activities of any of our family. The new era would not only elevate the families' already considerable reputation, but would herald a time when the dynamic of the family would both flounder and flourish in equal measure.

The Donnelleys had moved back to the West End and were living on the same street in Arthurs Hill as the Shottons, on

Vallum Way. Since Frankie Shotton's death, Vera had struggled to cope; not just with their five kids, but with the bereavement of losing her young beloved husband. She was dealing with things the best way she could, which wasn't all that well unfortunately. The fact that some of her family were just across the street from her should have been a blessing, but for her it turned out to be more of a curse.

There were eight of Muriel and The Growler's clan across the street from Vera, and both sets of kids fought like cat and dog. Vera had little control over her own litter, having lost much of her spirit after Frankie's death. The frequent fighting and aggravation over the road was taking its toll on her. Her oldest, Frank Junior, was always in trouble and in an attempt to steer her youngest child Stephen away from the same fate, Vera sent him to stay with us for a few months when we were still out of the way in West Denton. The girls Karen, Tina and Yvonne were left to deal with what was left of their bereaved family, and to cope with their troublesome cousins over the way. Vera had lost control of the kids it seemed, and she was in too much of a tailspin to realise it. Vallum Way became valium way for a while during that painful time.

Her troubles and heartache, however, were not burdens she had to endure for too much longer. By the December of 1982, Aunt Vera sadly lost her will to live without Frankie by her side, quietly passing away aged just 46, leaving her five kids to look after themselves. They were young, rebellious and understandably angry, having lost both parents so soon in their lives, but at least Vera was now with her Frankie, the love of her life and the one person that would probably have kept her family right. The girls, just like their granny and her sisters had done when Mariah left them, kept their family together as best they could, until such a time they found partners of their own, while the two boys were busy finding trouble of their own. Tony's family moved from his birthplace of Buckingham Street to Worley Close, just round the corner from the Shottons, spending a couple of years there before Uncle Peter bought the house on

Bentinck Road. In between times they spent spells back in a trailer on Hartford Camp.

At one time two families from this breed were capable of sharing a house together, now it was becoming difficult for two of them to live in the same street. Divisions were starting to come to the surface within our ranks, and not just on Vallum Way.

It wasn't enough for some of the chaps to be acknowledged as part of our family, some wanted to have their own reputation and be seen as a face within their own right, and not just because of what they were part of. The West End was full of people who lived outside the law, and all of them had dealings with, or became embroiled with, members of our family over the years. We had a strong presence there and made many lifelong friends and associates from similar backgrounds who had grown up with our family. Some of our breed, however, began to form alliances in the company of those outside of their own, particularly if they were earning with them.

Such familiarity can be a breeding ground for jealousy and contempt, and for some it was becoming all too easy to discredit one of their own amongst company, just to get a laugh out of people they were trying to impress in their pursuit of infamy.

Family rivalry can happen between two brothers, never mind between dozens of cousins, especially if they're chasing the same pound note, and for some, the pound notes of the 1980s were not to be found on the barrows or in the bars, but in the back of security vans or piled up in Post Office depots.

As much as we remember the 1980s for a multitude of reasons, not least of all the mod revival (which was a proper bit of me), punk rock (which was a proper bit of Tony) and the mobile phone (the first one we owned bought between us from Jimmy 'Roger' Moore – a big old Motorola 'brick') we mainly remember the 80s as the 'blagging' years. They were going off all over the place, and nowhere more so than the North East, in some part thanks to Legs' rise through the ranks of the local criminal fraternity. He was now placed to take things to the next level of family notoriety, with one or two of his younger cousins eager to emulate a new kind of role model.

They were influential years of our lives, and we had much to absorb from the world we lived in. Yet it's funny how seemingly harmless things, things that are no more than throw away remarks, could slowly seep into the psyche of young minds, knowing that they weren't entirely the right thing, yet failing to see what damage they could do.

One thing that had never officially been the case with our breed was the use of a universal family name that applied to all of us. The Percy Street thing had, for a while given many of the chaps the 'Sayers' label. For some that was no big deal, even if you weren't actually a Sayers, it was just a remnant of the fight with the Findlays.

For others it was a slap in the face. They wanted their own notoriety. As much as we loved our extended family, we were all coming out of different stables, and it became easy to have a pop at one of our own, highlighting any misgiving that they may have been guilty of, by putting it down to their branch of breeding, or lack of it. It was as if the bloodline we shared was being contaminated by new strains. Some that were not entirely in line with the one we all shared.

'That's the price of them Sayers,' you'd hear. Or 'typical of the Kellys.'

Other putdowns were common; 'only the Donnellys would do that,' or 'that's a proper Shotton's stroke,' 'Lennie's long suit,' 'a Hewson's caper' or 'a proper Patters move.' These, and more, were all common phrases throughout the various households of the family; we were all in the line of fire. It was harmless internal cross-kidding between ourselves.

We might grow up hearing stuff like that from our grannies and grandads, mams and dads, but it was never said in badness, and never said in the company of those outside the family. They knew full well they were referring to their own in condemnation, but because they had a different name it became a 'thing' to use their surname as the reason for them doing whatever it was that displeased someone, and they would only say such things in jest among themselves and never for the ears of others.

As a result, we as kids would cast similar aspersions on any of our own, and make it sound all the worse by suggesting it was just what their lot would do. It was cross-kidding of the cruellest kind really, but we saw it as harmless fun, even though we were having a go at one of our own. It was fine to do that amongst ourselves, because for the best part it was just light-hearted humour, with a little extra bite.

Once certain family members took to this sort of talk in mixed company, however, it became something that others, outsiders, got the idea that it was ok to do, and that was something which would serve to be the undoing of some of our breed. Loyalties were becoming misplaced and one-upmanship was the fuel that would fan the flames of any fire beginning to ignite within the family. The old guard were on the way out, and for all the good qualities they had instilled in us, their absence, the growth of our numbers, the changing times, and decades of changing attitudes and values were something we were all going to live to regret.

Peter Sayers had recently opened the shop in the Grainger Market, and business was good, however, he had more than a sweat on in the famous summer of 1976. There was a lack of potatoes available due to the record-breaking hot weather that year, and along with his brother John and other associates, he was arrested and tried in relation to an alleged fraud charge. The allegation was that they had carried out what they call a 'long firm.' Long firm fraud involves setting up a trading company for fraudulent purposes; the basic idea is to trade legitimately, buying goods and paying suppliers on the button in order to build up a good credit record. Once they are sufficiently well-established, the fraudsters then order the next increased round of goods on credit. They then upsticks with the goods and the profits from their sales. The goods would be sold or wholesaled elsewhere to eager punters keen to buy gear for less than they would normally be paying for it legitimately.

Regardless of the ins and outs of long-firming, Tony's dad, Peter, and our Uncle John, along with their associates, managed to evade conviction, not least of all due to lack of evidence. Although, evidence is something that plays only a small part in the real-life drama of cops and robbers, something time would come to establish beyond reasonable doubt.

So, while we were growing up, our parents were growing up too, in terms of maturity, with grandparents growing old, in every sense of the word.

The age of the dinosaurs who never left the country, or blacked out the tits on a Page 3 model in *The Sun*, were giving way to a generation that flew on airplanes to foreign countries to lay half naked *in* the sun, and coming up right behind that generation was us. We were a combination of the both new and the old testaments of our family, and both the good and bad from both of those worlds would find its way into us, in some distorted form or another.

Eccentric silly things, like Granny Liza, who would get a thick black marker pen (there were always plenty lying about as they were used for marking price tickets for the barrows), and she'd draw bikini tops on the Page 3 girls, put glasses on them or make them look cross eyed, draw a 'tache on them or black out some of their teeth and write things like 'dirty midden', or 'Jessabelle', with an arrow pointing to the poor topless model.

Old fashioned? Narrow minded? Yes. Yet wise and worldly. Naïve, yet as wide as a barn door. Conservative in many ways, yet liberal in so many others. But never labour.

Liza, and the last remaining members of her generation, were a reminder of what we came from, a curious contradiction of a clan. She, in fact, had taken her mother's Catholic practicing to the extreme. She attended St Mary's daily, hardly ever used bad language or bought anything even half crooked, and smut of any kind, such as those lovely girls on Page 3, was simply not tolerated. Such contrasting outlooks within a family can be a little confusing, but they are the strange idiosyncrasies you remember.

The labour reference earlier was a comment with regard to work and not politics, by the way. Politics were of no concern to our family, they were not playing by anyone's rules anyway so it didn't really matter to them which government was running the country. But work?

Well, as much as they went to graft, or even did a bit of 'hard labour' (courtesy of Her Majesty), it wouldn't take much to put some of them off doing the odd day's work for a day in the boozer. Just seeing a cross-eyed person in the morning before they went to work (whatever work happened to be that day), would be enough to make them throw the towel in before they even started.

Someone, somewhere down the line, had been nicked for one thing or another after seeing a cockeyed fella when they left the house in the morning. That was enough for them to lay the blame on that fact, simply because they'd looked at someone with crossed-eyes. Thereafter proclaiming it to be bad luck to see a person on their way to work, who had 'one eye going to the shops, and another coming back with the change', and that if they did then something bad would happen. Subsequently, they decided the safest thing to do in that instance, was to do nothing at all, and call it a day to avoid any shan mazel (bad luck).

A ridiculous notion, and an outrageous excuse to have a day on the drink. Silly, prudish, bigoted eccentricities like these are passed on and will stay with a young person because they *are* odd, and it's the old peculiar things that become embedded in your memory. Fortunately all of that generation had so many strange and unusual personality traits, that memories of them are rich, full and plenty, and in some strange ways have shaped our own behaviour.

We inherited some of those characteristics but we were also absorbing the more open-minded, hedonistic views of our parents, who'd done their growing up in the swinging 60s. We were exposed to the best of both worlds, and the worst, and the cocktail was a potent one. Old values, new rules. Not just one common enemy any more but many, and some from where you would least expect to find them.

This was to become a decade to remember for a number of significant reasons, and it was all going to happen in the spring of our lives.

We, your narrators, Tony and Eddie, were always close.

We had very similar outlooks, just like the rest of us lads born during the mid-60s, but we stayed close throughout our youth, our adulthood and remain so even now in our more senior years. Growing up within our family we were cocooned in a kaleidoscope of colourful characters. It made our way of life seem less different because our way of life existed in every household we entered. We'd see comings and goings and wheelings and dealings of all kinds, not just under our own roof at home, but under the roofs of all of our family, and we were always around our family.

The rich fabric of life that we were exposed to, although we didn't know it, was slowly coming to an end, and we were lucky, or unlucky enough to have it in our blood and get a flavour of what we were about as a breed. The street life was in us, and we loved it. Our family were synonymous with street trading in Newcastle, and as kids, we thought our way of life was going to last forever. We would finish up sly pitching on the barrow, then like our dads, probably end up with a shop in the market. But as we all know, nothing lasts forever, and the most significant changes in our family's history were going to take place on our watch.

Albert Sayers had really gotten his teeth into the campaign for legalising the barrows, particularly after Mariah had passed away and he was more determined than ever to finish off the job in her memory, almost a century after Sally had first set up pitch near St Andrew's.

Newcastle was almost unrecognisable by the end of the 1970s, much of the change being accredited to Thomas Daniel

Smith, or T. Dan Smith as he was known. Smith became a prominent figure in the North East, and his monuments to progress would shape the face of the city for decades to come. Elected to Newcastle City Council in 1950, the Labour member became Chairman of the Housing Committee and later, leader of the City Council during the 1960s. His idea was to rid Newcastle of its slum areas; putting in place regeneration plans which included building motorways and demolishing a large area of the city centre in order to make way for a new shopping centre.

Pledging to turn Newcastle into the 'Brasilia of the North', Smith gave the go-ahead to the destruction of many architecturally significant buildings; tearing down some of the region's Victorian schools, most of Old Eldon Square and the stunning Royal Arcade, as well as replacing much of the town's terraced housing with brutalist high-rise tower blocks. Many of the beautiful buildings of the city were eventually replaced with concrete monstrosities, although some of these did not appear until after Smith's reign as City Council leader came to an end.

Despite Smith pumping cash into various local arts institutions, many residents of the city resented his cold-looking, characterless buildings; one of which was the hugely criticised Cruddas Park housing scheme in the West End. Many felt that his regeneration plans would subsequently see our neighbourhoods become labelled as ugly, impoverished slums. While leading the redevelopment of the city, T. Dan Smith formed business links with architect John Poulson, which led to a 1974 trial for accepting bribes. The disgraced councillor pleaded guilty and was sentenced to seven years imprisonment for corruption.

Told you everybody was at it.

Albert saw the regeneration of the city as a potential Sword of Damocles hanging over the family, and felt the unity of the street traders was the only way forward. Not everyone in the town agreed with him. Even Albert's cousin, Georgie Kelly, felt he was capable of getting a pitch, once the town had been put back together, without the need for the newly formed Barrow Boys Association.

Hard to believe that some of their own, blood they'd worked with all their life, with the same street trading heritage, couldn't even agree on the way forward as a family.

Frankie Hewson Sr and his son Frank Jr teamed up with Albert alongside the Patter Brothers, Frankie Kelly and Billy Buck. Support came from Jimmy Holmes, the Drummond twins, Tommy Quinn (or Tommy Driver as he is known) and Ray Mouzon, all of whom co-operated with the plan, with Albert acting as the spokesman for the Association.

Sadly, even the Donnellys decided that the Association was not for them. Maybe they were suspicious of hidden agendas and pitches going to people that had not been in the game nearly as long as members of our breed had. It was a sign of the times that all of the family could not agree on such an important matter, especially when others were only too happy to do so. Following the Seppy Stuart incident, which was later almost replicated by Tommy Driver, some felt convincing the new local authority to comply with the desires of the barrow boys was going to be almost impossible.

The law which prevented Newcastle street trading was in fact an archaic bylaw, enforced by the police with gusto. The hope was, with forward thinking councillors like the soon-to-be Lord Mayor of Newcastle, Bennie Abrahams, having influence on city developments, they perhaps might find a sympathetic ear within the corridors of power. If Albert had known T. Dan Smith was crooked the job would have been done years earlier, but his unscrupulous behaviour was not revealed until he'd left office.

Albert presented a compelling case for the barrow boys, largely based on our family's longevity and tenacity within the game, not to mention the terrible persecution and generations of harassment endured by so many of them at the hands of the law. It had actually reached the point by then where some of the Old

Bill would nick you remotely. One persistent antagonist was in fact sitting on a bus, off duty, when he spotted a couple of the chaps working the 'front'. He knocked on the window of the bus, getting their attention as it passed them on the corner of Nelson Street, at which point he raised his wrist, pointed at his watch, and then felt his own collar.

The next day he landed at the 'front' to see the two same faces at work. 'You're nicked,' he told them. 'Now, and from yesterday at 2 o'clock.' That's why he wanted them to see him record the time by pointing to his watch from the bus the day before. It simply wouldn't stand up today, but it was, and always had been, open season on the barrow boys of Newcastle. The old trick of following a barrow on the move, like Sally had encountered a hundred years earlier, was still being employed, but now they'd do it from a moving police vehicle. Following you through the city until you were literally run out of it, or you simply got sick of pushing your barrow, at which point they'd nick you.

The SPG would drive down Nelson Street and even make a pinch through their loud speaker, 'You're all nicked,' would come the call, and they'd rattle off the names of whoever was out with a barrow, and these nickings would be upheld in the magistrates courts, which was also a crooked house since numerous shop owners, including Mr Anthony Bookless, would often be sat on the bench. They all had a vested interest in keeping the barrows off the streets, especially Bookless as he owned a chain of self-service fruit shops. The barrow lads never stood a chance, and were treated like common criminals, with blatant contempt and disdain from almost everyone in authority.

In a last ditch attempt to get some public support, Albert organised a peaceful demonstration late in 1980, which saw all the lads taking their barrows through the town, ending up at Pilgrim Street nick.

Following decades of lobbying and months of negotiation, the demonstration was a public show in support of the association's campaign.

It was only when the lads arrived at the nick and Albert informed the officer in charge that the press were on their way to document the proceedings and report on the ongoing plight of the barrow lads and lasses, that he was asked not to involve the press as it had been decided at the newly-built Civic Centre that legal pitches were finally going to be allocated. Our voice had eventually been heard, but the details of the decision were yet to be revealed. From the beat officers, to the desk sergeants, from the magistrates to the councillors, our family had been a constant thorn in their side. But victory was finally ours.

Ironically, it is doubtful any of the decision makers at the council had any idea that the plush red carpet which had been laid on the grand staircase inside the new Civic Centre, adorning their corridors of power, had actually been supplied and fitted by a former barrow boy. For that service, my father got to meet King Olav V of Norway when he came to open the Civic in 1968, little did he know he was shaking hands with one of our own, nice one Ed.

So that was it.

In the year 1981, 95 years after it had all begun, our family had finally made the good burghers of Newcastle relent, and they were about to legitimise generations of persecution and prosecution once and for all. No more wondering if you'd get to work each day. No more chancing your arm on a load of stock only to have it confiscated, or having to stand the rest of the day to sell it in order to pay for being nicked twice before lunchtime. No more indignity to suffer, getting carted away in front of a crowd of shoppers or dragged off like an animal into the back of a meat wagon. No more jail time, no more harassment, no more conflict.

A chance to become legitimate, part of the system, run a legal business and enjoy the liberty and the benefits that came with it. That was the dream. That was what the family had wanted for generations, and now that it was about to become a reality, all our problems might be over. Mariah would have been delighted that the tenacity and determination of the family had finally paid off, but victory always comes at some cost, and the reality of what was to unfold was more a case of them receiving with one hand, and relinquishing with the other.

The decade had only just begun and already a huge milestone had been reached, but at what cost to the family? While all of those that had unified with the Association were allocated pitches, those who had chosen to paddle their own canoe were hung out to dry. Uncle Georgie Kelly, one of the greatest characters of Newcastle street trading, was overlooked, as was Muriel Donnelly who, along with young Mariah and Liza, was resigned to working the pitch she had been allocated by the Watch Committee, which unlike the newly-allocated pitches, would die with them. Challenge the decision of the council and all bets were off.

Some of the latter-day barrow boys were allocated better pitches than some of our lot, qualifying the concerns that some of the family had harboured. The next issue was who would get what pitch? And that decision was never going to please everyone. Albert was awarded the best pitch in the town, smack bang in the middle of Northumberland Street, our equivalent to Oxford Street, with rates as high as anywhere in the country outside of there. In light of the seeming success, however, there was much to question after the event, and some people felt vindicated for suspecting an unfair outcome. But what was the option? To believe we were never going to get it all our own way was fair enough; but to not get our own way because we never all tried, wasn't something we could really complain about, and the initial allocation, after much discussion, was non-negotiable.

Take it or leave it. These pitches, or no pitches.

The victory wasn't entirely hollow, disruptive maybe, and not without far reaching implications. Every action, it is said, has an equal and opposite reaction, an observation made by another Albert, Albert Einstein, and this was definitely one of those situations. In another phrase, with showman origins; what you lose on the swings, you'll make up for on the roundabouts.

And that was now the hope.

Post legalisation, which I myself was a part of, due to me working for my grandad and Uncle Frankie by then, I become one of the handful of barrow boys in Newcastle that made the first and only transition from generations of sly pitching to being licensed. I was pipped at the post for holding the title of Newcastle's youngest officially-licensed barrow boy by one of my frisk-filled and favourite cousins, young Frankie Kelly. Bastard!

He worked the shite out of me for years about it. He knew I'd been sly pitching with my grandad and Uncle Frankie for about 12 months before we were licensed, while he still had another year in school. He walked out the gates and straight into a license, which was only right. He was Uncle Frankie Kelly's only son. He'd been given a license to work a pitch near the Clock Bar at the top of Nun Street with his brother, Billy Buck, and as part of the license agreement the stall holder's son could be licensed too. Buck had no kids, so our young Kelly became the youngest legalised barrow boy in this city, a title that will undoubtedly always be his.

So we were finally licensed, or 'slanged-up' as we say. Another condition, as part of the agreement, was that we were supposed to police our own streets as far as other grafters popping up were concerned, which happened a lot when everyone was sly pitching, because as much as it had open season for the gavas to pinch the barrow boys, it had also been open season for anyone else game enough to work the street here.

Once we had our own pitches, rent paid, straight, legit and above board, we were expected to protect it, instructed to in fact. Again, a poisoned challis, as we turned from street traders to virtual shop keepers. The action couldn't have been more equal and opposite. We were supposed to keep sly pitchers off the streets, what a fucking irony! But the bottom line was, deal or no deal? And we dealt. Once the deal had been struck, there would be room to manoeuvre, once the dust settled it could be scrutinised, but in the meantime, it was a case of half a loaf being better than none. Family dynamics had changed yet again, and the unity we had built our reputation on was beginning to crack under the strain.

Young Kelly and me just thought it was a bit of craic, wearing a badge for graft which effectively stuck two fingers up to the law, less concerned with the inconvenience of health and safety regulations, weights and measures, hygiene certificates and all the bollocks that came with legalisation. We were too busy having a good time.

The 1980s were our 1960s and, as young bucks coming onto the pub and club scene, with our own West End clique and family beside us, we were all set up to have the times of our lives.

FROM BOYS TO MEN

From the late 70s we were all running around the town as young teenagers. Ducking and diving, wheeling and dealing, and in some cases, choring and thieving, following in the footsteps that our family had left all over the streets of Newcastle for generations. The week from Monday to Saturday was for us, just like most people, all about graft. For Tony and me it was the fruit market at Team Valley early doors – great in the summer but not so clever in the middle of winter – followed by a day dodging around the Grainger Market in our parents' fruit shops or grafting the barrow. The main purpose for getting stuck into work, was Saturday night. But before you even thought about hitting Rick's Bar on the Bigg Market then Tuxedo Junction or Julie's, you had to have your tuggies sorted. Looking the part on a night out was paramount.

As disco music swept the nation, sharp-suited men and chicks with curly perms and shoulder pads were the style of the day when everyone hit fever pitch on Saturday night, and it was the time of our lives. Born into a 'family' with a reputation, we were running around the city streets like Angels with Dirty Faces during the week and hitting the clubs like little old men about town every weekend.

Legs was a face on the club scene, he had ten or more years on most of us, as did the firm he moved about with, all as smart as darts, and all chaps. So when we made our tentative appearance on the scene, at no more than 15 or 16, we not only had a style and image to look up to, we had one to *live* up to. Even as newcomers on the nightlife circuit, we got access to many places and entry into most of the clubs because of who we were. It wasn't an intimidation or fear thing, far from it, after all we were just kids really, yet we were respected. Some of the older doormen in the town had just been making their bones when our dads were in the town every night of the week. Some of the younger bouncers knew Legs and co (not the ones off *Top of the Pops* – my brother Tony and his firm), and as a result, we'd get a bye at the door, rarely had to pay, and never stood in the queue, and we were only kids.

Once you get that kind of treatment at such an impressionable age, it sets the bar at a certain level, and you begin to expect it all the time. That's why it was so important to look the part when we turned out. Not just so we stood out from the crowd and didn't look like a bums, but so we looked old enough to be in the fucking place. So half our wages went on the night out, and the rest was spent in Trelawney's.

Geoff was the guvner in there, and he took the very best care of us. Legs, Wilbo, Keith Kennedy, Big Zulu, Lawsy, Dicky Ford, Davey Lancaster, Alan Fisher, all the chaps used Trelawney's and they spent fortunes in there, so Geoff made sure he looked after them, and us. We, me and Tony, would pop in through the week and have a cup of tea with him in the back office of the shop, which was on the outside of the Grainger Market. We'd spend our dinner break in there and see what new schmutter (clothing) Geoff might have in for us to hit the town in at the weekend. Sometimes he'd dress you so well that you looked like you could own the club, never mind fanny (bluff) your way through the door. But even with a healthy discount, the bill for a black double breasted Van Gils blazer, pale grey Wexman slacks, burgundy leather weaved shoes, soft pink Swiss cotton shirt with matching burgundy silk tie and hanky; which you looked so fucking well in that you just had to have it for Saturday; could come to more money than we were due for our week's wages.

An average wage for a workingman was about £130 a week at the time, a bill from Trelawney's might be one and a half, and that was after Geoff had knocked a long 'un off, (£100). We might have picked up £15 a day in the town, topped up with selling a few trays or shopping a bit of gear from the fruit shops or the barrows to restaurants and cafés. W might buy a bit of hoist from a shop lifter and get a bit of wages off that, or get a bit of tom from someone like my granddad or Bobby 'Curly'

McGreevy, he was a tricky old character who could get his hands on anything and knew everyone worth knowing.

Curly ended up becoming a full-time lodger at Granny Liza's house on Westgate Hill Terrace, the perfect environment for a man like him. Frankie Doodles spent a while there around about that time but returned home to Lilly and his family after months of estrangement. His life of living on the edge and looking over his shoulder had come between him and Lilly, and they both carried the burden of losing Carol, which can have an impact, and causes some kind of pent up resentment within a relationship. Realising that if he was ever to be reunited with his family, however, Doodles knew he would have to change his ways. Family first.

Even if you need a few months to blow out before you commit to a whole new lifestyle, it is always family first, because when the chips are down, and your back's against the wall, family is all you have.

We had to make ourselves busy if we were going to get tuggied up off Geoff and still be poked up for Tux at the weekend. Life revolved around that routine for a while, and on the weeks when we could hit Trelawney's, land at Rick's looking a million, and then roll up to the door and get a bye off Paul Tucker or Ron at Tuxedo Junction, and still have enough money for 20 Benson, a skin-full of vodka, and even a bottle of Moet; if we copped on a bird, then we'd cracked it. If we didn't, we at least made sure we copped on some poor thing for a slow dance at the end of the night, smooching to the sultry sounds of Luther Vandross, Barry White or the Stylistics, and then spend the last ten minutes in a clinch singing *Three Times a Lady* down some poor things earhole, sounding less like Lionel Richie and like more like a sheep shiteing razor blades.

On the weekends when we couldn't cut the mustard, we'd be sat in the Balmoral on Westgate Road, The Greyhound on Pitt Street or the Dodds Arms on Elswick Road, as sick as a dog. Mind you, a night, or even a day, in one of those boozers could turn out to be more eventful than any Saturday night in the Bigg

Market. These were rough West End bars, filled with misfits and miscreants. Old local bars, half full of villains, and the rest made up of old characters, drunks, ponces, and stoners, with a handful of old sorts from the West End who were better fighters than half the men. 100% mad, and 100% crooked, not a straight goer in the place.

While we were pretending to be 21, and acting like we were 31, Legs was working his way through different little firms. We'd see them through the week if we called in to the Chalk & Cheese. Everyone would be in there at some point; Fish and Derek Tams, Young Scone Rigney, Spud Tate, Lawsy, Pie, Billy Mac, Kenny May (son of the bookmaker from the 69 Club episode), Zulu, Jimmy Peacock, young Lenny Conroy, Jimmy and Geordie Dillon, all the chaps, as well as a few straight-goers who loved the atmosphere in there. Big Cockney Alf was someone I befriended from those days, he was a fireman who had palled up with a lass from up here. He was a diamond geezer and got on well with all the chaps. I spent some happy times with him and his wife Heather when I worked in London, they actually put me up for a while, good people, decent people, salt of the earth. But the snooker hall was a villain's den, a world beyond our years, yet a world we were completely at home in.

We hadn't exactly led sheltered lives, and despite our tender ages, we were worldly wise; street life teaches you to be, and in order to survive the streets, you have to be.

We also knew that money was finding its way into some people's pockets even easier than it was in to ours. We went to graft every day and might have worked long hours in our dad's shops or on the barrows, even after a 5am start, but it wasn't exactly *hard* labour. We could sit and have a bit of craic in the front of Uncle Peter's Bedford TK, with a Devon slice from Milligan's bakers, washed down with a nice cup of tea (coffee wasn't really a thing yet), dart away for half an hour if we had a bit of business, or even go round and butter up Geoff for the weekend so we'd get more discount off him.

He loved us young 'uns, and why not? We were little old men spending money in the best men's outfitters in town, while kids our age were running around in Geordie Jeans and shell suits. Geoff loved the craic, and made sure we were looking aces on a night out, with a few quid's worth on our backs, and a few quid left on our hips.

But seeing the lifestyle of Legs and the other chaps in the snooker hall or in the clubs, who didn't seem to do nearly as much work as we did, spent most of their time doing what they wanted, and still had the money to fund their lifestyle, did make us think about doing other things. The 'easy come, easy go' merchants were all around us.

They were the chaps, and although our cash may not have come so easy to us, it was every bit as easy to spend.

I'd had about a year on the barrows after legalisation, it became a bit boring and stale without the cat-and-mouse game with the law to be honest. I was getting restless and needed to get my fingers into meatier pies, after all I was still only a grafter on the barrow; it wasn't my pitch, and I would never have one either unless I inherited my Uncle Frankie Hewsons', and he had two sons and a daughter in line before me, so that was a lifetime away from happening.

All our cousins were in similar positions. Joe Riley, Aunt Sylvia and Gypsy Joe's son, had worked for a couple of years with Uncle Albert on the pitch, but they parted company after we got licensed. The split was not entirely amicable, but it did Joe no harm as he turned his hand to the prop. Property maintenance was a trade of many Travellers, and Joe was very good at taking a bit of work. He became very successful and eventually set up his own company and still trades today, although it must be a 30-stretch since he picked up a tool or climbed up a ladder; he has plenty of workers to take care of that for him. He's no fool, Joe. His brothers, Frankie and Philip, followed in his wake and were also on the club scene with us, often bringing along a few of their Traveller pals, like Jim Wilson from Darlington or mad

Adam Hoppy, the Carpet King. We'd all turn out suited and booted most weekends, like something out of a mob movie.

We were always firm-handed on a Saturday night and the Grand Central bar in Tuxedo Junction was our pitch. It seemed the West End had a corner in every place in the town, and members of our family would always be in the thick of it. We'd see all the Stuarties from the East End in there, Pog, Anthony, Little Legs, or Brian to give his real name, and Chris or 'Big H' as we called him in school. They were just like us, street traders from a big family in Daisy Hill, all top lads and people who we have grown up with and still see regularly. We would all be in Grand Central on a Saturday night, and by the time we joined Legs and his firm, it felt like our team had just about taken over the gaff. They were the nights when we were kings, and in many ways were a throwback to La Dolce Vita days of the 60s.

On the work front, Tony and his older brother Peter took more of a role in their dad's shop as Uncle Peter now had an interest in a reclamation yard with his brother John and Ward Smith. My old man came out of the fruit shop after a couple of years following a second heart attack, leaving the job to my brother Tony, which didn't last long, eventually selling the shop to Scotch Ward. Young Frankie Kelly didn't really bother with the barrows that much, and did a bit of running around with a few boys from the West End, as did John, Stephen and Michael Sayers. Young Stephen Shotton was a wild child and ended up back on Vallum Way in the thick of the chaos, and in the heart of the Wild West End.

We were all of an age where we had just come out of school or were just about to. I had been at St Mary's Tech in Benton with cousins John, and later Stephen after it turned from a Tech to a comprehensive. Tony, Peter, Michael, Frankie Kelly Jr and Young Gun (Stephen Shotton) had all went to St Cuthbert's on the West Road. We all played truant a lot, because it was far more interesting and educational to be in the yard, on the barrows or at the market, learning the life skills needed to survive in the world, especially our world. But since sly pitching was no longer an option, as part of the deal with the Association, a livelihood on the streets was something that was no longer available to any of us. The victory, in that respect, was hollow; what we'd been born into was no longer viable to us as a means of earning a living. And we knew nothing else.

The schooling we had came from our family, from the street, and what was going on around us and, as a result, the temptation to follow a crooked path was not an easy one to resist. We certainly had every opportunity to have chosen a career in crime, and undoubtedly doors were there to be opened for us if we'd wanted to go through them. There were few other options really. None of us were going to get a job. We weren't exactly scholars and in all likelihood none of us could hold one down. Our lot weren't used to being told what to do or when to do it, and besides that, we had the wherewithal to go out and earn it ourselves in any case. So, decisions were having to be made, and even then as young men about town, we were making choices that would have far reaching implications on the rest of our lives.

For some of us, the temptation was too strong to resist. Legs was the oldest of our generation, the fifth generation of our family to earn a living on the streets of Newcastle. He'd gone crooked, despite having a trade and other options available to him through oud dad. It's just in some people. Nature or nurture?

To be fair, when it's going on all around you, in your family and in your community, it's hard not to slip in to it. Everyone likes to have money, to have nice things and to be respected (for doing whatever they did), so if there was a readily available route to those things, and you were game enough to gamble with your liberty, then there would only be one outcome.

Joe Riley was a little younger than Legs, but he was more inclined to wheel and deal, and had a good head for business. Our John (Sayers) joined the army when he came out of school. Not sure whether he really wanted a career in the forces, or whether he simply wanted to master the art of military planning for alternative use; but we know that's what the press and the law would love to think. We're speculating and being a bit facetious, but he certainly did don the purple beret of the paratroop regiment for about a year and a half, before rejoining civvy street.

Frankie Riley, born and bred in tin (a trailer), had lived the Traveller life and went to work on the prop with his younger brother Philip, although he didn't do the club scene as much as some of us; getting married at just 18 to a young Travelling girl who stopped on Lemington camp.

Peter Sayers, Tony's older brother, worked with his dad in the shop, but was more interested in women, motor scooters and CB radios than anything else. He did the mod revival thing with me, and we often visited the old Dolce Vita which held mod nights on a Monday. Tony was a careful chap, always has been, you don't get the nickname Hymee for nothing, but he was a good grafter and knew the fruit trade better than he might have done for someone of his age. I was a 'spieler', not the gambling kind, but the talking, always at the hurry up, and loved a deal.

Stephen Sayers, well, what can we say that hasn't already been said about him? (read his book). Stephen was a very shy lad, to the point where he'd go red if he was talking to someone he didn't know. But his shy exterior betrayed a violent and disruptive nature. He loved a fight, could certainly have one, and was as game as a pebble. His younger brother Michael should have been a comedian, as should have young Kelly, they are two of the wittiest people we've ever had the pleasure of knowing.

Michael was a very funny lad, and he and Tony, or Hymee as we all call him, were known as the 'gigglers' and the bane of their granny Liza's life, although they were probably two of her favourites as well. Michael was also a very bright lad, extremely intelligent, he had big ideas and was very ambitious. Young Kelly was just frisk on a stick. He was a laugh a minute and the life and soul of any party, not too keen on selling apples and pears for a living, he ran around with his own little firm from the West End, lads we'd grown up with like Luggsy and Bullas.

Young Gun (our Stephen Shotton), was the youngest of the group and would go on to follow in the footsteps of, and work alongside some of his older cousins as their careers developed. And that was our clique growing up. Of course, there were many associates from the West End that featured in our youth, but that was the nucleus of the young men in our family in the early 80s.

There were, of course, Doodles' boys, Thomas and Morry, but they were creating a stable and straight future for themselves and no one could condemn them for that. Albert Cruddas' boys Kelly and young Al kept themselves to themselves to some degree, and although we would see enough of them growing up, they tended to do their own thing. The Patters kids were much younger, as were Frankie Hewson Jr's two boys and Jimmy Kelly's. The Growler's brood were a law unto themselves, and they did exactly what they wanted to do, regardless of what anyone else might have thought.

On reflection, if we had all pooled our resources, combined our talents and screwed our loaves, we could have really done some damage, in a good way, in business, but there was simply too much rivalry and one-upmanship within in our ranks. We'd all been given the tools to take care of ourselves, the ability to survive, to provide and to stand on our own two feet, but whatever had happened along the way, we had lost the team spirit that Mariah had cultivated when she and her seven daughters were out on the barrows building a little empire.

Maybe it was because there was no clear figurehead any longer? Or maybe it was a man thing, now that the days of the strong matriarchs of the family had passed? Either way, we were about to take on the world, each in our own different ways, and the outcome of that would shape the rest of our lives, and in some ways, the shape of many others.

We dipped in and out of the town scene and spent a lot of time on the camp at Hartford, or the one in Lemington. We'd be running around with young Travellers in transit vans and courting young Travelling girls on the scene at the time, barri frisk, chavy! (which translates from Cant into Geordie as 'great fun, man!')

I ran about with Mark Lee for a while, a Travelling lad out of Scotland; we were in the oil business. Not as glamorous as it sounds. We simply bought or begged sump waste oil from garages and the like, on the premise that we needed a little bit to carry out some tarmac work we were doing.

Using a suction pump to fill up the 45-gallon drums we had in the van, we'd then sell it on to oil refiners like Amicoil on the quayside. It was a good earner, but I was never clean, and that wasn't a good state to be in. The crooked tanker drivers made all the difference though. One of them was happy to pay us for twice the amount of oil we supplied him with, as long as we split the profit from the transaction with him. Just another 'straight' fella, with his fingers in the till.

After a while jumping around with that and other things, I got approached by a friend from the East End, Christine Tate. She asked me to come to work with her and her fella Stu, a grafter out of Nottingham, and Johnny Cuff, my dad's old pal from the Dolce Vita. They were in the rag trade and ran a fashion show business in the North East and other areas around the country. They were buying all of the out-of-season catalogue fashions from the big mail order firms like Grattan, Kays and Littlewoods. They'd asked me to come and run a team for them in Scotland as they knew I could spiel. They'd book workingmen's clubs, women's institutes and village halls, bill the area and put on a fashion show and sale. They'd get a couple of good sorts to model the gear, floor staff to serve the punters and a top man to conduct the sale – That's where I came in.

It was a great game for me, sat at a table with a half of lager, 20 snout and a microphone, spieling about the dress the model was wearing as she paraded around the room. We'd serve the punters there and then from the stock we carried, and the punters loved it as we sold at a quarter of the catalogue price. I ran the shows in Scotland for couple of years. We rented a big old house in Uddingston, just outside Glasgow, with my team working Edinburgh and Johnny Cuff's pal, Collin Craggs, running the Glasgow team.

We had a great time, working evenings and spending all day in the Davis Snooker Hall in Hamilton. We were also getting a few quid too. It was around the time of the miner's strikes and hardly a week went by when I didn't get a tug off the Old Bill as we drove up the A74 to Glasgow from Carlisle, simply because I was driving a Luton transit (full of stock), which the law thought was full of flying pickets. Teams of striking miners were shuttled around this way at the time, to join their fellow miners on the picket lines all over the country. I shit myself the first time this happened as I didn't have a driving license at the time. Me and our Frankie Riley had taken our driving tests early as we had wanted to have a summer driving ice-cream vans in Jersey for one of Leg's pals, Abbey, who had a good set up over there, but I failed my test and unfortunately we never got to go.

I say unfortunately, but it is funny how things turn out. If Jersey had happened, Frankie might never have ended up married so soon.

Anyway, when we got pulled over on the A74 one Monday on the way up to the Scotch side for the week, I thought, 'this is it, I'm nicked,' but the old bill didn't even ask to see my documents. They did make us empty the contents of the van at the roadside though, as they thought they were transporting striking miners.

The impromptu fashion show at the roadside was a bit of a chew, as all the tea chests we carried gear in had to come out so they could see we weren't carrying bodies on the move. I was busy fannying (sweet talking) for my life, and as God is my judge, I ended up selling one of the bizzies a blouse for his wife before they let us go on our way. I'm still proud of that deal to this day.

I drove that route for 12 months before sitting my test again and must have been stopped a dozen times before I got my licence in Hamilton, in an old clapped out Audi belonging to Colin Craggs. Eventually I became tired of working away, I was missing the town, so after parting company with Stu and Christine , I returned home and set up on my own and ran shows around Northumberland and Durham for a couple of years. Stu tried to put the block on me of course, unsuccessfully. It's a big wide world out there, and as my granddad used to say, 'never educate a mug.'

Not that I was a mug. He meant anyone outside of your own, and I'd been given an education by someone else, and made the most of it. Point proven.

By the time I was back in town, Hymee had found himself back on Hartford Camp. His parents had moved back there after selling the house on Bentinck Road and retiring from the fruit game in the market, it had become very hard in there, too many fruit shops and everyone going at the slaughter with their gear made for slim pickings. Hymee would commute from the camp to the fruit market in Gateshead every morning, as he was running a fruit shop on the West Road at just 19 years of age, and doing a pretty good job of it. Just like me, he was doing all of that, driving loaded wagons up and down the place long before he'd passed his test.

John was out of the army and he, Stephen and Michael, were gaining a fearsome reputation, even among the crazy natives of the Wild West End. More than any of us, they had grown up in the shadow of villainy with their dad, Uncle John. He'd been in trouble with the law all his life and his boys held the authorities in the same disregard as he did.

They hated the law with a passion. They were running around thieving and going from petty things like screwing motors and vans, to crimes of a more serious nature. They could all have a fight and nobody in the town, or even the West End, fucked with them.

Young Kelly was a live wire and didn't want to play second fiddle to his cousins, so he and his little firm did their own thing. The Gypsy crew were in the town most weekends, staying Granny Liza's, and clubbing with us, but spent their week hawking for graft or up a ladder.

Liza's house on Westgate Hill Terrace had, for many years, been the main meeting place for all the family, we referred to it as Vallance Road, a tongue in cheek reference to the home made famous, or infamous as the case may be, as the residence of the Krays. The Donnellys were very much in the mix as far as activity in the town was concerned and, of them, Peter was the one that would make the most impact and try to steal anyone's thunder.

Although, his brother Frankie brought the house down in 1981, the public house that is. In a comic yet potentially life-threatening fashion, Frankie burst into the Greyhound on Pitt Street with a shotgun after a disagreement with another relative by the name of Frankie Slater. After letting a couple of rounds off, and everyone hitting the deck, Frankie took off just before the law arrived on the scene. But being the West End, they got zero information from the inhabitants of the bar about what had went off. One bystander claimed that they thought the gunshots were coming from the television in the bar.

Looking out for your own was the norm in such a community, and if it ever came on top then you just kept your mouth shut. But funny as it may be, Frankie somehow managed to get a five-stretch over that debacle. Straight people with licensed premises can't afford to have that sort of stuff going on, and the law eventually caught up with Frankie.

It seemed that everyone wanted to be the top of the tree. The big earner, the big shot, the man about town, a face. The small band of men that had been our grandads had set that stall out, but they were less in number and had worked alongside each other for the main part.

Our fathers had all grown up as young men with different surnames and this, in some way, may have had some bearing on the gradual disenfranchising of the family, although the Percy Street thing had thrown a banner over them all for a while. So, without a common interest, without the barrows, our generation seemed to splinter into different fields. We all wanted to succeed, to achieve, and to be respected for whatever it was we did. We may all have been in one boat, but we were not all rowing in the same direction.

I had come home and was doing ok. I was driving a nice BMW and had enough money to be a regular in Trelawney's as well as Tux most weekends, or Julie's, which became the club of choice on a Tuesday or Thursday. These were the things our money went on when we were in your late teens, and when you didn't have the money to be on the scene, you felt you were failing yourself in some way.

Our lives could be a famine or a feast, sometimes you're poked up to the hilt, and other times you're on the bones of your arse. When you did have a tickle, you were out and about, looking sharp and holding court in the clubs. And when you weren't, but your cousins were, it made you even more determined to get your finger out. So for some of us, when the opportunity came along to get rolled into a bit of graft that could change your life, for a while at least, then it was very easy to take the next step and take your criminal career to the next level.

Fortunately, me and Hymee were getting it straight, and we'd never really had any designs on a career in crime.

I had had seen how much her son being jailed had upset my mother, and it affected me each time he went on a visit and couldn't bring my brother home. So I put myself to good use, and opened a café on Westgate Hill, famed for its motorbike shops, and just around the corner from my Aunt Liza's house. I called it Fast Eddie's. That was a nickname some people referred to me by at the time. The name also worked well with all the bikers on the hill, as there was a famous off-road motorcycle star of the same name.

I also opened a swag shop further up the West Road, selling mail order clothing alongside the fashion show business, and all before the time I was 21. My brother Legs was now very much an active villain and had elevated to the ranks of being a 'Face'. The 80s were a decade of wide spread violence on the streets, with riots all over England, and the constant threat of terror from the IRA. They were also the 'blagging' years, and post offices, security vans and wages blags were very much the flavour of the time all over the country. Legs never tried to tempt me into his way of life as he knew I had my own thing sorted, and after all, he didn't want to see his kid brother in trouble. Even though I probably had as many friends in jail as on the pavement, I simply didn't need that lifestyle. I was earning, and just like all of our breed before us, I was spending. I had a nice motor, I went to Tenerife for a month every kipper season, and I treated himself to a nice three-stone diamond ring for my 21st birthday, bought from brother-in law 'Roger', for £1,200. Not bad for a street lad of 21, when in 1986 a working man was only picking up £130 for a week's wages.

Hymee was fiddling away in the West Road fruit shop and like me, didn't need the agg of villainy. He was happy with the single life and living under the stars on the camp with his mam and dad, getting a few quid, and having very little exes (expenses), right up his street. Cousins John, Stephen and Michael, however, were looking for the fast track way up the criminal ladder, and with Legs at the forefront of the local underworld, they had just the ticket to get them there.

The ultimate goal of any villain worth his salt is to secure enough dough to set themselves up in business, or to skip that bit and go straight to retirement, but a successful business is often the goal, even if that meant rolling somebody in to account for the money. Other villains, however, are career criminals, and simply love doing what they do, and that usually ends up with them doing loads of bird or winding up potless after years of being a champagne Charlie and not putting their ill-gotten gains to use, the curse of 'easy come, easy go'.

In spite of the chaos all over the country, the town had really come to life again in the 80s, and the club scene was reminiscent of the swinging 60s. There were half a dozen good clubs on the go, but Tuxedo Junction was the place to be, and be seen. You had to have a collar and tie on to get in at one point, or at least a shirt and blazer or a suit. Even the local press had some headline about there being a ban on white socks in Tux. It was a classy joint. There was a shark tank in the foyer, three bars in the main club with a glass-encased restaurant, island dance floor and telephones on all the tables so you could call a bird sitting across the room and make a meet with her at the bar.

Through the corridor, near the toilets, you entered Grand Central, a smaller and more intimate setting with a podium for the dancers, who were a throwback to the go-go dancers of the 60s, and forerunners to the pole dancing girls of today, wearing skimpy bikinis or sexy lingerie. Lesley Park, a half-Venezuelan girl was the stand out one I remember. There were two bars in there, and our firm always commandeered the top bar. Downstairs was Manhattans, which is where we would plot up with a sort for a drink in a dark corner, if we got lucky.

Everyone was out on a weekend. You could turn up at Rick's by yourself and be in company for the rest of the night, usually finishing up in The Godfather on Market Street, owned by big mad Alex Cuscani, or Vamps on the Quayside. Vamps didn't have a late license, but cheekily sold pots of tea (white wine) and pots of coffee (red wine), and all the chaps, birds in tow, would end up in one of these gaffs in the early hours of a Sunday morning.

We were living the dream. As young bits of boys, Saturday night was like a fantasy for us. We got free entry in the clubs, no queues, the DJs made a fuss over the mic when they saw us roll in, and we looked and spent well. Everyone in our circle was a chap, no straight-goers, all wide-boys and villains and, by the time you'd shaken hands with everyone, showed out or had a drink with them, you could have easily been recreating a scene from *Goodfellas*.

Santino's in the Bigg Market was another gaff we all used regularly. It was owned by Rossano Arcceri and his younger uncle, Adriano, another large and mixed-up family with uncles younger than their nephews. They were two Sardinian lads whose family were big in the restaurant game on Teesside. Ross is one of my oldest friends, and I first encountered him when I used to call to their place with boxes of tomatoes, lettuce, mushrooms, lemons or anything we had to clear from the barrows or the shops.

I could have only been about 13 or so at the time, and I marched in to Santino's with my cap on, looking for the boss. They were good punters and they really took a shine to the cheeky little wide-boy who talked them into buying whatever he had to sell. I remember serving them up with a parcel of jumpers one time, Italian ski wear called OneUp. All the staff wanted to be in on the act, so I encouraged Ross and Adriano to buy the parcel and serve all the kitchen and front of house staff themselves. They agreed, and I made off with his poke, my Saturday night money. I called in a week later with some lemons or something, and they were screaming about the jumpers. Some had come away at the collar, some had sleeves hanging off them. I'd spent the dough, so I simply asked what they wanted him to do about it. They wanted a refund. I told them it wasn't Marks & Spencer and I didn't have a return policy. It didn't wash very well, just like the jumpers.

'Ok,' I conceded. 'Give me a needle and thread and I'll fix them for you.'

They looked at me and laughed, but I walked out of there without returning a penny, and give them the box of lemons as a sweetener. They loved me, and that became mutual!
Good people and close friends to this day.

Santino's however, became the centre of the wrong kind of attention after an extremely violent incident that me and Hymee both missed by the skin of our teeth. Doormen in the town were starting to take liberties with lots of people during that time. There had been a major shift in security in the town's clubs and pubs, largely down to one man, and what a man! He hailed from Rowlands Gill, and he could fight for fun.

Our firm didn't bother with many people from over the river, they had their own chaps running around over there. Two ageing tearaways from that side of the river were Paddy Leonard and

Billy Robinson, good old boys with long-term reputations in the North East. They got to know about this handful from Rowlands Gill and took him under their wing. By the time they'd gained his confidence and explained to him how someone with such a talent for knocking people out could serve him well, they were ready to present a force to the streets of Newcastle that would change the dynamics of the town for a long time: Viv Graham was that force, and what a force to be reckoned with; and he did plenty of wrecking in his time as a major face on Tyneside, slowly taking control of much of the door security across the region.

If Viv was looking after your gaff, you weren't going to get any more aggravation from would-be troublemakers and pests. He also cleared out much of the drug use in the clubs and pubs, which didn't go down too well with the people who were supplying them. Another outfit that didn't take too kindly to Viv's emergence onto the scene, was the West End firm. They weren't used to being told what they could and couldn't do by anyone, least of all the doormen under Viv's protection, and various violent episodes broke out during that time as Viv and his army aimed to seize control of the city's venues. Much of what happened in the town came to the attention of the West Enders, and they were cautious about this big, raw-boned country bumpkin coming onto their manor and laying down the law.

Legs had been in Julie's one night and got into a disagreement with a couple of doormen on Viv's firm and, not content with giving him a bit of a tightener (beating), they decided to smash the windscreen of his motor with a scaffolding pole as he drove away from the club. A week later, Hymee and me were in Rick's bar with a couple of girls when our cousin Peter Donnelly came marching in, as loud as ever, he was after all, The Growler's son. It was toward the end of the night and we'd all had a drink. Peter told me that the lad on the door at Rick's had been on the door at Julie's on the night when Legs had taken a beating.

Maybe Peter was making the balls for me to fire, but he knew of my reputation as a bit of a cheeky Charlie and knew that I'd have something to say to the bouncer. Knowing Peter, he probably just wanted to see a bit of frisk unfold. Charged up with cheeky juice, I confronted the bouncer, about twice my size, and told him in no uncertain terms that he and his friends needed to pull some money up to fix Legs' motor.

Peter was laughing about his cheeky little cousin dishing out a coating to the big bouncer as we walked down from Rick's towards Santino's, at which time he pulled his usual stroke and got me in a bear hug. He loved to demonstrate his physical strength, he was a big enough lad and well put together. Once he had me in his grip, he squeezed and squeezed, until I virtually went limp. Ignoring my pleas to let go, and unable to speak any further due to shortage of breath, I seized him by the nose with his teeth and bit down as hard as he could without taking the end of it off. There was no other option, he had me trapped. This caused Peter to release his hold, but not before sticking his finger into my eye, down to the knuckle. We were stood there effing and blinding at each other over this unnecessary behavior before I told him to fuck off just as a taxi rolled up. Peter tried to stop from me getting in.

'Howay, cuz,' he pleaded. 'It's only a bit a frisk. Come down to Santino's and I'll buy youse a pizza.'

I could hardly see. So me, Hymee and the two girls jumped in the cab and left the scene... after telling Peter to go and fuck himself. Peter went onto Santino's alone. It turns out that Viv was in there with a couple of big burly doormen. Peter immediately about turned, before they could spot him, but returned a short while later armed with a shotgun. Peter marched through the crowded restaurant to the backroom dining area where Viv and his crew were sitting, away from the general public.

Once in there, and totally contrary to any plan Peter might have had, he was quickly overpowered by one of the bouncers, who was stabbed during the struggle for the gun. Once Peter had been relieved of the weapon, Viv proceeded to give him the hiding of his life, leaving him for dead in the back lane after pummelling him repeatedly with empty beer kegs. As the place was full of punters, it wasn't long before the Old Bill arrived, along with two ambulances, one for the bouncer who had taken a knife wound to the heart, and one for Peter who had taken the lickings of a dog from Viv.

Peter was subsequently charged with attempted murder, and remanded in Durham for nine months, the doorman thankfully pulled through and Peter was eventually acquitted of any offence when the victim failed to testify. That finger in my eye was the best thing that could have happened to us, and thankfully the only injury any of us incurred on that fateful night.

Peter was a West Ender, he was making a name for himself and had little respect for anyone who stood in his way. Viv knew the West End firm was his biggest threat in Newcastle, and the events of that night in Santino's reinforced his concerns about having to take them on in his battle to control Newcastle's doors. By this time the whole town was on its toes, as incidents flared up almost nightly. Viv was gaining a great deal of control, but very little respect from the West End boys, who were a painful thorn in his side. They didn't take notice of the police, so they weren't about to take notice of some knockout merchant from the sticks. Viv was dealing with hardened criminals, people who simply did not give a fuck, and would never cow down to anyone, especially on their own manor, and one of Viv's main venues was right in the heart of the West End.

The social and workingmen's club scene during the 1980s was as equally vibrant as the nightclub scene, and there were some fantastic groups and show bands doing the circuit around the North East. One such group went by the name of Zoots Navaro, and such was their popularity that they opened up their own venue on Waterloo Street, right in the heart of our family's old stomping ground, a hundred yards away from our beloved St Mary's Cathedral.

Zoots, as it was called, became an extremely busy club, regularly frequented by West Enders. Viv had the door there, and it gave him first-hand experience of how people from the West End performed. They were a law unto themselves and moved as a pack.

They watched each other's backs, took no nonsense from anyone and never backed down from anything or anyone. They were a nuisance to him, and he didn't know how to deal with them. Like our family, people from the West End were clannish, and outsiders were always treated with suspicion.

To perplex Viv even more, he got to witness first-hand just how his nemeses performed when they stood side by side with him against a common enemy one night, rather than standing toe to toe with his bouncers, which was usually the case.

It may have been Viv's door, but it was a West End club, so on one occasion when the club came under threat from a crowd of out of town revellers on a stag weekend, strong in numbers and hell bent on smashing the place up, the West End firm stood their ground, shoulder to shoulder with Viv's team and protected their gaff for all they were worth.

Had those boys not done so, the club would have certainly been trashed and the door staff would have been outnumbered hugely and fighting for their lives. Such a show of solidarity when faced with a common enemy, only served to qualify Viv's notion that this West End firm were a different proposition to anything else he'd encountered.

Away from the nightlife, it was time to take business to the next level. Legs had built up a good reputation and was a game grafter. He'd worked with several little firms over the years, some good, staunch, trusted and brave men. But there's no better insurance policy than working with your own, especially when your own are like we were. You might believe whole heartedly that your work colleagues would never twirl (grass), but until they are facing a 12 or 15-stretch for something, you can never be entirely sure.

Many villains are first generation bad boys. We, however, had a pedigree that was unmatched. Our fathers, their fathers and even our grannies had served time behind bars. Some had done so when they were not even the right person in the dock, yet not once, never in five generations, had one of our breed twirled. Grassing was simply the one single thing that would cast you out from our world, and no one in our family had ever been guilty of such a thing, not under any circumstances. Whatever happens, you say nothing, and you keep your mouth shut. It's not rocket science, it's the law; the law in our world.

If you went to work with your own, you knew for a guaranteed fact that if they got nicked, no matter what the threat of conviction might be, you would be safe in the knowledge that they would ever, ever give you up, not even to save their own skin. So when John, Stephen and Michael were making their bones, it seemed inevitable that Legs would put at least one of them forward the next time a firm had to be put together.

By the mid-80s we were out of our teenage years and were laying the foundations for the lives we had chosen to lead. Women were on the scene and we were clubbing the weekends away like we didn't have a care in the world, a world in which we were known, respected, and in some quarters feared. It wasn't like everyone knew us by our face, apart from those that lived in our world, or ran the bars, clubs and restaurants. The general population were not the kind of company we kept, but there would be times when we would overhear people at the bar or on the next table mention the name of one of our own in the context of some conversation they were having, which usually consisted of comments like, 'naughty fuckers them' or 'you wouldn't want to get on the wrong side of that lot.' The reputation was escalating.

There was, however, lots of hearsay due to the amount of activity that was going on. Our family consisted of a core nucleus, and a legion of long-term trusted associates, loyal and staunch. But there were also other families in the West End that were busy making a name for themselves, only too happy to put their heads above the parapet and take on all comers in their race to be the top dogs on the streets of Newcastle. Viv Graham had blown the whole game wide open, upsetting so many little firms along the way that retaliations and reprisals were almost a weekly occurrence.

The Harrisons and the Conroys were making themselves very busy at the time and didn't come under the protection, rule, or wing of anyone else from the West End. They, like us, were sizeable in their numbers, and like us, knew that their strength was in their number. They were certainly not people you'd want to mess with, yet for decades before this our family had been the biggest team, particularly in our manor, but that was about to be challenged in a violent power struggle that would shock the city.

BATTLES, BALLIES AND STICKY BUNS

During the 80s, there were blags going off all over the place, and the North East was right up there with the best of them for armed robberies on post office depots and security vans. It was also the birth place of ram-raiding.

There was a certain breed of criminal that carried out these types of robberies, the two former ones in particular, and they were the men at the top of their game. Neither of us two are villains. We never have been, nor do we profess to be, but we do know plenty, and this little city had some of the best. As the size and scale of each headline-making robbery increased, both in daring and execution, the law had certain members of our family firmly in their sights whenever something major went off up here. There were, as we've said, many other families that were making a name for themselves at the time, but the type of jobs being pulled off around the North East carried the hallmarks of what the police and the press called 'a new breed of criminal.'

Daring, cunning, vicious and professional, and as far as the law was concerned, there was only one firm that fitted the bill. When something seroius went off, it was, among others, the doors of some of our family that got kicked in. With or without justifiable cause, the Old Bill would come down on a handful of members of our family, usually doing little to further their investigation, whilst inadvertently enhancing the reputation of those under the spotlight.

Coupled with this, small time crooks were running around using other people's names to further themselves, while other even less scrupulous toerags were putting some of our family names down to things which had nothing to do with them, or to things that the informants knew nothing about; happy to do so, so long as it got them out of a pickle. This didn't deter those among our ranks that had chosen to forge themselves a career in crime. It did, however, embellish much of what they actually did, and in the underworld that can have a conflicting effect.

As well as serving to enhance a reputation, it can also make someone a marked man in the eyes of the law, quickly becoming a target criminal. It also gives the public a distorted perception of the people under scrutiny from the police. The likes of Legs, John, Stephen and Michael gave the Old Bill plenty to keep them busy, and the press plenty to write about. The truth is, much of what has been written about their exploits, John, Stephen and Michael in particular, was highly sensationalised and clearly orchestrated by the law. Our family had been a nuisance to them for decades, in one way or another, and they must have hated the fact that we still were, now more so than ever. They also knew from old that we always stood strong, never once being co-operative with them in any of their investigations.

Coppers love a grass, it makes their job so much easier, and whenever they had any of our lot in custody, they knew they were never going to get any change from them. This no doubt incensed them, and along with the reputation that was being created in the press, much of it the law's own doing; the bizzies, it seemed, really did have it in for some of our lads.

One such incident that qualified beyond any reasonable doubt my opinion of how we were viewed by the police occurred around 1986. A few of us from the town had gone up to the sticks to have a night out with the Gypsy crew at the Pegswood Club, they ran a great disco night on a Sunday. After a heavy night out with everyone, me and our Stephen decided to spend the night on the camp at Hartford with cousins, which was a mile or two from where we'd all been drinking. The next morning we jumped into my jeep, (I'd swapped the BMW away) and we drove through to the town, picking up a bird I was knocking about with at the time, Dawn. As we left the East End with her on board, we drove up the central motorway towards home and the West End. We were driving across the flyover, just past the turn off for the Civic Centre, when we were surrounded by unmarked police cars, about three of them.

We were boxed in, and dramatically pulled over before five or six plain clothes gavas jumped out with sticky buns (guns) at the ready, and started screaming at us to get out of the vehicle. We were spread-eagled across the bonnet and sides of the motor, with the bizzies screaming and shouting the whole time as motorists passed by in amazement. Within minutes three squad cars appeared, one for each of us, and they promptly carted their three suspects off to Gosforth nick. It turns out there had just been an armed robbery carried out at a bookies on Shields Road, about a couple of miles from away, and the culprits were seen making their getaway in a red car, same colour as my jeep.

It was all quite laughable really, especially as we had done nothing wrong.

The two can-bottles in the front of the squad car I was in were as twitchy as fuck, and one of them tried to inject a little humour into the proceedings in order to defuse the situation, asking me to remove the barrels of the shotgun from his neck. Funny cunt.

Once at the nick, we were led to the reception and greeted by the desk sergeant, a copper by the name of Slaughter; Sergeant fucking Slaughter, you couldn't make it up.

One by one, the coppers checked each name and read us our rights, informing us that we'd been arrested on suspicion of armed robbery. I was in absolute shock and Dawn was in tears, as was Stephen, but his were tears of laughter; this was water off a duck's back to him.

We were then taken to the cells, although they did let Dawn sit in the holding area as she was visibly upset. Obviously, they knew exactly who Stephen was, and as luck would have it, or not as was the case, good old Sergeant Slaughter knew of Legs and my old man, having previously nicked the pair of them during his career. He must have thought he was a friend of the family, he knew us that well.

I sat back in my damper (cell), thinking about my briefcase which was in the back of the jeep, containing paperwork, about two grand in readies, and around £1500 in cheques made out to my fashion show business. Stephen could hardly talk for laughing, shouting 'Fuck' em, cuz'. 'We might be here a while' he shouted, 'so try and get ya nut down'. He refused to speak to them at all, and didn't even give his name, but they knew who he was. He knew the drill and knew it would take a while. We were still a bit hungover and Dawn was still distraught.

The bunk was stinking. There was no chance of anyone getting their nut down on that thing.

After a couple of hours, two CID entered, and their little play act went something like this:

'Well you're in big trouble this time, Lennie.'

This time?

'We've got you bang to rights.'

Silence.

'You'll get a ten-stretch for this, and so will your bird.'

Again, no reply. There was no comprehending the stupidity of these two middle-aged professional men coming out with such bollocks.

'You all think you're clever you lot, don't you? Well we've got you now, you and your cousin.'

'You're are going to jail for this, son. So you better have a think about what you wanna tell us,' added the other.

Did they really think these remarks were going to make a difference to the situation? Where was the money? Where were the stickies (guns)? Why would there be a bird with us? Generally solid evidence is needed for such accusations. It was fucking laughable, yet it showed me just how much they had the needle with our lot, and the fact that we were nicked together undoubtedly made matters all the worse. The Old Bill were known for fitting people up, and I was praying that wouldn't be the case, but they eventually realised it was a non-starter.

We were left to stew all day before they released Dawn, but stuck to me and Stephen until the evening, before slinging us both out without charge. The truth of the matter was, they pulled us over on suspicion, and by chance Stephen Sayers was on board, making it simply too good an opportunity for them to miss: a bit of harassment and an opportunity to let us know that they were on our case, and by 'us', I mean Stephen, because that was what it was all really about. This is how it has always been for Stephen, and sadly it was only going to intensify over the course of the decade.

The thing that really made the difference, however, and brought the spotlight right on the chaps, was Sunderland. Other tasty jobs had gone off in the 1980s, but Sunderland was a turning point.

Orchard Street Post Office Depot was the scene of a highly efficient armed robbery, in fact it was the largest PO robbery in the country at the time, taking place on 12th of August, 1987; the first day of the grouse shooting season, known to many as the Glorious 12th, and also the date of Stephen's 22nd birthday.

Various sums of how much had been stolen were bandied about before the press announced that it was just short of a million quid in unmarked notes due for payment to Post Office staff around the country; this was a time before wages were paid direct to employee's banks by electronic transfer. Within a couple of days of the news breaking, the law started kicking doors in, and inevitably our lads were at the top of their list. They hit family homes: our home on the West Road looking for Legs, as well Uncle John and Aunt Yvonne's on York Street looking for Stephen, and they did this in a manner that made sure all and sundry knew they meant business.

They also raided our John's home, but unlike Legs and Stephen who were not present at either of their addresses at the time of the raids, our John was sat at home, and duly got nicked on suspicion, and subsequently charged with the armed robbery. They also arrested a good friend of the family, known as Little Ken, and both men were remanded in custody while the Old Bill hunted down the people they believed made up the rest of the gang. Without any real evidence, and we know how unimportant that is if they want you, both our John and Little Ken were remanded in Durham for over a year while the investigation continued.

It became clear, very quickly, that they meant to capture Legs and our Stephen in relation to this thing and, fearing a fit up, they both decided it would be better for them to go on their toes. You might ask why someone would go on the run for something they didn't do, or for a crime with zero evidence against them, but if the Old Bill had four or five high profile villains in the dock at the same time on the same charge, then for all intents and purposes they had their 'gang' and a far better chance of getting a guilty verdict once they'd choreographed their fit up, regardless of any guilt. Legs and Stephen knew this, such was the pressure on the law to get a conviction in relation to what had went off in Sunderland, so they both went on the trot.

The law knew we had family connections with the Travelling community. Aunt Sylvia and Uncle Joe lived on the camp at Hartford Bridge in Bedlington, along with their kids and extended family. My sister Michelle and her husband Jimmy also lived up there, as well Hymee and his mam and dad, Peter and Rita, who now had a chalet on there.

Maybe the police were tipped off, or maybe they just assumed Legs and Stephen would head to the camp. Either way, a raid of disproportionate measures was carried out on the camp, and it shook the residents to their core. It was a dawn raid and they hit three or four trailers simultaneously.

We're talking about 90 armed-response, snipers in the paddock near the trailers, several squad cars, riot vans, and two ambulances parked at the gate. They meant business! Hymee was on the camp at the time and vividly recalls waking up on the bunk, on that bright summer's morning in August, to the sound of every dog on the camp barking. Peering out of the window, he watched the whole episode unfold.

Marksmen in full body armour had taken up positions around the ground with automatic weapons. Looking up to the gate, he saw the glut of police vans and ambulances, unable to enter the site as they couldn't fit underneath the barrier. Hymee whispered through the chalet as loud as he could to mark his dads card. As Peter stumbled out of bed and reached the window, an unmarked vehicle pulled up outside his sister's place, and several plain-clothed, pistol-wielding serious crime squad piled out in the direction of Sylvia's door.

Uncle Joe took months to recover from having the barrels of a gun shoved up his nostrils when they crept into his trailer, waking him up at gunpoint, as he recalls, before speaking over their radio 'negative, negative, target absent.' They did the same to my brother-in-law, he had dark curly hair just like Legs, and they were double twitchy when they saw him come to the door of his trailer. Peter was targeted within seconds though, only just giving him time to lock his chalet door.

He refused to unlock the door. Besides Hymee, Peter's wife and daughter were in the chalet with him and he didn't want nervous gavas waving guns around the place, so insisted they disarm before he let them in.

'We'll smash the door down if you don't unlock it,' came the reply.

Within minutes, Hymee and Peter, both only half dressed, and half awake, were being arrested on suspicion of being involved in an armed robbery. They, along with Hymees' mam Rita, were handcuffed and carted off in full view of everyone on the camp, and as the car Hymee was in spun round at the bottom of the ground, he remembers seeing 'Roger' stood outside his trailer, with his two young boys, my nephews Jimmy and Thomas, by his side, aged about six or seven at the time, all looking shell shocked and understandably shaken.

Strangely, Hymee remembers the fact very well, as he recalls thinking to himself, 'Why have they all got suit trousers on?' Funny the things that stick in your mind.

Even the warden, Robert Riley, Uncle Joe's brother, who had never done a wrong thing in his life, was traumatised by the whole experience that morning, it made the man a nervous wreck for a long time after, God rest his soul (his passing was many years later and had nothing to do with this event).

To say it was on top, is a bit of an understatement! And both Legs and Stephen knew that, until John and Ken had been dealt with, their only chance of survival was to keep out of the way, and keep what looked like a gang out of the dock.

So that was that, they both went on the missing list for the next 12 months, and the exploits of that episode are well documented in our Stephen's book, *The Sayers: Tried and Tested.*

As far as I was concerned, it was a time when I could hardly leave the house on the West Road without getting followed or pulled over by the law. If I was on a night out with a girl, or with another couple, we'd get a tug. If I went to the shop for a pint of milk there'd be an unmarked car on me, not that I was a suspects, but eyes were on me because they thought I might be shuttling my brother around under their noses.

If we were off out somewhere and they were plotted up, we'd give them a wave as we pulled away and they would put their heads down as if we couldn't see them, it was laughable. Hymee had been locked up for three days in Houghton-Le-Spring following his arrest during the camp raid. His mother and father were also held at other police stations in the Durham area for the same period. They were the only ones to be removed from the camp, probably because of their name. Sayers. That much was obvious.

In remarkably similar circumstances to the time I was nicked with Stephen, the law confiscated money, approximately four grand, from Peter's chalet which were takings from the fruit shop that Hymee ran on the West Road. In this instance, however, the money was not returned for over a year, as Northumbria Police suggested it was a bung from the robbery in Sunderland. The fact that it could be accounted for without question as takings from the shop did not prevent the money from remaining in the custody of Northumbria Police until the case was over.

And similarly, while in custody, Tony encountered the same kind of juvenile scare tactics the CID used when they'd questioned me. He had to sit and listen to that sort of bollocks all weekend, before being released without charge, as were his parents. Not the most pleasurable way for a family to spend the weekend, but it was what it was, and they all just got on with it.

Legs did contact me often during this period obviously, and that consisted of visiting numerous call boxes, speaking in Cant (Romany dialect) or some unfathomable mix of slang that the law wouldn't understand. I would provide my brother with telephone numbers for other call boxes for our next conversation, again using slang to relay them, all done so that the law never had a clue what we were talking about, or the time to put a trace on a call box, also never using the same phone box twice. It was a surreal time and an episode that became a major turn in the road for some of us.

Like me, Tony was earning an honest living running the shop his dad had opened on the West Road along with the help of Big Stevie Baxter, who has been a loyal and trusted friend of the family since our childhood, and still stands the barrow today with Albert Sayers. The fruit game was in Tonys' blood and he turned the pitch into a cracking little business, despite having four grand taken out of his cash flow over the Sunderland thing. Even the early starts and the long hours weren't enough to make him consider alternative means of supporting himself, although the opportunity to do so was always available, but some people prefer to sleep with both eyes closed and not have to worry about who might be coming to their door.

Like we said earlier, the choices we were all making would mould the shapes of our lives, and like all men of the world, you live and die by the decisions that you make, especially when your livelihood, your liberty and your survival depend upon them.

I continued to work on building a business and was based at a shop on the West Road, about fifty yards from Hymee. Yes, we were always as thick as thieves – without being either! Tony was selling fruit and veg, I was selling schmutter. Both in our early 20s. Life was good. Straight money was being earned, and we were well-known around the town because of who we were.

Older people had watched us grow up and knew our dads and granddads, and the people of our generation knew us because of the exploits of our cousins and my brother, as well as the historical reputation of the family. However, for all the good times we were having as the new young men about town, some of our role models, the men and women who had made us who we were, were rapidly becoming figures of the past; each passing was like removing a building block from the foundations upon which we stood as a family.

Many of them lived to see the fight for legalisation of the barrows come to its conclusion, and for all it was considered a victory for us, it was in many ways a poisoned chalice. As a result, those who didn't live to witness the outcome of that life long battle weren't around to see the ramifications of it either.

Albert had secured the best deal he could in relation to the allocation of pitches, and what they agreed in 1981 was to be the status quo from that day to this. No additional pitches, and nothing left for our family on the streets. Even if we'd wanted to pull a barrow onto 'the front' at Nelson Street, like our family had done for generations, the new agreement prevented us from doing so.

In the mix of all of that, there was dispute about who got what pitch, and some shuffling about was done in order to try and appease all parties. Trying to please everyone is an impossible and thankless task (we know that from writing this book), but the deal had been struck, and we had to lie in the bed we'd made.

The self-policing thing became an issue, as many of the would-be grafters who wanted to pop up on Northumberland Street at the entrance of Eldon Square were friends of the family, either from the town or further afield. We didn't want to be responsible for putting the block on them, even if what they were selling didn't conflict with our costermonger livelihood.

No one would dream of sly pitching with a barrow any more, but plenty of swag grafters and plunder merchants would still try and have a go with a bit of gear, and the authorities didn't want that either.

The Mouse (Michael Carr) had teamed up with another great friend of the family, Terry Milligan. Terry, or Little Legs as he is known (everyone seemed to be known for their legs?), had been instrumental in bringing lines like the Rubik's Cube to Newcastle, a line that Albert Sayers and Georgie Kelly had gotten a nice few quid with. Terry volunteered to police that aspect of sly pitching, provided he was granted a license for a pitch of his own.

And so it came to pass that he and The Mouse were given a pitch right outside of the Eldon Square entrance on Northumberland Street, to work fancy goods; swag and plunder basically. It was as good as having a shop, and a shrewd move on Terry's part. It also cured the policing situation for the council and nullified a compromising situation for Albert and the Association.

With Terry and The Mouse now running their own pitch selling swag, they were only too happy to protect their right to do so. Everyone was a winner. But it wasn't nearly as much fun as it had been in the past. Street trading was now legit, constrained and mundane. Of course, just being on the cobbles selling a bit of gear was still a buzz, but the element of danger, the fact that you were bucking the system and dodging the law had always given it that bit of extra spice. It wasn't until that element was removed that the lads realised that the real fun part, the thing that set them apart, was no longer an ingredient in what they did for a living. Sometimes in life, getting the thing you want isn't nearly as rewarding as you'd imagined, and similarly, you never really appreciate what you've already got until it's gone.

Sadly, that was frequently the case throughout the 1980s. The arrival of each new member of the next generation of our family, five times removed from Granny Mariah, seemed to be matched by the loss of a member of the old guard; each passing felt like a piece of our history was dying with them. Of Mariah's remaining daughters, of which there were six to Billy Fleming and two to Big Tom, several were lost during these turbulent years, as well as Albert Cruddas. The closest to home was Tony's granny, Liza Sayers who died aged 74 on the 24th of June, 1984, and my granddad, Old Frankie Hewson, on the 6th of February, 1986. Both were immense characters who'd had a huge influence on our lives and the lives of all our family.

Once again, Newcastle saw funerals of spectacular proportions as cortèges 40 or 50 strong would weave their way through the streets they had worked all their lives. Barrows blanked with black cloths and white crosses on them, bystanders coming to a standstill as the processions crawled round the Grainger Market passing 'the front' on Nelson Street. Even the press would cover these events, and in Old Hewson's case they sent a news crew out to film the proceedings. Interment at Elswick or the West Road was the tradition, following a requiem mass at St Mary's Cathedral. We were, in spite of everything, God-fearing people, strong Catholics that practiced our faith; a faith that absolves you of your sins and conveniently wipes the slate clean after a hearty confession. Very convenient.

This was something Mariah had done religiously all her life, even in the wilderness years when she was a stray from the flock due to her relationship with Big Tom. It was an important thing for us, our faith, and those like Big Tom and even my father, had to convert to Catholicism in order to marry into the family under God's roof.

In a demonstration of our respect for the Church, the press, for once, reported a positive story involving John and Stephen Sayers, even if they did take a cheap shot in the paper, headlining the article in the *Evening Chronicle* with 'The Sayers Brothers involved with a famous Crook'. Very clever. The story, however, reported how the lads had retrieved a priceless, heavily ornate ceremonial staff, or crook (See what they did?); returning it to the Bishop's representative Canon Peter Strange in 1987. There had been an outcry after the valuable piece was stolen from a place of worship, and an appeal for its return was made in the press. The chaps had got to hear about this unscrupulous act, learning of the item's whereabouts through the grapevine, the street Telegraph, and using whatever means necessary, got their hands on the priceless artefact and returned it to its rightful place.

The 'crook' had been presented to the first Bishop of Newcastle, Rev. Ernest Wilberforce back in 1883, and had been described as irreplaceable by the Church following the raid on the cathedral in 1987. Thanks to John and Stephen, that same 'crook' is now back safely where it belongs. I know one swallow doesn't make a summer, but it does demonstrate that hearts and values were in the right place. Unlike so many criminals, our family knew there were certain lines that should simply never be crossed. The 'new breed of criminal' that the press were so keen to describe some of them as, were in reality the 'old school breed of criminal'; something the authorities failed to realise.

During the 1980s we suffered the loss of Liza and Old Hewson, Joss the Boss, Chrissy, both Muriel Donnelly and The Growler, Pow Patter, Old Coronation Kelly, and Aunt Bella, who died just four days after my wedding on the 30th of November, 1988. And just five days before the decade came to a close, we said our farewells, in traditional style, to the one and only Billy Buck, all of them the original old school.

We were dropping like flies, and that period claimed the lives of many of the people who had formed our foundation, and although many of their ways were now outdated, many of their values still remain as strong among some of us today as they did when they were on the pavement.

Funerals are a big part of life for members of a large family, and when you are from a family like ours, one that is known so well and in turn one that knows so many people, it often feels like you spend half your time paying your respects. Sadly, this is often the only time that a lot of people get to see each other, something that is always remarked upon by everyone on such solemn occasions. Some people our age have attended no more than two or three funerals in their lives, yet from the age of early adulthood it seemed we were never away from the West Road Crematorium or Elswick Road Cemetery.

In the 1980s alone, we attended ten direct family funerals, many in quick succession, and when you throw in the funerals of close friends and associates to that mix, the number could easily double or treble. We must have attended over 300 funerals each, mostly the same ones, from Glasgow to Gravesend, but mostly on our manor; professional mourners, but it comes with the territory. Respects must be paid, respect is important, and not just in death.

The decade had served up much heartache, many new challenges, many new faces, and many divisions. We may still have been close as a family, in as much as we were all still based in the West End, but cracks were beginning to appear, even though by this time many of us were literally living within shouting distance of each other around the Stanhope Street area, just up from the hallowed ground of St James' Park football stadium.

At one point, as well as myself, Tony (Hymee), his brother Peter and sister Dionne, Stephen Sayers, Young Gun (Stephen Shotton), Uncle Jimmy Kelly, his twin Frankie and his son, young Kelly all lived in old Tyneside flats on the back to back streets that snaked their way across Stanhope Street. We were always in and out of each other's homes, like one big dysfunctional family, and in the winter of 1988 there was cause to celebrate as one big happy family, which came as a welcome reprieve after so many funerals.

I, despite some controversy, got married in the November of 1988. It was a big affair, with the full Catholic ceremony at St Mary's. I had my cousin Tony by my side as best man, cousin Lisa on my other arm. Lisa was the sister to Joe, Frankie and Philip; daughter to Uncle Joe and Aunt Sylvia and was a Travelling girl born and bred. Now just to make things clear, and as we've stated before, when we refer to each other as 'cuz', it matters not to us whether that cousin is a first cousin, a cousin once removed or a second cousin, in some cases not even a cousin at all but just a very close friend of the family. As far as we're concerned, we were all just family, and if you weren't a cousin of some description then you were most likely either an uncle or an auntie, even if not a proper one by definition of bloodline.

Lisa, however, was the daughter of my mother's full cousin, which I believe made her my second cousin and, in the eyes of the Travelling community, marriages of such a nature are common place.

Marrying your own kind is not only a way of ensuring that you both knew what to expect from each other, but also a way of keeping the bloodline strong, and if it was good enough for the royal family, it was good enough for us. We had all seen how marrying straight goers or rank outsiders had unravelled over the years, look no further than Mariah and Billy Fleming, and numerous others who had come into the fold with unsuccessful outcomes. More importantly, however, such a union had to be accepted in the eyes of the Church, and gladly we received its blessing.

Lisa had come to work on the fashion shows with me as a model, and then later in the clothes shop on the West Road. We had known each other all our lives, we were family, and we got on like a house on fire. Such close proximity over a 12-month period from 1987 to '88, however, resulted in us developing an attachment towards each other. This scared both of us and we were unsure as to what we should do about it. But, love they say, conquers all, and after much deliberation and attempts to quell our mutual feelings for each other, I decided to make a life-changing decision. There was no way we were going to have a brief relationship and then just move on to the next boyfriend or girlfriend, that would simply not have been acceptable, and would have been disrespectful to not just both our families, but to our collective breed.

Travelling girls are chaste. They don't have casual relationships, it simply isn't done. Once they become involved with a man, it usually turns into marriage. No Travelling girl worth her salt wants to be known as a 'handy lass' or a luvney (a woman of questionable morals or ill repute), jumping from one man's arms to another. Their first love is usually their last and only love, and I was fully aware of the rules.

Lisa also knew this and knew that if we were to make our relationship public, it would have to be with honourable intention. It would be hard enough for us to get the blessing of every one of our family as it was, as there were still some of the old guard on the scene, and old-fashioned values would be difficult to overcome. I decided that if I was of a mind to settle down with someone I loved, someone who spoke my language and lived life the same way as me, then maybe this was the time to do so. I'd been out with a few sorts up to that point, had a couple of lengthy relationships even, but they were with regular girls, girls from a different background; 'gorja hantle' as we would call them, people not from the Travelling community, and certainly not people from our background.

Although I don't consider myself to be a Traveller as such, it's in my blood, and I had decided that I was about to pop the question to a full-time one. After a weekend in the Lake District in an old trailer with a few pals, one of them being my good friend Anthony Stuart, a fellow street trader and old school mate in whom I confided during our three days getting drunk and stoned with the boys in the lakes, I returned to Newcastle and had a word with Lisa.

I explained that I was aware we couldn't have a relationship for all of the obvious reasons, and that the only way we could was if I was to ask for her hand. She accepted the situation and resigned herself to the fact that we were not going to be together. What she didn't expect was for me to say that I was prepared to take that chance, if she was prepared to as well. We were both a bit shocked to say the least. I was only 23 and Lisa was just 19, but we knew we were in love and we knew the gravity of the decision we were about to make. Lisa, thankfully accepted my proposal, sat in a transit van on the yard of my parents' house on the West Road, very romantic. Gypsy style.

Within the year, we were married, in what became the wedding of the decade.

The news of this reverberated throughout the family and the people in the town that knew us, of which there were plenty, and not all of them agreed with it, but our family was never too far away from controversy. Once I'd been up to the camp and asked Uncle Joe for Lisa's hand, it was, and had to be, accepted by everyone. I remember he asked me for two horses, a dog and half a dozen chickens as a dowry, funny old fella Frenchie (his nickname).

So, the pews of our beloved cathedral were overflowing and the place was filled to the rafters as 500 daytime guests arrived from far and wide to celebrate our wedding. It was the full works, with us men in silver mohair morning suits, top hats and gloves, and Lisa, a vision in white with her cousin Dionne and best friend Pamela Rose as maids of honour. I had my sister's two boys, Jimmy and Thomas, and Legs' oldest son Bradley as pages. His daughter Bianca and Frankie Riley's baby girl Chantelle were bridesmaids. We were married on a Wednesday, as was tradition, and the ceremony took place in the dark as it was pissing down with rain by 3pm on that cold November day.

The idea was to have a wedding that went straight through. None of that daytime separate to the night-time bollocks. Once we'd jumped the broom (married), we were going to party, all day and all night. We had deliberated over a venue for the reception, and as we had specific requirements and needed to cater for 500 wedding guests and a further 500 who attended in the evening, we were somewhat limited to where we could hold it. We had friends in the catering game so we wanted to use them, Big Stan and Brenda who ran the Falcon in Prudhoe at the time, and we also wanted to take over the entire chosen venue for the duration; and it had to be in the town.

I'd been to see Zoots Navaro perform a couple of times and got on well with their front man Dave, and his female sidekick

Charlie. They were a Motown review band and did all the stuff we had grown up on. They had also taken over a venue on our manor and it seemed like it might just fit the bill. The only issue was, it was also Viv's gaff, and we all knew how he felt about the West End firm. Fortunately, I made Dave see the sense in allowing us to use the venue, it would be a huge earner for him, and I personally assured him that there would be no trouble on our special day.

He agreed to the plan, and even agreed for Zoots to perform at the reception at no cost, the fact that I placed an order for a hundred cases of Moet & Chandon probably tipped the scales. I also spoke to Viv about it on a night out with Roger, The Mouse and David Tate, the brother of the girl I'd worked the fashion shows with, when we bumped into him at Maddison's nightclub. Viv knew Roger and The Mouse, and was involved with David's sister-in-law. Knowing that I was not one of the West End types that were troublesome to him, Viv consented to the reception being held there and even agreed to us sorting out our own security on the door, truth being we didn't need any.

No one was going to cause trouble or attempt to gatecrash a thousand-strong wedding party full of fist fighting Travellers, target criminals, and every face in Newcastle; although Viv did put in an appearance, just to make sure we were treating the place with due respect, which of course we were, and also to raise a glass to me and Lisa, fair play to him. There was a mutual respect with Viv, despite all that was going down on the pavement, and although there were a few sticky buns around the place that day, they were only ones of the eating variety.

It was an incredible day, and night, as we danced and sang our way into the early hours, a gathering of cultures and a time to celebrate 'family', especially since we were all one family on both bride and groom's sides. Legs and Stephen were back off their toes, having handed themselves in for questioning and thankfully getting released without charge once John and Little Ken had been acquitted of any involvement in Sunderland. They, and every other face in Newcastle, as well as several from further afield, were out kicking their heights in full celebration with us and all our family of all generations.

The only one of the chaps unable to attend was our Michael, who was serving four years for an affray that took place in Bentley's nightclub in the run up to the wedding. Apart from that, it was a full squad, and a wedding that is still talked about to this day.

But the good times were short lived, as just like everything else in our family, what we get in one hand, is quite often taken away from the other, and after cause for celebration, the decade was about to end on a much more solemn note.

MEAN STREETS

With Billy Buck, Chrissy, Bella and Muriel Donnelly all passing away within a year of the wedding, and with the decade coming to an end, we had every right to think the 80s had served up enough heartache for us all. But one more member of our family, one from our generation, was taken from us during that fateful 12 months, and this time it wasn't by the Grim Reaper.

Within a year of the wedding, our cousin John Sayers received a custodial sentence that would set the bar higher than anyone could have ever imagined. Following his 12-month lie-down in Durham and subsequent acquittal over Sunderland just over a year earlier, John found himself in the dock once more on another serious armed robbery charge. The law weren't going to let him slip through their fingers this time, and following a lengthy trial for a £350,000 raid on Pritchard's Security depot in Durham, John found himself staring down the barrel of a 15-stretch.

The shockwaves could be felt all over Newcastle, and we were all stunned and devastated by the length of the sentence. John, at that point, infamously became elevated to the ranks of a serious career criminal whose reputation now spread far beyond the streets where we'd grown up. Such was his standing, and such was the trepidation with which the system dealt with him, he served his entire term as a Cat A, or Double Cat A prisoner, in some of the most notorious jails in the land.

The Sayers name was now becoming acknowledged as one of the most infamous family names in Newcastle's criminal underworld, both inside and outside of prison population, and the ramifications of that notoriety would have far reaching implications.

Legs had returned home from his time on the trot and was doing all he could to hang onto his marriage. He had three kids by now, but Legs' year of absence on the run, his philandering, and flamboyant ways, had worn so thin with his wife that she threatened to leave him unless he straightened out. From that point on, Legs made every attempt to turn himself around; however, it was a decision that tortured him for the remainder of his life and all who knew him and his legendary crazy ways could see that his decision to toe the mark in order to keep his family together was sucking the very life out of him. Legs had been an active criminal, his choice and his life. But he had responsibilities and other lives to consider now.

Living out the rest of his life without the buzz, the tickles and the kudos that comes with such a colourful career was hard to swallow, especially when he'd been used to it for so long, and especially when his cousins and pals were still at it. It was a tough and brave choice for Legs to make, and it was the beginning of the end for him as the Jack the Lad he had always been. It was, however, the honourable decision and one that we all ultimately make when it comes to family, because whatever the circumstances are, family comes first.

Never for us to be too far from each other, Hymee came out of the shop on the West Road about the same time as I came out of Catalogue West (my shop along the road from his). Hymee started working in the ice-cream business with the Gregorio brothers, a family of Italian school friends from the West End, good boys and good friends to this day, before returning to his roots and taking up on an offer from another good fella, Big Peter May, to help run his fruit and veg wholesale operation on Mill Lane.

Peter was another son of the bookmaker that fronted the Krays with Lucky Joe Lisle and my dad back in the 60s. Tony had also produced the first two Sayers boys of the next generation in 1990. His girlfriend, mother of his identical twins, was sister to Legs' wife. That lot must have had a real taste for our breed, as another of their sisters was knocking about with our Stephen at the time.

They both went on to produce kids with them, Becky Liza was born to Stephen, and Hymee had the twins, Tony and Jack. Lisa and I, however, were in no such hurry to start a family of our own, living on the camp for the first year of married life, before travelling the country working gaffs (markets) all over England.

I cashed up the shop and the fashion show business as the recession kicked in, and decided to go back to my roots. I loved the street life, and if I couldn't work the pavement in my own town, then I had to work elsewhere in the country. We grafted markets from Inglestone in Scotland to Torquay on the south coast, and everywhere in between. I was a capable grafter, having had the best of teachers in the shape of Old Hewson, Albert Sayers and Georgie Kelly, and I knew how to pull a pitch and work a hedge.

It was while doing so on Catterick Market that I was approached by Dennis was offered the chance to go to London with him to work the R.O (the Run Out) or 'ram' as it is known. But I made it clear that there would have to be a role for Lisa too.

The Run Out shop on Oxford Street was not due to open for a few months, but Dennis's son Elliot was already grafting out of a pitch there with watches, perfume and a bit of dreck jewellery. So, we packed up the Escort van that we virtually lived out of and set off for the Smoke. But not before we experienced the arrival of ecstasy, and 1989's unforgettable summer of love.

The new love drug wave, and the culture that went with it, was the most incredible time, and one that changed the face of the club scene beyond all recognition in the 1990s, as well as the face of Newcastle's underworld. Charlie (cocaine) had always been around, and the 60s had been the pill-popping decade of purple hearts, LSD, blueies, uppers, downers, and any-other-way-you-likers, but nothing compared to the impact of ecstasy.

No matter how much people wanted to kiss and cuddle each other, express love and emotion for each other, male or female, in the middle of a dance floor when one (an E) come on you, which usually happened within half an hour of dropping it; there were some people who wanted to kill each other in their battle to control its supply. Equal and opposite reactions in perfect synergy once again. Together with other mind-altering substances, drugs were taking over as the business of choice for many villains with the arrival of ecstasy. The blaggers were up against it, with surveillance techniques and police detection systems becoming more and more sophisticated; and like any other city, town or even village at that time, power struggles emerged between rival gangs in their battle to control the supply of ecstasy.

Newcastle was no different, and it already had a history of high-profile crime, with more than its fair share of 'gangsters' keen to capitalise on this new line of business. It also had a new Sheriff in town in the massive shape of Viv Graham. There were plenty of fighting men on Tyneside, one or two of them came from within our ranks, but Viv was special, and now had a legion of pumped-up, steroid-taking doormen at his command.

Besides his firm being the common enemy of all the drug dealers (apart from the Old Bill), there were more than enough rival firms keen to take control of this lucrative new business. As the tidal wave of love, peace and ecstasy swept over the youth population with illegal raves and warehouse parties popping up at a moment's notice, the law had more than enough on their plate, before they had time to even contemplate tackling the gang warfare that was about to ensue.

Hot summers, hot clubs and hot tempers were the tone of the late 1980s and early 90s, and even without the burgeoning drug problem and all that went with it, the country was in the grip of what seemed to be an all-out rebellion against the state, as a heatwave of riots sparked off in hot spots up and down the land.

The Meadow Well Estate in North Shields, just outside of Newcastle, was the catalyst for a spate of 'youth uprisings' around the city as disgruntled teenagers held pitched battles with the law on the streets of the town during the first two years of the 1990s. Some of these were fuelled by incidents that sparked unrest, like the ones in Meadow Well which were in response to the death of a young joyrider who lost his life after being chased along the Coast Road by the police.

Others, particularly those in the West End, were riots simply for the hell of it, as the place really began to live up to its Wild West reputation. Some suggested that the mini riots in the West End were orchestrated by certain notorious families on the manor at that time, in a display of how they could command a group of would-be soldiers to carry out their bidding; a group of fucking cowboys more like.

But whatever the reason, and on top of everything else that was going on, several flare-ups occurred during the summer of 1991, and in one particular riot in Elswick, the Dodds Arms, a long standing and favoured watering hole for West Enders, was completely burnt to the ground. It might not have been such a bad thing in fairness, and probably prevented a few more unsavoury incidents if the Doddsies had continued to live up to its nickname of The Stabbers Arms.

In contrast to the mindless violence and disorder that was being reported from riots all over the country, the love drug had changed the club scene beyond all recognition, as sharp suits with collar and ties went out the window, and baggy tops, jeans and trainers became the dance craze dress code of the E'd up raver, while the music became as potently hypnotic as the drug that everyone was on. Our Saturdays changed beyond all recognition. From getting suited and booted and posing the night away in Rick's bar then Tux, to meeting in the Biz Bar at the bottom of Westgate Hill, a seedy little basement bar and an out and out West End drinking den, where everyone would meet in preparation for a night of loved-up ecstasy in Walkers.

The club of choice for the West End firm was Walkers, formerly La Dolce Vita, which in turn had stood on the site of Mariah's warehouse many years ago. And just like the Dolce, and the warehouse, Walkers saw plenty of action during the euphoric weekends of the early 90s.

We could often be 30 or 40-handed by the time we left the Biz Bar, and everyone in the place would be on one, or two, or three. We'd weave our way up to Blackfriars where the queue would be down the street and round the corner as hundreds of young ravers clambered to get in the place. It was standard for us not to queue anywhere, but when you're mob-handed, and there's about 200 punters waiting in line, getting our mob in could easily trigger off a bit of bother if the security were seen to let 30 of us waltz straight through the front door. Like a modern-day scene from *Goodfellas*, the side doors that lead through the kitchen would be opened for us, and we would be ushered through to the club by the doormen, and immediately head to the first floor and the top corner bar.

Just like all other venues of choice for the West Enders, we always had our own section, and unless you were on the firm, you weren't getting anywhere near our bar. Not that many people tried it, although the odd park ranger (stranger) would stray into our section, but they rarely hung round long enough to get a drink.

It was the strangest of times, and seeing people you'd grown up with, rough and ready people, lads who were violent and loved a fight, all dancing, cuddling and telling each other how much they loved each other, was truly something to behold.

Even our cousin, Joe Riley and good family friend Adam Hoppy and their crew from the sticks, who were still turning out in suits and using other clubs that hadn't really embraced the E scene, came along to see what all the fuss was about. I can recall about half a dozen of them turning up at Walkers one night, all looking aces and dressed to the nines, while everyone in the club was jumping around like lunatics, rushing off their nuts, some sucking dummies, some with Vicks inhalers sticking out their noses, or snorting bottles of poppers, pumped-up and sweating as the music and euphoria of the ecstasy turned the club into a rave before your very eyes. And what an eye opener it was for Joe's firm.

They hung around for a while, but when it started to heat up in our corner and some of our team started swilling each other with pints of water and ice buckets, they soon shuffled out the way to avoid their tailor-made suits from getting drenched. Some of them were a bit weary of the new scene and it took a while for them to ease into the culture that eventually swept the nation, but mad Adam, who was never seen out in anything other than a suit, silk shirt and hanky, turned up the following week wearing baggy shorts, sweatshirt and sneakers, got off his nut and started swilling with the rest of them to the chorus of Legs' rallying cry 'you cannot get wetter!'

After months of back on, and back off with his missus, Legs had reappeared, and for all his legendary exploits, he burst onto the E scene, bigger, better and madder than ever. He was never going to let this era pass him by.

Even people like The Mouse, and our older cousin Frankie Donnelly, men with 10 or 15 year on us, got sucked up and swallowed in by this intoxicating era, and they 'kicked it' with the best of them. The swilling job came about as a result of having to cool down in the hot, thumping nightclubs, and what better way to do it than to have your pal drown you with an ice bucket full of water. But Legs being Legs, he had to go one better, and one particular Saturday, as the crowds filed out of Walkers and into the street for the ritual car park parties that always took place after the club closed and people were still off their nuts, he pulled one of his crazy Legs like stunts, one that has since gone down in club folklore.

It didn't matter which flight of stairs you used to get down from the first floor where our schmeck (particular place) was, you'd be in a bottleneck to get out the door of Walkers, in fact it was harder to get out the place than it was to get in, even if you weren't a straight goer. On this particular night we were all shuffling down the main staircase with hundreds of others. The staircase went down one flight to a half landing and doubled back down the last flight to the lobby and the exit. The place was gridlocked as the heaving crowds sang and bounced in unison, even turning waiting in line into a make shift party.

We would all be looking around for each other to make sure we were together on leaving, before deciding where to go next, which was usually somewhere like the Bay Horse at the Big Lamp, or the Balmoral further up the hill which was ran by Pat

Younger, whose son Sean, a good lad and a close friend, invariably had the spare keys on him, which meant we had a venue in which to finish off the night. God bless Sean and may God rest his soul, as he sadly passed away a few years back.

Anyway, we were all crammed on the staircase when Legs appeared at the top landing. He must have looked at the mob of popeyed clubbers all heaving and sweating as they struggled to escape to the car park, when he decided to let out another of his rallying cries, 'EVERYBODY LOVES IT!' The jam-packed crowd responded in unison, however for Legs, nature was about to call, and when you've got to go, you've got to go; even when you can't move, you've got to go.

Faced with either wetting himself, or coming to some other arrangement, Legs proceeded to relieve himself all over the gridlocked crowd below, which we were all fucking part of. With no one able to move in any direction, Legs continued to shower the crowd while shouting, 'Yi cannit get nee wetter!'

The screams and shouts of disgust, the effing and blinding and hurling of abuse were short lived, just like his latest moment of madness thankfully, but with everyone already soaked with sweat, or covered in drink and water anyway, he somehow managed to get the heaving crowd shouting the same thing back to him. It was unbelievable. Maybe there was just so much love in the air with the Es, or maybe the fact that no one could move out of the way, and they didn't give a fuck by then anyhow, the potentially volatile situation simply turned on its head. Whatever it was, to see your crazy brother doing what he did, and somehow managing to get the crowd on his side as they all chanted back to him, 'Yi cannit get nee wetter!' was incredible and completely unforgettable.

Legs got got locked up that night when the law broke up the car park party, which they always did, and if it wasn't that night, then it could have been any one of many Saturday nights in the summer of 1989, when he would get carted off in a meat wagon, as the Old Bill turned up to disperse the car-park parties; pissing on everybody's night out.

Street trading was in our blood and I was now working Oxford Street. That was about as good as it gets for any street trader worth his salt. It was a time just after the recession of mid-80s, and within a year or two shops were closing down all over the country. With such extortionate rent and rates on Oxford Street, the property owners were only too happy to let someone take over a place in order to cover the expense, regardless of their credentials. They became far less stringent with regard to who they were leasing to, as long as you had the money to pay the R&R, you were in. So, Lisa and I landed there in the spring of 1991, raring and ready to go to work. We had a great time down there and went to work with Elliot and Sascha, Dennis's son and daughter. Working the MOT with the watches for a few weeks, lumping up with the perfume and snide jewellery before the shop was ready to open, and working Oxford Street was a real buzz.

I will never forget pulling a pitch one time, with Lisa at the front working as 'rick in', when I looked up and saw a familiar face in the hedge. It was Dennis Norden of *It'll be Alright on the Night* fame (a popular TV bloopers program that was running at the time). He watched with great interest as I drew the hedge in and got them tee'd up for the sale. Pulling pitches and twirling a hedge is basically a performance, and when it's done well it's a pleasure to watch. As soon as I delivered the 'bat' and Lisa dropped in with the first 'Yes' and pulled up her money, that was it, I couldn't have given a toss if the Queen was spectating, it was time to take the dough, and we didn't half take some too. Oxford Street was not just a great experience, it was a gold mine and we had some great times there.

The opening of the shop, however, was not without its problems.

A rival firm was about to open up just a few hundred yards from us on the other side of Oxford Street, and although a mutual agreement had been met by both parties, it soon became apparent that the other firm were less than noble when it came to upholding their side of the deal, and on the first day of opening a serious wakeup call suggested all was far from well with the opposition.

I remember clearly:

A meat wagon full of Old Bill turned up just as I was in the middle of pulling our very first pitch, apparently responding to a complaint about the noise from the speakers we had placed outside the shop front on the pavement. I'd only been at it five minutes, although they did tell me I could be heard in Marble Arch. They made us clear the shop while they read the riot act. They hadn't long left before we got another visit as I attempted to pull the second pitch. This time from someone with far worse intentions.

I'd been spieling for about 10 minutes, drawing punters into the store, warming them up for our first sale. There must have been a hundred eager bargain hunters in the shop as it was filling up nicely, when I noticed a big lump lurking at the door, looking more than a little conspicuous. Continuing to get about my job, I kept an eye on him as he muscled his way down the front. By the time he reached the counter in front of the rostrum, on which I was standing, he seemed to be twice the size again. I just didn't fancy this fella at all, and my suspicions were qualified when he pulled out a machete from inside his leather jacket and shouted to me, 'Are you Dennis?'

I didn't even have time to reply before Dennis darted out the shop screaming blue murder. The crowd of punters scattered in abstract panic. Fortunately, the big lump took off as well, but not before letting everyone know that what he was waving about in his hand was for Dennis, and that he'd be back to serve him up with it.

The frighteners had been put on us in no uncertain terms, and it affected the dynamics of our time down there from that point on. The store closed for the day, and we didn't return to graft for a week while Dennis tried to straighten things out. Thankfully he did, and we were back to work, but by now he had a new partner, and a corner of the take had to go in their direction every week from then on. The firm Dennis enlisted to protect us were one of the most notorious in London at the time, and one whose path I would cross again some years later when I lived in Tenerife, but that's another story.

Suffice to say, the addition of another partner made life much harder for Dennis, and it took the dairy off the job in many ways. For my part it was a case of only going to graft if I knew we had the best firm on our side. Had this been happening in my home town, then I would have known exactly who we were dealing with, and who the best firm was, but I was not on my manor, however, we were saved by the 'A Team' and I was happy that they were capable enough to iron out any problems we might have encountered with the opposition."

Dennis was under mounting pressure as he was parting with a huge corner of his take to get protection, and feeling that it was time to move on, I parted company with Dennis and co after the summer and went back on the gaffs, before returning home to Newcastle for the Christmas.

"We moved back into the West Road house for a while and enjoyed the company of Aunt Mariah for a short time. She had been poorly following the passing of Coronation, and my mam had offered her to come and convalesce with us following a spell in hospital, rather than go straight back home to her bachelor boys, Georgie and Thomas. The West Road house had become another open house for the family, and many good times were had there, and I remember fondly those months with Aunt Mariah under our roof, as we'd sit of an evening and listen to tales of the 'good old days.' Mariah was a character very much in the mould of her mother and name sake, witty, cheeky and sarcastic, yet charming with it. She loved a glass of stout, just like her mother had, although she stopped short of heating it up with a poker. We all made a fuss of her during that time with us, and it was great to spend such quality time with her. I'd never know my own granny Sarah, so spending a few months under the same roof as one of her sisters was a pleasure. I learned a lot from her about Sarah, Granny Mariah and our families past. It was the time when the seed about writing this story was planted.

An entire book could be written just about the tales she told us, and she agreed every time I told her she should have written a book. 'Aye' she would say, just the same way Old Mariah did, 'I'll have to learn how to write first, son.'

Aunt Mariah planted the seed and set me on this path before she sadly passed away in the autumn of 1992 aged 80. A great loss, and yet another procession through the streets we'd traded on for over a century took place as the press paid tribute to yet another 'Barrow Queen of Newcastle', in similar homage to her infamous mother. Even though that was over a quarter of a century ago, I knew this would someday have to be done, however, the story was still unfolding, and I knew the time wasn't right. Life for me was about to become very real and overtake any plans that I might have had to do anything about it, and the story, after all, was never going to go away. In fact it could only unfold even further, and it did, as life for all of us took over and many plans, like those made by mice and men, went completely awry."

On the streets of the city centre, life was more stable, for the barrow boys at least, as legalisation became the gateway into the system. My old man, Tony's' dad , and now Uncle Albert all had legitimate business interests and had shown some of our generation the way ahead. Living outside of the mainstream was becoming far more problematic, particularly if you were ever to own your own home or have a successful business. This was a massive leap in mindset from the old ways when everyone dealt in cash, and what you had and where you got it from was under far less scrutiny. 'The life' was in some ways becoming diluted, and for those among our ranks who chose to continually buck the system, life was about to become very dangerous. The Wild West End became wilder than ever, as rival families started flexing their muscles, and literally began shooting lumps out of each other.

Viv and his firm were vying for outright control of the doors in Newcastle, and his anti-drug approach was not received well by those with a vested interest in its supply. He was cautious about the West End firm, because unlike any other enemies he might have made in the region, the West End firm was made up largely of active criminals, and some very violent ones at that, people who'd shoot you as soon as have a row with you. Viv had already been the victim of a shooting in 1988 and lived under constant threat during his time as a major force on Tyneside. There was, however, a degree of mutual respect between Viv and our family, although some people around the town went out of their way to promote bad blood between both parties.

Prevention is always better than cure, and bloodshed can be very bad for business, so while other families in the West End were running around shooting up the place, and each other, conflict between our lads and Viv was skirted around with mutual caution.

Several of the Harrison brothers became gunshot victims during those turbulent times, and the Conroys were also on the receiving end of frequent gunfire, as tit-for-tat reprisals became a weekly event in the scramble to be recognised as a serious firm. Buildings were shot up, drive-by shootings and vicious assaults became common place, and the West End really wasn't a safe place to be anymore, even civilians got caught up the middle of the copycat riots of the same time. Viv was knocking people out like it was going out of fashion, and lots of people didn't like it. Keeping friends close and enemies closer was the way forward and, despite the events in Santino's with Peter Donnelly, the other chaps in our family tried to maintain the status quo with Viv. They even joined forces in an incident at Hobo's Nightclub on Bath Lane, near the bottom of Westgate Hill, which had formerly been called Change Is, and had been owned by Bob Monkhouse.

The violent assault on a doorman at the club resulted in Viv and one of his associates receiving a custodial sentence along with our Stephen and a couple of his firm. Contrary to popular belief, there was a mutual respect and friendship between Viv and our lads, and their time shared behind bars cemented that, although involvement between them fizzled out following their release from Durham in 1993.

One episode that could have altered the status quo, however, was the fight that never happened. A young giant of a fella from Teesside called Lee Duffy had burst onto the scene, and his reputation was spreading throughout the North East like wildfire. Lee had run into our John in jail and they became friends. John had asked Lee to look out for his brother Michael on his moves around the prison system. And so it came about that Lee Duffy and Michael Sayers got to know each other as they crossed paths in the prison population, having met while both serving a four-year sentence.

They had both been sentenced on the same day, for separate offences of affray, and were due to be released at the same time. Lee, however, received a further six months for bashing a screw and, as a result served, a half a stretch longer than Michael. Upon his delayed release, Michael and Hymee (the gigglers), were asked by Stephen, who had yet to meet Lee, to go down to Eston with a bung for him to help him get on his feet. The Duffer, as we called him, ended up spending many a weekend in the town, often in the West End. He was a fearsome individual and like all hardmen, he feared no one, least of all this Viv Graham he was hearing so much about. It was on one such weekend that he decided he would take a walk into the city centre and 'put it on' Viv there and then, right on his own doorstep.

Fuelled by a two-day bender holding court with the crowd who'd been on it with him, he marched his pumped up drinking partners down the town like the Pied Piper, in search of the Big Fella, with one thing on his mind. He sparked half a dozen doormen on Viv's firm that night, and let them all know that he was looking for their guv'nor.

Viv didn't put an appearance in and Lee felt he'd won a moral victory. It did little to ease the tension between Viv and the West End lads and served only to put more distance between them. The lines were becoming blurred as the mutual respect between Viv and our lads was being tested by the actions of others, people who were in our orbit, and in some cases even people from within our family. God only knows what might have happened that night if Viv had fallen into the trap of fronting up The Duffer. It was a potential fight that everyone talked about, but one that never came to fruition, but if it had, it would have been a fight to end all fights, and with hearts the size of those two, it might well have been a fight to the death.

In spite of everything that was going on in Newcastle at that time, we can only speak as we find, and although Viv made countless enemies in his time as a serious figure on Tyneside, he had always been civil whenever we met him, and for every enemy he undoubtedly made, he made twice as many friends, not least of all from within our ranks.

Unfortunately however, the pressure cooker that was Newcastle in the early 90s was about to explode for Viv. On New Year's Eve 1993, he was violently gunned down on Wallsend High Street, virtually on the stroke of midnight. He was shot three times by an unidentified gunman and died in the early hours of New Year's Day, aged just 34. RIP, Viv.

A huge investigation ensued and many people were dragged in for questioning, including some of our lads, but with such a string of obvious enemies left in his wake, Viv's murder became one of several unsolved crimes that occurred during that turbulent decade.

Although many of these events were not directly part of our lives, they were explosive events which were going on around us, typical of what was occurring on the mean streets of our city.

It's easy to *bullet point* much of what was happening on the streets back then, a violent and terrifying period of warfare that has gone down in gangland folklore:

- Howard Mills: Boxer, doorman; leg blown off by shotgun, 1989
- Michael Sayers: Shot several times through a window while drinking in the New Darnell public house, 1993

- Harry Orange: Caught in the crossfire of the attack on Michael
- Viv Graham: Assassinated, New Year's Eve 1993
- Frankie Kelly Jr: Shot in Macey's Bar, 23 December 1995
- John Brian Sayers (John Sr): Shot in the face at close range, 1995
- Paul Logan: delivery driver; shot dead in Shotley Bridge, December 1995
- Freddie Knights: Shot dead on his mother's doorstep, 20 September 2000
- Peter Gowling: Shot dead in his flat, Valentine's Day 2001

We're not speaking out of school in relation to any of the dreadful incidents that took place during that period. They are all well documented and the details we've outlined are available in the public domain. However, with the exception of one of the above, many of those incidents and tragic losses of life remain, to this day, like so many other violent crimes at that time, unsolved mysteries.

In the midst of all this, two of the new feared West End families were doing a great job for the law by almost cancelling each other out in a free-for-all feud that spilled onto our streets, bringing the spotlight well and truly down on the Wild West End.

The war between the Harrisons and the Conroys in the early 1990s is now also part of Tyneside folklore. Brothers James, Joseph and Andrew Harrison were all jailed for ten years in 1995 after they were found guilty of orchestrating a terrifying gun battle in the West End, staging an armed attack on the Conroy's Happy House Hostel on Westmorland Road, the heart of Harrison territory. But members of the rival clan fired back at the Harrisons from inside the building, forcing innocent passers-by to run for cover.

The shoot-out was said to be revenge for a petrol-bomb attack on a caravan belonging to their father, Trevor Harrison, one time partner in the scrap yard with Uncle John.

The 'Harras' believed their reputation would make them untouchable, suspecting no one would dare come forward to give evidence against them in court. But the accounts of three witnesses led to their conviction at York Crown Court, although all the witnesses were forced to change their identities and start a new life away from the North East.

The Conroys were also in a spot of bother when Paddy Conroy was jailed for just under 12 years after he was convicted of kidnapping and torturing Billy Collier, a relative of the Harrisons, as part of a reprisal attack. Collier was allegedly handcuffed and tied up, before having the sides of his nostrils ripped off and his front teeth pulled out with pliers.

The attack was said to be revenge for an arson attack on one of Conroy's properties, and for the Harrison clan desecrating Conroy's father's grave. Paddy Conroy was convicted of torture, kidnap and false imprisonment along with associate David Glover, in 1995.

Again, all documented publicly, and all part and parcel of what our streets had become. A long way from the days of back street 'jump ups' and selling a bit of hoist to a barrow boy, some of whom had now also become bad boys themselves.

The local newspapers were full of what was going on, and the publicity only served to fuel speculation and enhance reputations, as shootings, stabbings, back stabbings and double crossings were rife, and more and more risks were being taken in the fight to become the main players in the city. Because of such bravado, because so much crazy stuff was going on, and because so many lies were being told, Stephen and Michael somehow became embroiled in a plot to extort money from a wealthy individual, a former nightclub family friend back in the Tux days. He had unfortunately befriended other members of the criminal fraternity in Newcastle, and the mix was being put in by certain individuals with hidden agendas.

Consequently, Stephen and Michael were foolishly baited into a trap that resulted in them both receiving what turned out to be the lengthiest prison sentences in British history for the charges they were found guilty of; a so-called '£50,000 blackmail plot', for which Stephen received 10 and half stretch, and Michael got a 12.

The sentence was an outrageous disgrace. It was absolute mayhem on Tyneside, and one shock just seemed to be followed in quick succession by the next. While many of our family had made valid attempts to blend into society and become part of the system, including me and Tony, one branch of our breed had elevated themselves and their name to a whole new level of notoriety.

The reputation they now possessed would go on to be one that would definitely be 'tried and tested at the highest level'.

DAMAGE DONE

The die was well and truly cast by now. John, Stephen and Michael; the Sayers brothers, born to Uncle John and Aunt Yvonne, had all acquired fearsome reputations, thanks not only to their many dangerous and violent exploits, but also the sensationalised press coverage dedicated to them. The Sayers name carried weight like none before them on Tyneside ever had, and none ever since have come close to.

The barrow boys had seen their day with the authorities, and the century long battle for licensed pitches had been brought to a close once and for all in 1981, yet both evolutions came at a price. What had happened, had happened; history was written, and the clock could not be turned back. The damage had been done in many respects, and some of that damage would become something that still haunts many of our family today.

The shooting of Uncle John occurred as the two of us were training with Stephen in the makeshift gym we'd put together in the basement of the hostel on the bottom of Westmorland Road, owned by Uncle John. This was at the height of the gun-toting days of the 90s, so when we got the news by phone and drove frantically to the hospital, we were at a loss for who might have been responsible, since so many incidents of this nature were going off at the time. We arrived at the General Hospital on Westgate Road to find Uncle John's car parked outside A&E.

He'd driven himself there after the attack on his life, and I remember pulling up outside the entrance with Stephen and Hymee and seeing his BMW parked awkwardly with the driver's door still wide open. There were bits of flesh, bone and blood splattered all over the inside the motor. It transpired that he'd been shot through the jaw at pointblank range by someone he'd been talking to as he sat in his car with the window down. It wasn't a gang related incident, but a macabre and sinister set up. It was an attempt to take his life, as well as some of his money, which he was going to hand over in exchange for some computer discs that allegedly held information which could help release his son John Henry from jail and the 15-year sentence he was doing as a result of the Pritchard robbery.

In his attempt to clear his son's name, Uncle John almost lost his life, and the tense time that followed while he received hospital treatment, was spent vigilantly by many of us guarding him from a possible follow-up on his life from anyone hoping to finish off their botched assassination attempt.

The other horrifying incident that remains firmly imprinted on our minds, was the shooting of our lovable rogue of a crazy frisk-filled cousin, young Frankie Kelly.

Frankie had been out drinking in town on the run up to Christmas 1995, and I will never forget receiving the call at the West Road house, from Hymee.

'Cuz, our Frankie's been shot! He said.'

I was shocked, but again, since shootings were the flavour of the month, I wasn't totally gob smacked. Not until he told me that young Kelly had been found dead at the scene. I dropped the phone and went cold. I couldn't believe what I was hearing. My heart sank and I screamed and shouted uncontrollably on hearing about my dear cousin. For all he was no angel, he was certainly not involved with all the crazy gun warfare going on in the city. To meet with such a brutal ending in the prime of his life, aged just 28, in full sight of a bar full of Christmas revellers, was completely unthinkable.

I miss Frankie massively, and from that day to this I place a wreath on his grave every Christmas. It's no big deal, but it's my way of letting him know how much he meant, and that he will never be forgotten by me. May you rest in peace, dear cousin."

The seemingly continual heartache endured by the family was thankfully punctuated with relief of some description.

For all the madness and sadness of the 1990s, it was also time when much new blood was being brought into the fold, and the happiness that comes with the arrival of new children somehow seemed to compensate for the blood we'd lost; a positive distraction from the senseless amount of blood being shed.

We'd thankfully all grown out of the rave scene, which for us came just in time as we were all starting to settle into lives with children of our own. This would be the new generation of our family. But what kind of breed would this generation be? There would be no street trading barrow boys amongst them, that avenue had been closed to us the day we achieved legalisation, and the agreement with the council had put an end to that chapter. In one hand, and out the other.

Some of our fathers had made the leap from spaceman to business man since the 1970s. 'Spaceman' is a term used to describe someone that doesn't exist in the system, has no discernible occupation, pays no tax and receives no benefits, existing only by the merits of their own survival tactics. Many of us now, however, had become tax-paying, service-providing, contributing members of society. Our generation had caught the tail end of the 'good old days,' and the streets were not just in our blood, but the place where we had grown up, been educated, and knew the rules of.

For myself, it was all about business. I jumped from barrows to the run out, from fashion shows to shops and a café, and in 1992 took over yet another premises on the West Road (it's a long old road that West Road) and opened a carpet warehouse with my dad and Legs. It was still impossible to keep Legs motivated about going to work, and the only thing he could be relied upon for was his unreliability.

Me and Lisa were living in the bosom of our family, in the heart the West End, when we were blessed with our firstborn child and son, Louis, in 1995, before moving out of our ground floor Tyneside flat and into a nice big house in Wideopen, on the outskirts of the city. I was 30 years old, and we'd been married for seven years before he came along, during which time we'd worked hard, played hard, and gotten everything out of our system. Preparation over, it was time to settle down and start a family, and life for me at that time could not have been much better.

Hymee was running the show on Mill Lane at the wholesale fruit and veg warehouse with Peter May. Single once more, he had a healthy relationship with his twin boys, moved back in to the West End, and was enjoying the best of both worlds: singledom and parenthood simultaneously.

We both still hit the town occasionally, usually with Joe, Adam and the rest of the Gypsy crew and, just like the old times, we would turn out looking aces, suited, booted and looking the part. The crazy days of the rave scene were long behind us, when everyone went mashugana (silly, crazy) and dressed like bums.

Trelawney's had long since closed its doors, and the new destination for all the chaps was Leaf, a high-end outfitters on Pilgrim Street, just across the road from the nick. The place was opened by a good friend of the family and the man behind the famous Sergeant Peppers jeans brand, Brian Smith. He and his lovely wife Josie still serve the best dressed people in Newcastle to this day from the same shop, although an outfit for the weekend costs a lot more now than it did from Geoff, even after Brian looks after you. You see, some of the old habits die hard, and just as our granddads and our dads had always been the men about town, unpolished diamonds, sharp-suited, gentlemanly and charismatic, loveable rogues, we instinctively carried ourselves the same way, when we weren't full of E.

Our views, our street smarts and our outlooks were inherent qualities that filtered down through the generations, however, the reputation that our forefathers had cultivated over the decades had culminated into a new reputation that was now far greater than the sum of its parts.

John, Stephen and Michael, now all behind bars serving a total of 37 years between them, had become public enemies in the eyes of the law, all sadly leaving sons and daughters behind them to endure the heartbreak of being separated from their fathers for such huge chunks of their young lives. Much of the latter half of the 90s was spent touring the country's high security prisons in order to visit our convicted, high profile cousins.

Time was spent driving up and down the country, on the train or, on the odd occasion, in the sky. Joe 'the pilot', a friend of Uncle John's, had a small light aircraft in which he shuttled some family visitors to and from Parkhurst on the Isle of Wight. It really was planes, trains and automobiles for a while.

As well as Parkhurst, the lads spent spells of time in Frankland, Full Sutton, Wakefield, Whitemoor, Belmarsh and Brixton. That's an additional punishment as well you understand. Housing a prisoner as far away from their loved ones as they can, is simply an attempt to make visits costly, complicated and time consuming; the hope being that the prisoner gets fewer visits and is therefore more isolated. For the majority of their time in those places, they would be Cat A, or even Double Cat A, usually locked up for 23 hours a day. And often housed with some of the most dangerous people in the land.

It was a sad and a hard time for everyone involved, not just the lads, but also for the families they'd left behind. Years of travelling the country to see their family in some of the most inhospitable environments imaginable, was not a pleasant experience, but rightly or wrongly, the punishment is meant to be for everyone, not just the convicted.

We were all that much older by now. Lives were mapped out for some of us, at Her Majesties pleasure for the foreseeable future at least, but for those of us with lives still to manage, supporting our cousins in their time of need became something we would have to do. So, when Michael called Hymee from Whitemoor and asked him to round us up to come on a visit, suited and booted for the frisk, we were only too happy to do so.

We landed at the Central Station early doors, dressed like two Philadelphia lawyers, and five minutes later our cousin Joe Riley, Mad Adam, and another relation of ours, Frankie Slater, turned up looking just as sharp. We'd not all been together in a while, having grown out of the weekend club scene, so spirits were high as we were all out again suited up, with a full day in each other's company ahead of us. Although we were going on a visit and not a jolly, we ended up making it a visit to remember. Put half a dozen of us together, and anything can happen.

By the time our train arrived at Peterborough, we'd already had a drink with our breakfast, slipping into first class for a bit of scran, and plotting up there 'til we reached our destination. With an hour to kill before our connection to March, the nearest station to Whitemoor prison, we fired a couple of vodkas into us in the hotel near the station. The craic was good in Cricklewood, or March in this case, and we were on top form by the time we reached the nick.

Now warmed up, but not so much that the screws would put the block on us getting in, we were taken through the security routine, finger printed, and sniffer searched. Once we arrived at the main waiting room for regular visits, we were ushered through another set of doors, along a corridor and through further security procedures, before being led into a small visiting room with only four tables in it. This is where we were to have our visit, under the noses of half a dozen screws and a handful of other people visiting their high security friends and family.

As luck would have it, everybody was on top form that day. With the screws in earshot, able to hear every word we said, we had to be mindful of what we talked about, but such was the free-flowing wit, that we ended up giving *them* plenty to talk about. With everyone fighting to hold court and rattle off a tale, the craic and the cross-kidding ricocheted around the room like gunfire. The screws, and even Lord Longford who was there visiting some other dangerous individual, as was his want, couldn't help but laugh at our comical antics.

We regaled our incarcerated cousins with tales of Billy Buck, Doodles, and other dearly departed members of our family and characters from our past, as well as kidding about many of those still alive, like Legs, and especially those in the room that day. But it was all just a bit of fun and taken that way by everyone on the visit. We weren't offensive or disruptive. We weren't a load of toerags giving the screws a hard time, we were well dressed, reasonably well behaved, and naturally charming with it; probably a welcome relief for the screws, who often dealt with far less cordial visitors. They got plenty of entertainment into the bargain that day. All we were doing was making the best of a bad situation, given the circumstances. The hijinks of that visit reverberated around Whitemoor thanks to the screws, who never stopped talking about the performance they'd been party to, much to the amusement of the cousins we had to leave behind after only a couple of hours in their company.

What set us apart, however, went much deeper than how we looked, or how we carried ourselves. We had a history of this shit. We had breeding. It may not have been aristocratic, upper class breeding, but even within our community and the world we lived in, we were far from being newcomers to the job. I'm not suggesting for one minute that because we'd all grown up around family in the jail, that we were better than anyone else, or any worse for that matter. There were far more dangerous people in some of those prisons, more violent and notorious by far.

One time, a few of us were sitting in the SSU (Special Secure Unit) at Full Sutton Prison on a visit when Michael pointed out the little bespectacled fella sat holding his wife's hand at the next table. It was Donald Neilson – The Black Panther, at one time the most wanted man in Britain and public enemy number one. An armed robber and serial killer who'd murdered and mutilated over half a dozen poor innocent victims, and whose deadly and horrific exploits were headline news on a national level while he was at large. Hard to believe when we seen him up close. But besides the likes of him, many prison inmates are what you might call first generation villains. Sons of factory workers, dockers, teachers or bus drivers, straight goers of all descriptions. Orphans, or kids from troubled homes perhaps, yet largely people coming from seemingly straight backgrounds, tough ones maybe, but straight ones, where a rogue or a villain, or a complete nutter had somehow squirted out. The jails were all full of such first-generation criminals. Today they are just full of junkies

But sometimes you come across people like us. Families with a longstanding reputation within their community. Families with history, whose notoriety stretches far back into their lineage. People who live by a certain set of rules. People who have proper values, and old school morals. It is these kind of villains whose presence within the prison population commands respect.

The tales continued as we left Whitemoor in high spirits, following such a memorable visit. Knowing how much we'd all laughed together despite our surroundings, and how much it lifted the morale of our cousins, made us feel good about our *Reservoir Dogs* day out, and it just felt like it was going to be one of those days. After a short taxi ride back to March, we jumped the train to Peterborough, and had an hour to kill before our connection. Still buzzing from the visit, we decided to have another drink in the nearby hotel. The drink was going down like pop, and so much frisk was being had that we decided to miss the train and jump the next one an hour later.

By now, the cross-kidding was getting nearer and nearer the bone. A day in each other's company and the 'mad dog' was making an appearance. Now we weren't teenagers any more, we were grown men, with children of our own. But somehow, considering the circumstances, intoxicated by the events of the day, as well as the drink, we were having fun, and boisterously boarded the train for the final leg of the journey home.

There was standing room only on the 17.35 from Kings Cross to Edinburgh, as we wobbled about in the area between compartments, our volume levels going up, as the wind-ups continued on board the train. Noticing a few stares from other passengers, Frankie Slater decided to slope off to first class, away from the rest of us. But by now Joe and Hymee were getting me and Adam at it. As the train rattled on the track, Adam stumbled towards me, helped on by a shove in the back from one of those two. I neatly stepped aside and gave him a further shove, sending him headlong into the adjoining carriage.

His double-breasted suit jacket was up by his shoulders, and his long, dark, curly slicked back hair cascaded across the floor, coming to an abrupt halt as his face made contact with the rubber matting. A vision that makes us laugh to this day, although maybe you had to be there.

Nevertheless, our unruly behaviour had not gone unnoticed, and as luck would have it, for the other passengers at least, there was an off-duty police woman on the train. So, when an announcement was made over the PA system that our train would encounter a 15-minute delay at York, we sensed that all was not well.

As we pulled to a halt, we quickly tried to get off, not knowing what to expect, either on or off the train. Our door failed to open, and as we moved through the carriage to check the next exit, we clocked the off-duty police woman on the platform talking to several uniformed officers. We shuffled through the carriage as she pointed us all out to the waiting coppers, and by the time we reached the next exit, they were all there to meet us, and duly escorted us away from the train, much to the approval of the other passengers.

Slater thought he'd got away with it, but that train was going nowhere 'til Mrs. Off Duty had pointed him out. He was finally dragged off the train protesting his innocence, while we were being charged with disorderly conduct by British Rail Police.

Once they were satisfied the train was safe to leave, we were escorted from the station. We explained that we had to take a train back home but were banished from the premises and told to go and sober up.

Shameful!

So, we walked off up the road to the nearest bar. After two or three more drinks, before getting ejected from the bar, we staggered back to the station, fighting amongst ourselves on the way by this time. When we landed back there, we were in a worse state than when we'd been sent on our way to sober up. They must have heard us before they saw us, because the law were at the entrance when we rolled up, looking a lot less like Philadelphia lawyers than we had at the start the day.

After much drunken persuasion, Hymee and Joe managed to talk their way onto the next train, while I was busy refereeing Adam and Slats, who had now started ricking with each other. This continued all the way home in a taxi from York, as the Old Bill barred us from the station completely.

What a day, and what a state of affairs. It had all started off so well, the visit had been great, we looked a million dollars and the craic had been just like it used to be, but it had gotten out of hand, almost as if it were some kind of reminder that when we're together, anything can happen, and usually does, when the mad dog puts an appearance in.

It was a day to remember, even though court appearances and fines followed thanks to our ridiculous behaviour. That trip to Whitemoor gave Michael, John and Stephen, even though he was in a different jail, something to laugh about for a long time after. For that reason alone, it was worth the blisters (fines), and even the black eyes.

So, the new millennium was dawning, and lots of the old ways were becoming obsolete, especially on that mad visit.

Many of the old school morals and values may have still been intact among some of us, but the world that was opening up for our children was not one for the dinosaur. Technology was the future, and a proper education was paramount. We could always provide the real education, the type needed to survive on the street and stand on your own two feet, but if real success was to be achieved, success within the mainstream, then we would have to guide our kids through a maze. One that we had crawled through the hedges of, in order to navigate our way out of trouble, although for some of our breed, the shortcuts they took were more trouble than they were worth.

So, with the prospect of bringing our children into a family with a long standing tradition, a history within the city, and now a notorious reputation, in most cases by relation and association;

pointing our kids in a completely different direction was certainly going to be a challenge.

Legs had his own personal challenge, trying to live a straight life in order to keep his family together. He was in a tail spin he couldn't get out of, estranged from his wife, with long periods of time from his kids, unable to resurrect his marriage, unlike one of his trail blazing uncles, Frankie Doodles, who following his return to the marital home after a few months at Westgate Hill Terrace, retired gracefully from his career of crime and became a highly respected old time face from a bygone era.

Hymee was estranged from the mother of his two boys and dealing with being a part-time father. Young Frank Kelly had sadly left a widow and two young daughters behind, while John, Stephen and Michael were contemplating life behind bars for the foreseeable future.

Uncle John had various business interests, but had eventually split from Aunt Yvonne, while Peter remained happily married, still living on the camp, keeping his hand in with a deal here and there, and an interest in a motor pitch in Blyth.

Georgie Kelly was more or less made redundant as a familiar face and street trader around Newcastle, reduced to nicking a living in the bars, selling little bits of tom. Frankie Kelly gave up the pitch after Billy Buck died, and Thomas and his brother Jimmy spent their days at the prop.

Young Frankie Hewson continued to work the barrow outside Marks & Spencer near the Haymarket bus station, his daughter, Sharon, by his side for much of the time. The mad hatters as we called them, Michael and Terry Patterson, had the only licensed pitch on 'the front' and Albert Sayers stood his pitch, smack bang in the middle of Northumberland Street.

Fortunately, we had been spared the frequent loss of the family members encountered during the 1980s, and with the exception of Aunt Mariah, for the best part of the 1990s our numbers only increased. As many times as we have tried, the pair of us still can't manage to do a full roll call of the family, never mind the ones we're not supposed to know about. But just as life was starting to shape up nicely for me, with the new house fully decorated, the carpet warehouse doing well, and a sunbed shop just about ready to open for Lisa (they were all the rage back then), my life, plans, and entire world, and that of my wife and young son, was about to be turned on its head overnight.

On the 16th of March, 1998, we entered the maternity ward at Newcastle's Royal Victoria Infirmary anticipating the arrival of our second child.

Louis had been a big baby, weighing in at nine pounds on delivery, and this one was even bigger. A big bouncing baby boy was what we were expecting, and we'd already chosen his name, Sonny. But what should have been one of the happiest days of our lives, turned out to be the worst nightmare of mine, and almost the end of Lisa's. As a result of serious complications during delivery, which had gone on all day, Lisa catastrophically suffered a placenta abruption, causing our unborn son to drown in his mother womb.

As the delivery suite went into panic, an emergency C-Section was carried out, during which Lisa lost almost all of her blood in a matter of seconds. As she faded in front of me I held her hand, pleading with her to hold on, as our boy Sonny was brought silently into the world.

My memories of that night still haunt me, and I try not to think about it for that very reason, however, somewhere in the midst of the ensuing aura of panic, and the surreal tranquillity of life slipping away from Lisa, our Sonny Boy gasped for air. With a dozen doctors and nurses surrounding him, life was breathed into the nine and a half pound bruiser that entered the world without a murmur. Having already died in his mother's womb.

Sonny had now been without oxygen for almost 20 minutes that we knew about, while the medics tried to revive him, and on the cusp of the time when doctors are legally entitled to give up attempts to resuscitate, my boy gasped for air. He wanted to be here, he was a fighter, and he came back to us with that single heart-lifting breath. I spent the night between the ITU, where Lisa was receiving blood transfusions; and the special care baby unit where our Sonny Boy was fighting for his life, not knowing if either of my loved ones was going to make it through the night.

I'm glad to say that they both did, and though Lisa made a full recovery, for our Sonny Boy, the damage had most certainly been done. Life was never to be the same again, and a whole new set of challenges faced me and my young family, as the shockwaves reverberated through the entire breed and generation of our family.

Our challenge now, was raising a special needs child. I don't think I'd even heard of Cerebral Palsy before then, and for the first year of his life rarely a day went by when he, or we, didn't cry continually. Our hearts, and those of our immediate families were broken. Like many parents we came to meet in our situation, they informed us in the months that followed, that what we had gone through was a bereavement. The loss of the son we were expecting, which is exactly how it felt. Yet while coping with such a tragedy we were faced with raising a totally different son, a disabled son, with very special needs, all without having had any previous exposure to anyone with such serious complications, and all while caring for our firstborn, two-year old Louis.

That event altered the course of mine, and my young families' lives in ways I could never have imagined, but once again; if it doesn't kill you…

We were not the only ones of our generation facing challenges before the millennium came to a close. With broken marriages, dysfunctional households, prison and frequent harassment, even for family members that were minding their own business, guilty of nothing other than association; feelings of bitterness, jealousy and contempt started seeping in to our breed, and it was beginning to corrode many of the family values we all once shared, and we were in danger of becoming a breed that was slowly falling apart.

What the future held for us, the rest of our mixed-up generation, and the next one we were introducing to the clan, only time would tell.

Lives had to be rebuilt, readjusted and resurrected. If our upbringing had taught us anything, however, it had taught us how to survive, and it was that instinct above all others which truly made us a breed apart.

BETTER THE DEVIL YOU KNOW

The dawn of the 21st century genuinely felt like a millennium away from the time that our great-great-grandparents crossed paths aboard the Albert, en route to the port of Fleetwood from Belfast in search of a better life with nothing more than a hope and a prayer, a will to survive, and an instinct for keeping one step ahead of the game.

Sally with the 10 bob note she had tucked in her blouse, and Paddy with a book he couldn't read. They brought their primitive ingenuity to the streets of Newcastle and were persecuted for their entrepreneurship from the outset. Their passion to succeed in what they did, served only to antagonise their agitators, and the battle lines were drawn up early in our history.

Through the decades, and even the centuries, those battle lines, although now blurred beyond recognition, are as deeply drawn as ever. The cement that held our breed together, however, began to crumble with the passing of time and the passing of family members.

Just where and how Paddy and Sally's ancestors would ultimately fit into the scheme of things may not have been quite as they imagined, but despite the bloodline that has been vilified and persecuted beyond reasonable comprehension since the end of the 20th century, our stock have successfully, and eventually, blended into all walks of life, and now contribute to society on many levels.

There are military and medical personnel from within our ranks. There are performers and entertainers, social workers and council workers. There are young men working in the industries that supply your gas, or whose air conditioning cools your office down in the summer.

There are young men and women working in just about every sector you could think of, even the legal profession; and legitimate business men and women with their fingers in all sorts of pies, from the motor trade to catering and anything in between.

Much of this, however, has only been the case since our kids have reached adulthood, and many of the millennials from our family are fully embedded in straight society. The generation that we came from, was the last of the 'old school', and because our way of life was still somewhat viable by the time we became teenagers, our stall was set out, no pun intended. But with the victory of legalization came the end of the game that had been the birthright of our family. We'd missed the opportunity, and dismissed the necessity of an academic education, by which time we only had two options available to us besides poverty. One was business, the other was crime, and we have lived and died by whichever of those choices we made.

There is little room in society for our kind any more. It has outgrown our kind of people. Communities, and the spirit they generated, are almost a thing of the past, and unless you live in a ghetto, which is what most of our communities have become, you tend to keep yourself to yourself. Family and loyalty are almost qualities of the past, and the world we live in now is virtually unrecognisable, regardless of where you live or who you are.

The West Road is now the Curry Mile, and spot the white man is the game most people play whilst driving along it.

Tension across all communities is rife, and he riots we grew up with are still going on today, all over the world. We live under the constant threat of terrorism, while entire cultures live side by side in restless distrust of their neighbours. You don't even have to leave your home to get robbed any more, today they can hack into your bank account while you're sitting watching *The Chase*. Hooded bike-riders will snatch your expensive devices while you walk down the street, and the gangs of immigrant corner standers are intimidating enough to stop you walking to the local shop.

'A New Breed of Criminal' the term the press and the law used to describe members of our family, was a misnomer of huge proportion. The new breed of criminal is chatting to your kids online. They're grooming your daughters and trafficking them around *their* community. They are stood in groups on every inner-city corner, and the streets that many of us grew up in are no longer recognisable or safe to walk on. Crimes against the elderly and the young are common place and respect is a word that no one seems to give a second thought to.

Not in any way were our chaps the new breed of criminal. What they were, and what every city had at one time, when people felt safe enough to walk their own streets, was the 'old breed of criminal'. Yet so much effort, so many resources and so much time has been put into getting certain members of our family off the streets, that our town has become the hunting ground for the real new breed of criminal, and we know which was a safer place.

For example, whose door do you knock on these days if your kids are getting groomed and bullied, or you're scared to leave the house for all the delinquents terrorising your neighbourhood?

Don't say the police. They neither have the time, the resources or the inclination to take care of such matters, even if such matters interfere with your quality of life. It's a cliché, but we've all heard that old chestnut about how people in the East End of London will tell you that the streets were so much safer when the twins were around. That's not nostalgic cobblers. They say it because it's true. Why else would they? It's not as if Ronnie and Reg are still around to give them a slap if they don't say it?

So now we have a new criminal underworld, and it's one that affects us **all**. Not just those involved with crime in some way, or those employed to protect valuables and money for a living. Crime today is predatory. Cyber-crime, identity theft; stuff that wasn't even on the radar as little as ten or twenty years ago. It is crime that touches every one of us, civilian or otherwise. The moral compass no longer exists. The lack of 'old school' honour, morals amongst their own, and their blatant disregard of where to draw the line, endangers everyone. So, with their eye off the ball, terrorism a constant threat, and resources at an all-time low, the police have allowed our streets to become more dangerous and deadlier than ever before, and the communities under the most threat and in the most need of protection are the communities that used to have families like ours in their midst.

Sometimes, you really are better off with the Devil you know.

In almost parallel comparison, the very streets our family have worked for over 130 years, have become a place for all and sundry to get a living, while the old street traders have become a thing of the past, and would get nicked in a minute if they rolled up on Northumberland Street to work a line. But so long as you're on a unicycle, up a tightrope, or wearing a strait jacket that's been set on fire, while your pal juggles half a dozen chain-saws, blindfolded; you can plot yourself up and cause as much obstruction and disturbance as you like. Sally, old Mariah, and every one of her daughters would turn in their graves. They spent time behind bars in Dickensian prisons, enduring horrific conditions and the harshest treatment, all for breaking an antiquated by-law prohibiting obstruction of the public highway.

Ob-fucking-struction if you please!

These clowns bring the street to a standstill! You can't even hear yourself speak for the racket they make, never mind walk past them; even the buskers are all wired for sound, as if they're doing an audition for the *X-Factor*, it's a fucking joke. Generations of our family have been prosecuted and persecuted for selling fruit and veg off a barrow, and their crime was obstruction of the public highway. Yet rather than permit us to ply an honest trade, they drove us underground, slung us in the nick, giving us little place to turn, other than against them. Now any Tom, Dick or Harry Houdini can roll up on Northumberland Street and bring the place to a halt, without so much as a quiet word from an onlooking copper.

Maybe if they had been a bit more lenient with us back then, things might not have turned out the way they did. We will never know. So, as they say in the movies, 'fuggeddaboudit!'

If ifs and buts were bolts and nuts, I'd build you a bridge to China. It was what it was, and it is what it is.

So today, what say we about our breed?
Well, many of our lives have turned out to mirror much of the controversy, tragedy and heartache of our past. History and people, they say, have a tendency to repeat themselves. A fact which rings true, at least for those of our generation.

For certain members of the Family the witch-hunt continues.

Our cousin John is currently behind bars, and not for the first time since his 15 year sentence back in 1989. On more than one occasion suffering lengthy lie downs (time served on remand), for charges which failed to secure conviction. He has served almost 2 years on remand whilst waiting to stand trial on a conspiracy charge over the much publicised Tup Tup Palace drive by shooting in 2015.

Following an eight week trial at the Old Baily in 2018, John was acquitted of any involvement in the incident. The suggestion being that he instructed the attack to take place in response to his son being forcibly removed from the club. The details of the case are readily available to view online, and you can judge for yourself whether or not it was a plausible thing for a man in John's position to even consider, or whether it was yet another attempt to put him away solely on the back of his reputation.

Plausible or not, however, it was sufficient enough for them to keep John off the streets for the best part of 2 years, reinforce his already notorious reputation and perpetuate the myth, on yet another trumped up charge which failed to get the conviction they wanted. The second prize for the law, however, was that John's attempt to prove his innocence from any involvement in the incident, resulted in him receiving a custodial sentence for allegedly perverting the course of justice. So they got something for their troubles. It is an extremely bitter pill to swallow however, and at the very least makes life difficult for John, keeping him from his family for months or years at a time, which is precisely what they want.

Following a recent family bereavement, similarities can be drawn to when his Uncle Peter had to grieve in prison when his father (John's Grandad) Morry passed away. Although this time round John Henry was refused permission to even attend his half-sister Joanne's funeral, after she lost her life suddenly in the November of 2018, aged just 45. With just 9 months of his sentence to do, the powers that be felt John, still a Cat A prisoner, was too much of an escape risk? He had been facing a possible life sentence during his trial at the Old Baily. Yet having received only 5 years for perusing his line of defense, and having served 20 months on remand and thereby due for release in August 2019, they, in their infinite wisdom felt that John is an escape risk? The decision begs not only belief, but its very own question.

I state these facts not to drum up sympathy or empathy, but simply to illustrate that the persecution of certain branches of our bloodline is as prevalent today as it has ever been. The question is, will it ever end? Until they have the last laugh, some fear it may not.

These are only our views, however, they are echoed by many people, not just those within the family, and maybe John will give his own views, and tell his own story someday.

Stephen, thankfully, is keeping his hand in, and his new literary project is underway, so look out for that one. I know personally that he is a much happier individual these days, enjoying the delights of his children and grandchildren, as is Michael, and John, when he is allowed the chance to.

Hymee, has a new young family, with Nancy and Little Frankie Doodles to keep him on his toes. Yet once again straddles parenthood with life as a single father. He can keep hold of money far better than he can hold on to a woman. Like me, Tony is a great believer in the part which circumstantial impact has played in our family history, and the outcome of our breed, and thankfully he was only too happy to help map it out and record it with me.

For me, life has been eventful to say the least. Spells living in Tenerife and New York were extremely interesting, full of adventure and excitement. The years, however, have also been plagued with heartache and tragedy. I've dealt with divorce, and all the dreadful ramifications that it can have on 'family'. I've watched my father and my brother loss their battles with cancer, and even suffered the sudden and devastating loss of my Little Saint, Sonny Boy, tragically at the age of just 18. All of these, events have shaped my life in ways I could never have imagined. I've suffered health issues, both personal, physical and otherwise. I've been by my mother's side, and still am, as she battles with breast cancer for a second time. She, like her mother, her aunties and her granny, is a fighter, and she just gets on with it. If it doesn't kill you, it makes you stronger. That's the way we have to look at such things. It's in our genes. Strangely, however, all of this inspired me to finally put pen to paper, before it was too late, and record as much as possible of our families' unconventional history as we could for posterity. Everything, they say, happens for a reason.

So the dramas continue to unfold, and whilst the exploits of some of us are more comprehensively documented than others, we have all continued to live lives that are far from ordinary, managing for the best part, to keep our noses clean and stay out of trouble in the process. Our lives go on, eventful on many levels.

Our stories are still unfolding, on many levels, and what has gone on since we chose to end our story is, quite frankly, a book in itself in many ways every bit as interesting as you may think this one is. But for the benefit of our family yet to arrive, we like to think we've done our job.

Our kids have been around since the turn of the century and are contributing members of the millennial generation. They know what has gone on since we concluded our story, now with many of the blanks that punctuated the 100 years and the five generations before them filled in, and they and their children will have a better idea of who, and what they came from. This will hopefully serve as a document that gives them a true representation of their 'breed', rather than the legacy that has been created by some, and sensationalised by others, in various forms.

Hopefully, this will become something which might help repair some of the damage time has done to our family too. With each generation we become more diluted and further estranged, as our numbers now are truly uncountable. Without knowledge of our collective history and our shared heritage, the glue which kept us together for generations will be in danger of losing its grip, and unless we are very careful, we risk becoming A Breed very much Apart.

Life has taken all of us in very different directions, yet we all have certain traits in common, something to do with the mad dog probably.

But whether you have read this and feel that people like us are in some way different from the norm, or are in many ways like yourselves; or you feel that what we became was a result of circumstance, survival, station or some other contributing factor, and on reflection you feel you may have made some of the same choices. Or indeed you still have an opinion of us as bad people. Whatever your view, we hope we have at least painted a more realistic and understandable picture of our place in the community than the only one offered up by the press.

We are barrow boys and barrow girls at heart, we are people of the street, and we have suffered and celebrated, laughed and cried and lived and died by the decisions we've made along the way. And if you were to question our legacy and our place within the history of Newcastle and Tyneside, then consider this:

Over 130 years after Sally Kelly pulled the first of the family's barrows onto the streets of this city, there is still direct blood selling fruit and veg on those streets. Sadly, Albert Sayers, now in his 70th year, is the last man standing from our family, and although there are various pitches still being worked today in Newcastle, Uncle Albert is the only member of the breed upholding our tradition, and with no son to take the reins from him, our standing on the streets of the city will soon be resigned to history.

Amazingly, it all started on The Albert back in 1886, when Paddy met Sally (surely there's a movie title there?), and now, two centuries on, it is Albert who remains the last reminder of our family's presence on the streets of Newcastle, as the most well-known street trader in the city. However, our heritage has already been thankfully consigned to the history in a positive light.

His original barrow, the one used by his Granny Mariah, has proudly been rehoused in Beamish Museum, preserving our legacy for future generations as part and parcel of the fabric that makes up the history of our city. So, whether or not you, or we, think our family is part of Tyneside folklore, the administrators of the world-famous open-air museum feel that we have made mark enough to be part of North East social history, for all the right reasons.

It is up to you to make your mind up about our breed, but the people that know us, and the people we care about, know exactly what we are: a breed with proper morals, proper codes and proper values. Proper people!

AFTERWORD
EDDIE LENNIE JR

In 1839 Edward Bulwer-Lytton first coined the phrase, 'the pen is mightier than the sword'.

The much-used adage suggests a man can solve problems or achieve a better purpose with greater efficiency through communication with words than by violence with weapons. It is quite a noble sentiment, true in many ways, and a contradiction in terms to the equally well-known ancient proverb, 'live by the sword, die by the sword'.

A lesser-known sentiment is that some men live by the sword, but die by the pen. Some people live a violent and dangerous life, only to swear someone else's away when the shit hits the fan. I am proud to say that in relation to this sentiment, I have neither lived by the former, and will never succumb to the latter.

With regard to any of these ideals, it is fair to say that most of us believe there is a book inside us, even those who have at one time wielded the sword. Believing so and demonstrating such, however, are two totally different things.

For over a quarter of a century now I have wrestled with writing this book. I have been asked to tackle the challenge many times, by many people. Members of my family across all generations have championed the cause to document our heritage, not least of all in order to record our family's history for posterity, and for the young, upcoming generations whose life in the modern world is so far removed from that of their predecessors that *their* heritage is in danger of being forgotten forever. I am, surprisingly, not the first of my family to enter the literary world. My cousin, Stephen Sayers, released his memoirs back in 2015 after turning his back on a life by the sword with his first publication *Tried and Tested at the Highest Level*. I am pleased to say that more is expected from him in the future as he maintains his course along the straight and narrow. Strangely, both his and this book provide some insight in to the mindset and mentality that can breed someone like my cousin, his brothers, my brother and other relations, as well as many people like them.

So why write a book? My belief is that you will write a book if it is something that you *must* do. That's it, really. If you've spent the last 25 years feeling like you want to, or that you probably could write a book, then you will most likely never actually do so, as it is a lot easier said than done. But this project became something I simply had to do, even if it meant the book was only read by our family.

My co-conspirator on this project, Tony Sayers Sr, and I are products of a family with a remarkable history, and this is something we have recognised since we were children. Not simply because of the stories we were told, but because of the people and the way of life that surrounded us. We were also fortunate enough to have lived a lifestyle and benefited from a certain kind of education that is sadly becoming a thing of the past.

We have been lucky enough to have had support and input from members of our family throughout the process. From uncles, aunties, cousins, family friends and most thankfully my amazing mother Mary Lou. At the time of writing, she is now the oldest living member of our breed, aged 86, and thankfully still as sharp as a tack with a wealth of history and memories to rely on. Her powers of recall and captivating story-telling have been instrumental in helping the writing process, and made much of it as enjoyable and rewarding as I'd hoped it could be. Without her help and input, much of the detail would have been left out, as there are not many of her generation alive to remember the bygone times. I am eternally grateful for her assistance and for the fact that she is still around, and I hope that this book reflects the world she grew up in, as accurately as possible.

I'd like to thank our Uncle Frankie Hewson Jr for his support, and Uncle Albert Sayers for his continual encouragement and invaluable contribution to the cause. I also thank our cousin Stephen for breaking the mould, dropping the sword and picking up the pen for all the right reasons. For even he understands, after a life by the sword and the damage it has caused, that there is much truth behind the sentiment of Edward Bulwer-Lytton's famous adage.

Finally my cousin, who's more like my brother, Tony Sayers Sr must be acknowledged for his assistance in the compilation of this book. We have grown up together on the streets of Newcastle, born into a life and a family that have brought the words on these pages to life. We worked the street together as kids, a thing of the past these days. We discovered bars, nightclubs and women together. We earned together, holidayed together and stood side by side on the day of my wedding. Like me, Tony knew from an early age that we were different. Products of the swinging 60s, Tony, with me and all of *our* generation, caught the tail end of a life that is now a distant and romantic memory. A life that would no doubt be forgotten if we were not to have embarked upon this project.

For those of you that are from similar backgrounds, we hope you appreciate our honesty and our perception of the kind of world we lived in. For those of you that walk the straight and narrow, we hope you enjoyed an insight into another way of life, and understand how circumstance, opportunity and environment have a huge influence on the decisions you make in order to survive. We never set out to change your opinions, or to justify actions you may not conform to, but we did hope to present an alternative understanding of how people like us tick.

The story we've told, brings us up to the end of the 20th century. Yet so much more could be said about what has happened since then, and in most cases is still unfolding, not without drama. Our lives and our families' lives have continued to be every bit as colourful in the 21st century, as they had been up to that point. Once you've lived your life in the kind of world we grew up in, it becomes pretty hard to switch off the drama, and what was in-store for us and the rest of our family after the millennium, was to be stranger than any fiction we could have imagined. And regardless of how things turn out, our lives have been far from ordinary, and the truth of the matter is that every one of 'us' would rather have it that way; wolves for a day, rather than sheep all our lives.

Of course, there are regrets, anyone would admit to that in all honesty, but what is meant for you will not pass you by. If our lives had been less colourful there would have been far less to tell you. We all have a place to fill in this world, and our family existed as they did, just as you and your families fill the roles that are meant for you and them. It is all part and parcel of the wonderful fabric of life.

So we will watch this space, and if we feel it is something we 'must do', and if it is something we feel you'd like to know more about, then who knows, after another few evenings strolling down memory lane with a couple of bottles of red, we may well pick up the pen once more and bring you up to date.

In the meantime, we sincerely hope you enjoyed our story, and we thank you for getting to this point.

Special thanks must be given to our friend, confidant and publicist Steve Wraith, whose support and assistance has been consistently positive. And to Neil Jackson for his time and patience in turning our book cover idea into reality.

Finally, we would like to dedicate this book to every member of our beloved breed, both past and present. Without them there would be no story to tell.

Special dedications are made to my father, Eddie Lennie Sr, my brother Tony 'Legs' Lennie and my Little Saint, Sontino 'Sonny Boy' Lennie. You are all loved and missed more than you will ever know.

Ed x